# EVEREST
# SURGEON

*Yet again, for Beth*

# EVEREST SURGEON

## MICHAEL WARD AND THE EXPLORATION OF HIGH ASIA

### RIAZ DEAN

PEN & SWORD HISTORY

AN IMPRINT OF PEN & SWORD BOOKS LTD.
YORKSHIRE – PHILADELPHIA

First published in Great Britain in 2026 by
**PEN AND SWORD HISTORY**
An imprint of
Pen & Sword Books Ltd
Yorkshire – Philadelphia



ISBN 978 1 03619 214 3



A CIP catalogue record for this book is available from the British Library.



Typeset in Times New Roman 11/13 by
SJmagic DESIGN SERVICES, India.
Printed and bound in the UK by CPI Group (UK) Ltd.

The Publisher's authorised representative in the EU for product safety is
Authorised Rep Compliance Ltd., Ground Floor, 71 Lower Baggot Street,
Dublin D02 P593, Ireland.
www.arccompliance.com

*For a complete list of Pen & Sword titles please contact*
**PEN & SWORD BOOKS LIMITED**
George House, Units 12 & 13, Beevor Street, Off Pontefract Road,
Barnsley, South Yorkshire, S71 1HN, England
E-mail: enquiries@pen-and-sword.co.uk
Website: www.pen-and-sword.co.uk

or

PEN AND SWORD BOOKS
1950 Lawrence Rd, Havertown, PA 19083, USA
E-mail: uspen-and-sword@casematepublishers.com
Website: www.penandswordbooks.com

# Contents

# Maps

# Illustrations

# Foreword

## by Sir Chris Bonington

During the British Mount Kongur Expedition of 1981, after a long and exhausting climb, I led a team of four on the first ascent of that peak (25,326ft), the highest in the Pamirs and a northern outlier of both the Karakoram and Kunlun ranges. It lies in the Xinjiang province of China, a country which had only recently opened its doors to foreign climbing parties after the end of its Cultural Revolution.

The other notable side to this expedition was that it included four scientists who undertook important medical research high on the mountain itself. This second group was led by Dr Michael Ward, who was nine years older than me and the overall expedition leader. As Chairman of the Mount Everest Foundation at the time, he had instigated the expedition after working tirelessly with the Chinese Mountaineering Association. He and I had also been part of a reconnaissance of Kongur the previous year. But even before that, almost a decade earlier he had begun lobbying the Chinese authorities to permit such an expedition, and that it finally became a reality was primarily due to his efforts.

Although on this occasion Michael and his team chose to limit their focus to research, they were all accomplished mountaineers. He was the expedition doctor during the 1953 expedition when Mount Everest was climbed for the first time. He also assisted in the development of supplementary oxygen, which proved to be a critical factor then. More importantly, he instigated the 1951 reconnaissance of the mountain from the Nepalese side when a possible route to its summit was finally identified.

I first met Michael in 1963, when he invited me to join his expedition to what was at the time the last unclimbed peak over 8,000m, Shishapangma, but which unfortunately did not proceed. When I was frostbitten during my Eiger North Face Direct ascent three years later, Michael was my doctor in London, having become a specialist in the treatment of cold-related injuries. During our time together on Kongur, I came to know him very well and had a high regard for his intellect, as well as his mountaineering ability.

There was a time when Michael was justifiably regarded as one of Britain's foremost climbers, both on rock and on the highest of snowy peaks. He was also one of the first Westerners to explore and map parts of the Himalayas. A prolific writer, he published several books and countless articles for mountaineering and medical journals.

Michael Ward's accomplishments as a climber and a doctor of mountain medicine were significant and unique. Riaz Dean has written a comprehensive and engaging biography that will be of interest to mountaineers, outdoor medical practitioners and those keen to learn more about Himalayan exploration.

Sir Chris Bonington
Cumbria, 2025

# Introduction

On 29 May 1953 the world's highest peak was finally climbed after decades of effort, including many attempts falling short of the mark and more than a dozen lives lost. As the two successful climbers – Edmund Hillary and Tenzing Norgay – came down the mountain to lasting fame, one of the men who greeted them high on the slopes was Michael Ward, the expedition's doctor.

Ward is still best remembered for his role during that history-making event, but he achieved much more during his lifetime and this, in fact, was not his finest achievement. Later, in his book *In This Short Span* which was essentially an autobiography (although subtitled *A Mountaineering Memoir*) he wrote: 'Everest has changed men and Everest has killed men … As for me, 1953 consolidated my interest in investigating the relationship between men and the mountain environment.' But this 'interest' Michael spoke of could only hint at what was to come, since his memoir concluded soon after a journey into Bhutan in 1965, aged 40. When the second half of his life had played out, it would reveal the full breadth of his talents: as a mountaineer, a doctor-cum-surgeon, a scientist, an explorer and mapmaker, and a writer.

I subscribe to the view that the subject of a biography should, wherever possible, be allowed to speak for oneself. And since Ward was also a writer, I quote extensively from his works, which has the added advantage of demonstrating his writing ability. In the first few chapters, this is also through necessity as material from his early years is scant at best. Fortunately, for later years I had access to his expedition diaries when he travelled to Everest (1951 and '53), back to the Himalayas (1960 and '61), and then Bhutan (1964 and '65).

Ward did complete his memoirs with a second instalment, but unfortunately in draft form only, a month before he died. Notably, all 750 pages were laboriously handwritten in capitals and double-spaced, knowing his doctor's scrawl was barely legible to others (he never used a typewriter or computer). Ward intended calling it *Everest Surgeon* – hence my choice of title. In this biography, unless otherwise noted, quotations by him have been taken either from *In This Short Span* or his unpublished manuscript.

As a pioneer of 'mountain medicine' – today referred to as 'high altitude medicine and physiology' – Ward wrote *many* articles about the subject in medical and mountaineering journals. His body of work naturally contains a great deal of technical information and terminology, but here these have been kept to a minimum in the interests of the general reader. With them in mind, I have also tried to explain any mountaineering jargon used, which readers who are climbers will already be familiar with. Being British, the units of measure Ward used for height and distance were mostly imperial rather than metric; and since the conversion is easy enough, I have retained his use of 'feet' and 'miles' throughout.

It should be noted that although I too have a love for the mountains, not being a mountaineer myself, I often refer to others from this craft to describe situations and emotions which I obviously have not experienced. Nevertheless, it is worth mentioning that I do have previous association with Michael Ward through an earlier book of mine, having made use of his research into one of his lifelong interests. This was the clandestine mapping of high Asia during the 1800s by an obscure group of native Indian explorers known as the Pundits, of who a great deal more will be said later.

Returning to *that* ascent of Mount Everest in 1953, the story has been recounted many times, not only by the participants themselves but also by a host of other interested parties. However, their accounts reveal significant disagreements, particularly regarding *the* 'burning question': why did this expedition succeed when others before it had failed. Here, of course, this account is related from Ward's own perspective, both as a climber and a doctor.

Although largely forgotten today, even in Everest circles, this biography sets out the life of a man who went on to push the bounds of mountaineering well beyond that remarkable first ascent – and in more ways than one.

# 1

# First Peak

◇◇◇◇◇◇◇◇◇◇◇◇◇◇◇◇◇◇◇◇◇◇◇◇◇◇◇◇◇◇◇◇◇◇◇◇◇◇◇◇◇◇◇◇◇◇◇◇◇◇◇◇◇◇◇◇◇◇◇◇

As a child, Michael Phelps Ward did not have an upbringing typical of English boys at the time. And many of the influences that would shape him can traced back to a few early encounters, particularly certain people he met and a handful of books he read.

Born on 26 March 1925 in Hampstead, London, as an only child into a privileged background, he spent his preschool years with his parents in what was then the Federated Malay States (later Malaysia). His father Wilfrid Arthur Ward had joined the Civil Service there after the First World War, having served on the Western Front, Macedonia, and Palestine. His mother Norah Anne Phelps had been a nurse in London during the war, and the work ethic and discipline she witnessed in its hospitals made a deep impression upon her, which she did her best to pass onto Michael.

In Malaysia, Wilfrid Ward was part of a small team in the colonial service, administering a district as large as a typical British county. He lived there with his wife and son, although the family also spent much time in the capital, Kuala Lumpur. Other than being surrounded by many native servants, Michael grew up in the care of a Chinese *amah*, knowing few English children and mostly speaking either Malay or Chinese. When he was 7 years old, his parents sent him back 'home' to begin his schooling, in keeping with a longstanding practice of the British living in their colonies. Unsurprisingly then, he remembers his initial time at Sandown, a pre-preparatory school in Bexhill-on-Sea, as 'rather bewildering', and he found some of their rules strange. One such regulation was that at mealtimes he had to finish two pieces of bread with butter first, before another slice was permitted with jam.

After three years, Michael's English had improved sufficiently to be enrolled in St Edmund's, a preparatory school in Hindhead, Surrey. Here, the remnants of his Malay and Chinese were replaced with Latin and Greek, although to his frustration they were taught 'in the most boring manner possible'. Soon after enrolment, all new arrivals were assigned to one of four houses, each named after a famous Englishman. But the 11-year-old refused to be to put into one particular house, which reveals something of him then and in years to come:

> What I do remember is reading up about each and thinking that Scott was both a fool and a failure. Not only had he been beaten to the South Pole by Amundsen, but all his party had died while all of Amundsen's had lived … I was not interested in failure no matter how 'glorious' it was – I liked to win.

This competitiveness showed up again on learning he could gain extra points for his house by pulling up bracken from the school grounds. He proceeded to do so obsessively, at the cost of two painful hands, but stopped after one term upon realising it was the school's 'cheap and cunning ploy' to tidy up its grounds.

Through most of his time in primary school at Sandown and St Edmund's, Ward lived with the Walton family in the village of Underriver, near Sevenoaks in Kent. Sir Richmond, who was deputy secretary in the Admiralty during the war years, and his wife became Michael's guardian because his parents could only leave Malaysia infrequently. He got on well with their four children, especially the youngest boy who was eighteen months older than him. He remembers them building a tree house together and swinging between silver birch trees in a foolhardy manner.

In all, Michael would spend eight years in the Walton's care and recalls: 'I rarely missed my parents, my alternative family being quite enough.' Although on the face of it this lack of contact with his parents seems not to have affected him greatly, his only child Mark would, as an adult, write on his website: 'To me, personally, he was a remote figure in many ways, the result of his own emotionally undernourished childhood.'

At the Walton's home, Michael chanced upon a book which he read more than once. It began his deep interest in mountaineering and the challenge posed by its highest peak. Written by the legendary Frank Smythe, it was simply titled *Camp Six* and described his participation during the 1933 Everest Expedition. Eventually, climbing alone from the highest camp attained, Smythe managed to reach 28,200ft but knew 'the game was up' after coming up against conditions which he described as 'both difficult and dangerous, a fatal combination'. He went on to add: 'Those who have failed on Everest are unanimous in one thing: the relief of not having to go on outweighs all other considerations.' The sheer exhaustion in these words would one day ring in Michael's ears.

A second book he recalls being given soon afterwards was *The Complete Mountaineer* published in 1907 by George Abraham, a pioneer climber and photographer: 'The combination of pictures to which I could marry the text excited me … it showed men climbing steep snow and rock in the manner that I imagined mountaineers should.' As well as such books, maps of the Himalayas and Tibet contained in his battered student atlas were well-thumbed too.

At the end of the fourth form at St Edmund's, as an academic prize he received *The Pilots' Book of Everest*. It described the first flight over the mountain in 1933 by two RAF pilots, made possible by using bottled oxygen. After reading the book, Michael remembers longing to climb the peak. In the school library he found its companion book *First Over Everest*, which also happened to describe two secret journeys made in the vicinity of Everest around 1870 by one of the Pundits. Try as he might though, he could not find out more about these intrepid explorers, recalling: 'This really intrigued me and I never forgot about them.' Little did he know how often he would come across the Pundits' footprints during his exploration of high Asia in years to come.

While at St Edmund's, a passing incident made a vivid impression on young Michael: He recalls overhearing a conversation between two masters about a rock climbing accident which had just occurred involving an old boy of the school. Unable to draw himself away, Ward heard how the lead climber Wilfrid Noyce had fallen almost 200ft, and although seriously injured was saved from certain death after quick action from his partner, Menlove Edwards. By allowing the rope connecting them to run through his hands and across his shoulders, Menlove managed to check Wilf's fall gradually despite being pulled off his stance and dangling dangerously himself. He had thus effected, as the boy would later learn, a 'dynamic shoulder belay'; and even though the rope was severed to the last strand, it prevented the falling climber from crashing fatally to the ground. Michael would hear both names spoken many times again as the pair went on to became renowned mountaineers and, more so, after he had learned the craft sufficiently to join them.

Early in this process, one of Ward's most memorable experiences came in the Swiss Alps. While on holiday with his parents, he convinced them to let him join a family of three and their two guides attempting the Wetterhorn. The party left their Alpine hut the next day while the stars were still out and started walking uphill. In the opening paragraph of *In This Short Span*, Ward described how, after a sleepless night of anticipation: 'The brutal lower precipices looked impossible to the inexperienced eyes of a boy of fourteen.' But, as he learnt that day, finding a practicable route up a mountain can disarm its imposing faces, although in this case it involved almost eighteen hours of continuous effort by the time he returned home to anxious parents. At just over 12,000ft, the Wetterhorn was a worthy introduction to 'the hills'. Yet he ends this account with what would become his trademark understated style, simply recording: 'My first peak'.

Around this time, Ward began his years at Marlborough College, an old and well-regarded public school in Wiltshire. This time, he found the transition not as difficult since: 'I was very self-contained … not homesick, because I never had a permanent home to be sick about.' The college was noted for its emphasis on 'muscular Christianity', which Michael had mixed feelings about: 'I was happy with the physical and mental "muscularity" but not the Christian bit.' Students were required to attend church daily, with an extra-long service on Sundays; but although he liked singing and much of the service, 'its content left me cold and I switched off – vain repetition I did not like'.

He did enjoy the sports curriculum on offer, playing hockey and squash, cycling for miles, and going for long walks on the downs. Being wartime, Ward also joined the Cadet Corps aligned with the Royal Air Force and became engrossed with aircraft recognition. But he doesn't say whether this skill was in any way useful when a stray missile from a German bomber happened to land in a field adjacent to the Waltons' home.

Importantly, he liked learning and was full of curiosity as a student, but with so many questions that he became known as 'Mr Why' by his teachers. Ward was particularly fascinated with biology and recalls even at this early stage on deciding to become a surgeon. In this, he was influenced by his biology teacher Francis Knowles who, unusually for a schoolmaster at the time, was a Fellow of the Royal Society (he went on to become a distinguished scientist).

Ward's other big influence at Marlborough was a housemaster named Edwin Kempson. A mathematician by training, he also offered forestry as an optional pastime, which Michael took up eagerly in place of cricket, a sport he found boring. Together with a group of older boys, they helped clear many acres of scrub and woodland in the nearby Savernake Forest. His teacher was also a mountaineer of some note, having been to Everest with the 1935 and 1936 British expeditions. Known as the Walking Sahib by his Sherpas for the distances he covered at furious pace, Kempson inspired his young charges, sharing stories about tackling the highest of peaks. Ward would later write: 'The seed planted by the Wetterhorn climb and nurtured by *The Complete Mountaineer* was beginning to germinate.'

One particular experience Kempson described which stuck with Michael occurred in 1935, when their team was able to explore and map extensive areas in the Himalayas by travelling lightly laden and mostly living off the land. This was the modus operandi of their leader Eric Shipton, the doyen of British mountaineering, who detested large expeditions (this dislike later became a factor when he was controversially dumped as leader of the 1953 Everest expedition).

Finally, to Ward's delight, in his last year at college, aged 16, Kempson took him climbing. With a former pupil who was also a mountaineer, the trio headed to Scotland for ten glorious days on the Isle of Arran – although 'glorious' more in spirit than weather, as it rained the whole time and they never managed to stay dry. Moreover, the only respite the other two gained from the Walking Sahib's pace, regardless of the inclination of the slope, was by stopping him to indulge his other interest, birdwatching. Nevertheless, Michael did have a fine time and his description of this memory later as a writer is worth quoting:

> It was fun too to sit, perched on a rock buttress just under the black clouds, looking down on the sea. Sunlight lanced down to the surface through the gaps ever-changing in size and shape, making pools of light on the waves. Across these, myriads of gannets skimmed, soared and dived, making little blobs of white on the dark green surface. Towards the end of our holiday we had one partially sunny day when the mainland hills came into view as soft blue-brown shapes, indistinguishable in the distance from the sky haze.

On his return, Michael was fortunate to gain an introduction through a family friend to another climber of considerable stature, some forty years his senior. He later described Geoffrey Winthrop Young as the last Grand Old Man of Mountaineering. Losing a leg in the First World War did not stop him returning to the hills (using a specially designed artificial limb). His misfortune actually intensified his writing and poetry, which Ward greatly admired – hence his use of the first line from one of Young's verses 'The Cragsman' as the title of his autobiography:

> In this short span
> between the finger-tips on the smooth edge
> and these tense feet cramped to the crystal ledge
> I hold the life of man.

Ward would later regret 'that I was too immature not to have made more of this meeting', but before he left the 'Old Man' ensured some good did result from their encounter. He mentioned another mountaineer, John Barford, who would shortly be climbing around Langdale in the Lake District. Knowing

John was always keen to help young climbers, he suggested Michael write to John – which he promptly did and received an invitation to join him.

During the next two weeks Ward, then still a novice, learnt about the finer points of rock climbing from Barford, eleven years his senior and soon to publish the instruction book *Climbing in Britain*. The first thing Michael realised was that his old army boots, which he had previously put to good use in the hills, were not suitable on rock, despite being nailed with clinkers.

Higher up, another revealing lesson came as he struggled to find a handhold. He was advised to use what looked to him a miserable hold close by, but which John described as 'a good jug-handle'. Michael thus came to an early realisation: 'For the first time I was introduced to the gamesmanship practised by climbers on each other, especially by those standing at the top of the pitch.'

While the pair were in Langdale, they ran into the famous 'Little Man' of rock climbing, Alan Hargreaves, who had led most of the hardest routes in Britain, and he promptly joined them the next day. Ward struggled to keep up with this small man who hopped nimbly up the cliff face, but he learnt much in the process. Before they started climbing, he saw Hargreaves pull out a second pair of specially nailed boots from his rucksack, which were tight-fitting and designed for use on rock. And soon enough, Michael witnessed the secret of his speed: '[He] did the right move at the right time and in the right direction. There was no wasted scuffling, no coming back – all the holds appeared for him as if by magic.'

At the end of that fortnight, an aspiring young mountaineer went home having learnt from the best while undertaking some difficult climbs. One of these was a new route moving from tree to tree which Barford, recalling Ward's other efforts at Marlborough in forest clearing, named 'Savernake' in his honour.* Their time together signalled the start of a strong friendship – but the teacher was yet to impart to his pupil the harshest lesson in climbing.

---

* A new route, by convention, is named by the person who first climbs it.

**2**

# Bitten by the Bug

The early years of the war had not intruded greatly into Ward's life, but towards the end of his college years this changed as the conflict spread into the Pacific. Following the fall of Singapore in 1942, he was denied contact with his father for almost six years, after Wilfrid Ward was interned by the Japanese Army in the notorious Changi Prison. Michael's mother was lucky to secure a place on one of the last boats out of the port city with other desperate women and children. On returning to England, she rented a cottage in the Cotswolds where he joined her during the school holidays. He was in his late teens when all this occurred and so better able to cope with the long separation from his father, no doubt helped by the strong attraction he was developing for the hills.

After Marlborough, Ward was admitted to Peterhouse, the oldest college at Cambridge University and one of its most distinguished. Although he found his spartan room there cold and draughty, it had one advantage, being located directly below the roof. This allowed him to hone his skills at night on this and many other roofs on campus – dangerous though they were from neglected maintenance during wartime.

Michael had chosen to study medicine. Being a 'reserved occupation' this meant he was exempt from conscription in the military for now, but would be required to complete National Service after graduating as a doctor. His core subjects were anatomy and physiology within the Natural Sciences Tripos, although the undergraduate course had been cut back to two years due to the war.

As much as he was a keen squash player at Cambridge, making their second team, he was soon drawn to the university's mountaineering club. His first meet, organised by another medical student named Tony Worssam, saw their group climbing in North Wales. As the club was reliant on having members who could lead competently, Ward soon found himself out in front and 'feeling cock-a-hoop'.

However, when he tried a new route 300ft up a cliff face, he soon felt alone and anxious. Doubts began creeping in about his own ability, but it presented another learning moment: 'I convinced myself that if I had been only two feet off the ground this move would have been extremely easy. So I duly moved upwards and reached the top – but with quivering legs and hands.' Such situations helped Michael get to know himself better as a climber, finding on some days 'in an extraordinary state of physical and mental élan I could float up without any great effort', while on others he required the 'maximum of effort and will power' to complete even a simple route.

At the cottage where the club based itself, on the mantelpiece in the bunkroom sat two photographs, the first of Clogwyn du'r Arddhu. Better known as Cloggy and sometimes described as the shrine of British climbing, it looked 'brutal and uninviting' to Ward at the time. Nevertheless, he asked around about the possibility of there being a route up its impossible-looking cliff face, noting: 'I was fascinated, and came back to the photograph again and again to convince myself that I could actually see a way up it.' His recollection of trying to discover a feasible route to a summit with nothing more than an image to work off is telling; particularly considering the photograph sitting next to it, which was of Everest. (Less than a decade on, after poring over other images Ward would be sufficiently convinced he had found a way up this Himalayan peak to launch an expedition to reconnoitre its slopes.)

For now, climbing, and talk of climbing, became an obsession within his circle of student friends, and he recalls: 'The "bug" had truly bitten me then, and I wanted to climb every difficult route I could.' Although these challenges – often dangerous – posed by sheer cliffs were exciting, he writes: '[It] was mountain country that exercised the stronger hold over me … I had a curious feeling of personal passion and affinity with mountain country – it did not frighten me and I was content just to be there.'

This realisation, akin to a spiritual connection with the hills, was in itself an important one (just as it is, to take another example, with sailors for the sea). With hindsight he would observe: 'If this affinity is weak or lacking, the physical pleasure of rock-climbing wanes in time and the individual gives up climbing.' For Michael, though, as he would transition from the hills to mountaineering in the Himalayas, if anything, this affinity would intensify.

Like others mastering this craft, he soon learned the technique of total focus as a prerequisite for safe climbing, and the need to keep a tight control on any insidious fear of falling. But he also came to realise that intense concentration is impossible over long periods, observing how the best could 'switch off', talking or smoking in highly exposed and seemingly dangerous positions: 'The art of relaxation, I found, was as important as the art of concentration.'

Later in his first year at Cambridge, the club shifted its focus from climbs in Wales during winter to others further north into Scotland as the weather warmed. Ward was keen to attempt Ben Nevis, at 4,413ft the highest mountain in the United Kingdom. This eagerness was evident after he travelled there alone, despite suffering from an attack of influenza and a blazing row with his mother, who sensibly suggested he stay home in bed. Giddy and vomiting several times on the long train ride up, he continued doggedly with his heavy rucksack in falling snow, eventually sheltering in a barn at the start of the track. A good night's sleep nestled in the hay did wonders for his recovery, and the next morning, despite appalling weather, he clambered up towards the Nevis hut to join the others for some serious climbing.

His ascent of, or more to the point, descent off Tower Ridge and the summit plateau of Ben Nevis with Tony Worssam was certainly the most memorable of his efforts that summer. After some deft climbing, the pair successfully completed the ascent then stepped back onto the plateau, where a 'continuous low-pitched howl which ebbed and flowed' signalled what awaited them.

Here, they walked into the teeth of a howling Atlantic gale with gusts which made it impossible to stay upright, even with the aid of ice axes. Their plan was to locate a ruined observatory sited on the top and from it take a 140° compass bearing towards a snowy col leading back down to the hut. Finding the ruin before it got dark was their first imperative; then holding this bearing accurately as they staggered some 1½ miles along the summit plateau in the blizzard was going to be critical. Any deviation could easily see them fall off the cliff tops whose edges, compounded by the many cornices present, were tricky to spot in the gale and clouds.

Reduced to a slow crawl, the pair eventually ran out of daylight and could not locate the observatory. With little option now, they had to take a longer route down, but at least it was by way of an easier track lying behind the mountain. At this point, however, they were hit with a white-out and blinded by stinging particles of snow, barely able to see anything until they reached lower levels. Ward ends his account of this climb 'that I remember particularly well' by simply noting: 'Many hours later, and long after dark, we stumbled into the hut.'

His writing comes to the fore again, soon afterwards, describing better times in these hills:

> The weather began to improve and at least one day was sunny;
> I was then able to appreciate for the first time the wildness and
> stark beauty of the Highlands as I stood on top of the Ben just
> under the hurrying clouds, looking out on to mile upon mile of
> snow-covered hills stretching from the sea far inland.

On completing his medical degree as the war was coming to an end, Ward began work at the London Hospital (today, the Royal London Hospital). He also returned to climbing in North Wales, which was relatively close by, and often with Tony Worssam.

On one climb, Michael remembers Tony and another member sitting back chatting and smoking away while he attempted a new route up a narrow cleft. The pair were unaware how difficult upwards progress had become for him, with no safe way back down. Barely managing to secure even finger and toe holds, having earlier kicked off his nailed boots to get more traction, he was stretched to his limits. After being stuck at the same spot for almost thirty minutes and dangerously close to falling, Michael finally managed to haul himself over the top. This victory was a milestone he would remember well: 'It widened my mountaineering horizons. My attitude of mind changed. I knew I could do very hard routes and move up a class.'

Ward was ready now to take on new challenges, and the Alps was the natural pathway many British climbers took from rock to mountain climbing. However, it often meant having to get up in the middle of the night undertaking long and tiresome walks just to get to the mountain, before any real sport could begin.

A year after the war was over, together with John Barford and two others, he travelled to Switzerland to tackle some of its peaks. Their first, the needle-like Ago di Sciora (10,515ft), was accomplished in good time. Travelling further west to Zermatt, they completed a traverse of the Weisshorn, rising to almost 15,000ft, again without difficulty. In fact, no climb bar one tested Ward beyond his comfort zone, and that only because they took a wrong turn and strayed onto the imposing north-east face of Piz Badile. Rather than retreat, they continued up this wall and after some extreme rock climbing managed to summit, although Michael recalled: 'I was disconcerted by the tremendous scale and sweep of the steep rock walls on which I found myself … In time I learnt that fright is a very efficient defence mechanism in mountaineering for it should be always near the surface …'

Cautious though he tried to be, by this stage Ward was being noticed by his peers. Nea Morin, one of Britain's foremost female mountaineers at the time and twenty years his senior, in her autobiography *A Woman's Reach* writes: 'Michael was a brilliant climber with a style and grace of movement on the very hardest climbs (Monkey's Bow, for instance) which I have never seen equalled.'

Now in his early twenties, he had developed into a handsome man as well, with dark brown eyes, contrasting black eyebrows, and an olive complexion that darkened quickly in the sun. Standing two inches short of six feet and of medium build, he had a thick head of black hair which he kept smartly cropped. In old mountaineering photographs, he is also often seen with a beard to match, which he grew on longer expeditions when shaving was a luxury. Some years afterwards on Everest, Noyce would remark: 'His face too could be startlingly flexible, almost india-rubber.' The *Times* correspondent, James (later Jan) Morris, who joined them would describe him further:

> He was a slender, lithesome man, and it always gave me pleasure, even in those disagreeable circumstances, to watch him in action; his balance was so sure, and his movements so subtle, that when he turned his grinning and swarthy face upon you it was as if someone had drawn in a moustache upon a masterpiece by Praxiteles.

In August 1947, arriving alone at the Helyg hut in North Wales, Ward ran into the climber he had once overheard his masters at prep school discussing, whose quick reaction had saved the life of his partner. Here was the legendary Menlove Edwards himself, whom Ward regarded as one of two prewar British climbers that shone above all others (the other being Colin Kirkus). Menlove, who was fifteen years older, was also a doctor and had been a conscientious objector during the war. (Later, Michael learnt he suffered periods of mental instability, eventually taking his own life aged 48.)

The pair decided to do some climbing together, which soon stretched into a few days as they tackled some demanding faces. Ward took the lead when they attempted a new route up the West Buttress of Cloggy but was defeated, and Edwards fared no better. They switched to Longland's Climb, scrambling 400ft up the cliff face with Ward again out in front but now starting to feel rather exposed. Belaying him from below, Edwards encouraged him on, but in his own way, calling out: 'I can hold an elephant from here.'

After some fearful moments along Longland's Slab, Michael managed to work his way along a crack in the rock, taking a new direct route to finish. Hauling himself over the final overhang, he recalled: 'A surge of pleasure and relief went through me as I landed on top. Menlove took some time to follow, I noted with satisfaction.' The renowned British mountaineer Chris Bonington would later rate this climb 'certainly as difficult as anything that had been done at that time'.

Later that summer, Ward returned to Scotland looking to gain more experience on snow and ice. Fortunately, he was able to pair up with Bill

Murray, a leading mountaineer and writer of that country. His first book *Mountaineering in Scotland*, written in a German prisoner-of-war camp on rough toilet paper, would inspire generations of British climbers to head to the high country. In his autobiography *The Evidence of Things Not Seen*[*] Murray recounts his first meeting with Ward at the base of a near-vertical sandstone outcrop. His anecdote also illustrates how quickly Michael had learnt the art of gamesmanship from John Barford and others:

> There I met a slim black-haired youth of twenty[-two], who offered to show me some of the easier climbs first. I should have taken note of his bright sardonic eye. He instead put me on the hardest, and stood back grinning when I failed to get off the ground. He was Michael Ward, then reading medicine at Cambridge. We became friends.

The pair, teaming up with Barford, decided to attempt Ben Nevis over Easter by opening a new route up the Gardyloo Buttress. Meanwhile, the weather turned from bad to vicious. Cutting hand and footholds while snow drift poured over them, they climbed a steep ice-pitch and iced-up rocks to complete the route – described by Michael as 'terrifying' – which they named Easter Eve.

Murray was keen to join Ward and Barford that summer and attempt Mont Blanc, the highest peak in the Alps (and Europe), from the more challenging Italian side. But before they attempted it, recognising the difficulty of their planned route and Ward's lack of experience, they decided to first acclimatise by tackling a few mountains near Grenoble in France.

One of these involved a route up the Ailefroide via the Col de Coste-Rouge. If they were successful, it would be only the second time this route had been climbed by a British party, making its choice an added attraction. With no hut nearby, it also marked Michael's first Alpine bivouac at the foot of the glacier leading up to it. Starting out at midnight, they were at the mountain's base by dawn to begin their ascent. (Interestingly, in terms of the development of climbing footwear, Murray commented how the other two had an advantage by using the latest type of boots with corrugated rubber soles, which allowed them to move faster compared to his nailed soles.) After some careful climbing, including over verglas,

---

* Unless otherwise noted, quotes used by Bill Murray are taken from this book.

which was Michael's first experience negotiating such treacherous glaze of ice on rock, they finally overcame a steep wall to stand on the top.

As they descended, Ward recalls: 'I felt wonderfully elated – this was my first big Alpine route.' Two days later they planned to cross the Col de Coste-Rouge down the Glacier Blanc to attempt another nearby peak. But while descending from the col, disaster struck. Michael remembers nothing of what occurred. He woke up in a hospital bed with Bill lying in the one next to him, saying: 'We've had an accident and John's been killed.'

Bill's face was lacerated and bruised while Michael had fared worse, including a fractured skull and memory loss. It was at least twenty-four hours before he could piece together what had transpired and the events leading up to it, as described *In This Short Span*:* He had been in the middle on the rope as they descended from the Col de Coste-Rouge over steep snow and ice. Michael remembers it 'looked straightforward' and, as the sun was not yet up, the risk from icefall or stones 'seemed non-existent'. Halfway down, contrary to expectation, there was a large stone fall which hit John, who was bringing up the rear. He fell onto Michael, and they swept Bill along as they hurtled down over 500ft towards a crevasse, and fell partway in.

On regaining consciousness, Michael found his legs dangling over a 50ft drop and his broken ice axe lying beside him. He was bleeding profusely from his head which had been gashed during the fall by John's crampons. John's lifeless body lay beside Bill, beneath the lip of the crevasse.

Eventually, Bill was able to get moving again and help Michael struggle out. In his concussed state, Michael could not even recall his companions' names. Frustratingly, soon afterwards Bill signalled to a lone Frenchman passing by, explaining they desperately needed assistance getting down the slope. To their dismay, the mountaineer refused to help as it would take him away from his planned route. After offering them some wine, he simply continued on his way, oblivious to the sight of a dead climber and the others' dire predicament.

The pair struggled down the glacier and were eventually transported to the town of Gap, lying 35 miles south, where they were hospitalised for ten days before returning to England.

Over fifty years later, in his own account Murray shed more light on what occurred that day and a slightly different version of this confused event. He described Ward's actions during the accident, the reason for his

---

* A short note describing 'The accident on the Col. de La Coste Rouge' appeared in the *Alpine Journal* (1947).

broken ice axe, and how disaster had struck them in *two* separate stages after encountering soft snow lying on hard:

> [So] I stopped and warned the others to go slow and take care. 'Nonsense' cried Barford, and stepped down. Next moment he was flat on his back and hurtling down the slope – the snow had balled on his crampons. By good fortune, Ward was standing on a patch of firm snow frozen to the underlying ice. Quick as a flash he drove his axe and whipped the rope round it. When the jerk came the shaft snapped. The pair swept past me. I was torn off. But Ward had hung on to his broken axe-head and we all three braked hard … We had no sooner begun to move down again than a shower of stones fell from the wall of the Ailefroide. They came straight at us. We were all struck on the head and fell together.

Luckily for Murray, after the first fall he had picked up Ward's thick balaclava and pulled it onto his bare head, which cushioned the severity of his injury from the impact of the hurtling stones. Bill went on to describe pair's long struggle down the mountain. Michael had left his rucksack behind, whereas he had retained his in case they needed the food and clothes it contained:

> I was badly handicapped by the weight of my heavy rucksack. Michael following behind offered to carry it for me. He had lost much blood, still did not know who I was, and had been unable to lift his own rucksack from the ground. Yet, seeing me in trouble here he was offering help beyond all common sense. The contrast with the Frenchman was so marked that it gave me the energy I needed both to shoulder my own burden and to find the best route.

While recovering in the small and spotlessly clean hospital in Gap, they were well cared for by an order of nuns, but whose behaviour during their stay was at times inexplicable. They would not touch the injured pair nor wash their wounds, not even the encrusted blood on their faces. And when the time came for their discharge, they were simply handed back their unwashed clothes still covered in dried blood. Michael, with no change of clothing on hand, had no choice but to wear his bloodstained clothes on the ferry and train journey back home, to the startled looks of other passengers who gave the smelly pair a wide berth.

Murray ended his chapter on this incident admitting how lucky he and Ward were to survive that day in the Alps. In sharing his years of experience, he stressed: 'On the mountains, nothing better discourages luck from running out than alertness.' He went on to point out that 'fearlessness is a good companion – provided fear is there too as the watchdog'.

From Ward's perspective, at the time he experienced great trauma not only from his head injuries, but also the loss of a close friend. As he struggled to come to terms with what had occurred, he would reflect: 'I felt an extraordinary detachment about the whole event. John's death, which saddened me, remained strangely unconnected in my mind with the physical circumstances of our fall.'

Even after recovering, Michael was so exhausted from this experience he had to delay his final exams at Cambridge by six months. In terms of any future mountaineering, Ward recalls 'I had some qualms about returning to climbing'. After slowly working his way back and regaining confidence, starting with lesser heights, return he did, although noting 'I was considerably more cautious.'

# 3

# Groundwork for Everest

◇◇◇◇◇◇◇◇◇◇◇◇◇◇◇◇◇◇◇◇◇◇◇◇◇◇◇◇◇◇◇◇◇◇◇◇◇◇◇◇◇◇◇◇◇◇◇◇◇◇◇

The years following that fateful day on Col de Coste-Rouge, leading up to two Everest expeditions, were some of the most active and fruitful in Ward's life; not only as a mountaineer, but also in securing his career – first as a doctor, and then as a surgeon.

After the war, he had begun practicing clinical medicine at the London Hospital. This was demanding work and required long hours, particularly in the aftermath of war and the ongoing injuries, both physical and mental, from which many veterans and civilians were still recovering. What spare time he had was spent honing his skills as a climber, first on the lower rocky hills in southern England and then returning to the higher Alps. In 1949, Michael completed his training as a doctor and became a house surgeon at the London, before working in a similar capacity at the Ilford Hospital.

The following year, he came due for his two-year National Service and was assigned to the Royal Army Medical Corps (RAMC), attached to the Brigade of Guards in London. He started at their depot near Aldershot as a lieutenant, later rising to the rank of captain. Having been a member of the Cadet Corps at college, Michael found the course here and at the Field Training School in nearby Mychett, where he was taught army methods and drill, 'quite entertaining'. But he also recalls 'my main gain was the opportunity to recover from the fatigue of a year of continuous hospital work night and day'. He was hoping to land an overseas posting at this stage, but instead was assigned to a military hospital, the Royal Herbert in Woolwich.

Soon afterwards, a request out of the blue from a climbing acquaintance gave Ward the opportunity to at least get some excitement away from London and practise a skill which would be vital in years to come. He was asked to act as instructor to a group of army cadets from the Royal Military College in Sandhurst. Together they attempted a number of Glencoe peaks in the Scottish Highlands, despite the weather turning foul. This limited their efforts and eventually led to the group being snowbound for two full days. Direction finding became crucial and Michael rose to the occasion, recalling: 'I became expert at using a compass and even impressed myself one day when we all successfully traversed a group of peaks without seeing any of them through the mist and snow.'

Outside such diversions, he found work at the military hospital 'pleasant and life very lackadaisical' after his previous experience in London hospitals. During periods of inactivity, he began scanning the newspapers in the doctors' mess, which led to a startling find and became the trigger for his life-changing involvement in the Everest expeditions. Flicking idly through the papers on a Sunday morning early in 1951, he came across an article buried in the back page about a group leaving to reconnoitre Mount Everest. Although this was a small expedition party whose nationality he no longer recalled,* its members were certainly not British. Ward *does* remember his first reaction: he 'felt annoyed that we had been caught napping'.

Mount Everest was proven to be the world's highest peak in 1856 by the Great Trigonometrical Survey of India (the GTS).† Thereafter, it would forever attract the finest of mountaineers, many of whom would see it as the sport's ultimate prize. It had been controversially named after George Everest, Surveyor General of India from 1830–43, rather than being given a local name as was accepted practice, even back then.

In fact, the mountain hadn't been identified as being the highest while George Everest was stationed in India but occurred during the term of his successor Andrew Waugh. Knowing of no local name for this peak, Waugh chose 'to perpetuate the memory of that illustrious master of accurate geographical research', calling it Mont Everest (later changed to Mount Everest). In years to come, despite moves to have it renamed Chomolungma (meaning Goddess Mother in Tibetan) or Sagarmatha (Goddess of the Sky in Nepali), the initial name has stuck. Ironically, it continues to be mispronounced *Ever–est* rather than *Eve–rest*, which was how George insisted his surname be spoken. Worse still, although most people today can readily identify this mountain as being the world's highest, few know

---

* This was the clandestine visit by a Dane named R.B. Larsen that spring. Supported only by seven Sherpas, he attempted Everest from both Nepal and Tibet – see *The Mountain World* (1953) p.33.

† The GTS was initially a sister organisation of the Survey of India but absorbed by it in 1878.

of the man it was named after or the accomplishments that earned him this singular honour.

In a nutshell, George Everest was one of the driving forces behind mapping the Indian subcontinent, including the formidable mountain ranges making up its borders to the north. This map making was undertaken with a level of accuracy unsurpassed at the time, applying the recently developed technique of trigonometrical surveying from Europe. He was also responsible for completing what became known as the Great Arc of the Meridian, which his predecessor and founder of the GTS, William Lambton, had started in 1806 to determine the shape of the subcontinent's surface.

The measurement of this 'great arc' was of prime importance because, amongst other things, it was essential for accurately determining the height of mountains. The arc would span some 1,600 miles along a meridian of longitude from the southernmost tip of India to the foothills of the Himalayas at the 78-degree mark. When it was finally laid out, after almost forty years of tenacious effort and at the cost of countless lives, it was justly lauded as 'one of the most stupendous works in the whole history of science'.[*]

Straddling the Nepal-Tibet border but often hidden by cloud cover and its neighbouring peaks, Everest's height had been measured by the GTS not by physically reaching the mountain itself, but from a distance using a powerful theodolite. Around 1850, this instrument was used to sight the peak using six separate trig stations from within India's borders, each located over 100 miles away. Then, after applying the principles of trigonometrical surveying, its height was determined to average 29,002ft (updated to 29,032ft in 2020).

Initially, any thoughts of climbing a peak almost twice the height of Mont Blanc was beyond comprehension for most people but, mountaineers being what they are, this would soon change. Their first challenge, however, was to be able to locate the mountain among the jumble of other peaks lying deep within the Himalayas. This in itself was difficult because, at the time, Nepal had closed its borders to India. One of the first to venture there was a member of the Pundits named Hari Ram. Although he did manage to circumnavigate Everest in the early 1870s, he wasn't able to reach the mountain itself or identify it positively.

As mentioned earlier, while at prep school Ward had read a short description of Hari Ram's covert journey which sparked his lifelong interest into this obscure group of native Indian explorers. They were employed by

---

[*] As described by Clements Markham, then secretary and later long-time president of the Royal Geographical Society. For more on the work of George Everest and the GTS, see my earlier book *Mapping the Great Game*.

the GTS and sent into Central Asia and Tibet to help map India's northern neighbours. Europeans dared not venture across these forbidden borders at the time, even in disguise, for fear of being imprisoned and probably killed if they were discovered. Instead, the British trained the Pundits and dispatched them to secretly gather survey data using a technique known as 'route surveying'. On their return, the GTS turned the information they brought back into maps at its headquarters in Dehradun, located in the foothills of the Himalayas (where the Survey of India still resides today).

While undertaking their route surveys, the Pundits took bearings with a prismatic compass* and fixed latitude using a concealed sextant. It was the way they measured distances between places, though, which was remarkable and almost beggars belief. They did this by counting *every* pace they took – bearing in mind that the overall distances marched often amounted to many hundreds, even thousands of miles. For example, on one of his four missions, the best-known Pundit Nain Singh covered some 1,600 miles. Since the length of his stride was almost 2,000 paces per mile, this required him to diligently count out around 3,200,000 paces during this expedition alone. Ward would later apply these 'Pundit-style' techniques during his exploration in Bhutan, when more modern survey methods were impractical given the remoteness of the region and the difficult terrain he encountered.

The work of the Pundits took on added impetus because 'the Great Game' was in full swing during the 1800s. This evocative phrase (the Russians called it 'a Tournament of Shadows') came to describe the strategic rivalry between two of the largest empires of the day, Imperial Russia and Great Britain, as they jostled for influence and territory across Central Asia and Tibet. The rivals came close to all-out war over this 'game' on at least two occasions, though they managed to find a diplomatic solution each time.

However, it did lead to both the First and Second Afghan Wars flaring in 1839 and 1878 respectively, as British India moved to forestall Russia exercising control over its neighbour, which it regarded as a buffer state lying within its own sphere of influence. What is perhaps less well known, Britain also invaded Tibet in 1904 to stop Russia gaining a foothold there and threatening India from this flank too.

Britain's biggest fear during this period was that Russia wanted to wrest away its 'jewel in the crown' and, having recently lost its American colony, was not about to give up India under any circumstance. In this game of move and countermove, the mountain passes into India and surrounding

---

* A prismatic compass has extra attachments that allow sightings to be taken of distant objects such as mountain peaks.

territory took on considerable importance as the British feared they could provide gateways for the Czar's invading columns. These passes therefore needed to be mapped urgently, before being 'locked' from the inside. Indeed, if, as has been said, 'the first need of an army in a strange land is a reliable map', then the Great Game took the strategic value of the Pundits beyond just map making.

The longest of the Pundits' missions took over four years to complete; always travelling in disguise, as discovery by local authorities meant almost certain death. Yet their band of some twenty-one explorers (there may have been more) completed over fifty missions between 1863 and 1899. These were painstakingly catalogued by Ward in an article titled 'The Survey of India and the Pundits' which he published in the *Alpine Journal* (1998), and which represented the only comprehensive list put together at the time.

As individuals, a few Pundits would rank as high as other renowned explorers of this era. For example, when describing the exploits of Nain Singh, the famous Orientalist Sir Henry Yule stated: 'His observations have added a larger amount of important knowledge to the map of Asia than those of any living man'. Despite this assessment, Nain Singh doesn't even feature as an individual entry in *The Oxford Companion to World Exploration* but is listed generally under 'Pundit Mapmakers'. Nor are any of the Pundits listed in *any* capacity in many other books about eminent explorers.

After an extensive review of exploration in written records, my book *Mapping the Great Game* concluded: 'When considered as a whole, the Pundits were undoubtedly the greatest *group* of explorers the world has seen in recent history.' Of course, at the time their achievements were diminished in the eyes of many Westerners because they were Indian. Yet, as I pointed out, if success is measured not only by what one achieves, but also from where one starts in life *and* the resources at hand, then surely the achievements of the Pundits must be judged as extraordinary.

However, they remain unsung heroes of the British Raj, largely forgotten today even within India. This despite Nain Singh winning the highest honour bestowed by the Royal Geographical Society, its Patron's (Gold) Medal, which at the time represented the pinnacle for any explorer in the world. Moreover, it was the first time this medal had been awarded to a 'native', whose feats had to overcome inherent prejudices when being assessed and chosen above other 'European' explorers, which in itself gives a fair indication as to the magnitude of Nain Singh's achievement.

Ward, who would win a similar award one day, was fascinated by these Pundits and actively learned and applied their route survey techniques. In his efforts to get them the recognition they deserved, other than several articles he published in the *Alpine Journal*, he was planning to write a full-length book about their exploits. His unpublished autobiographical notes contain *many* pages describing the work of the Pundits. Unfortunately, his untimely death in 2005 meant he only got as far as writing a preface, which includes the following paragraph:

> My personal use of the Pundit style of mapping emphasised how important it was to have continuity of observations, and the observer must continue however bad the weather or however ill he felt. Also all observations must be immediately put in writing otherwise vital points would be forgotten or missed. No wonder the Pundits were uniformly exhausted after their journeys and had to have a long rest and lengthy debriefing sessions with their Survey of India case officers.

This book came to fruition when mountaineer and author Richard Sale, who had met Ward and knew of his vision for such a project, wrote *Mapping the Himalayas: Michael Ward and the Pundit Legacy*. Published in 2009, it was accompanied by forty-four large sheet maps, mostly illustrating the Pundits' individual journeys. There was also one which showed Ward's own exploration and mapping of northern Bhutan, Pundit-style; and whenever he could, Michael would retrace routes once travelled by his heroes.

In the text, Sale generously acknowledged Ward's founding role and included his preface together with many photographs Michael had taken in the Himalayas and Bhutan. In the book's foreword by Lord Wilson of Tillyorn, who years earlier had accompanied Ward on an expedition in Central Asia, he wrote: 'Michael Ward and his own feats of exploration fit well as a modern epilogue to those heroic memories of the Great Game.' He ended by describing him as 'the *last Pundit* and a person well worthy to carry that name'.

Following Pundit Hari Ram's initial foray around Everest, the first correct identification of the mountain from the ground was made by an officer of the Survey of India, Captain Henry Wood. At the turn of the century, from a distance of 100 miles or so he spotted the peak while in Nepal during 1903, and again from Tibet the following year. Chomolungma's towering summit makes it sacred to Tibetans, who believe such peaks represent a ladder, or cord, of sorts by which their ancestors descended to earth.

Once sighted, thoughts soon turned to the seemingly impossible: could this peak be climbed all the way to the top? It represented one of three last prizes of geographical exploration yet to be 'conquered' (a popular yet regrettable term) – the other two being the North and South Poles. Since these extremes were reached in 1909 and 1911 respectively, it left only Mount Everest, the 'Third Pole', as the final frontier.

The mountain lies within the Himalayas, a range which stretches some 1,500 miles across five countries and includes ninety-three peaks over 24,000ft. At such heights, Ward described what becomes 'the central problem of high altitude: for, as the atmospheric pressure is lowered, so is the oxygen pressure, and less oxygen gets driven through the lungs and less arrives at the cells'.* In the Himalayas, ten of its peaks reach beyond the 26,250ft (8,000m) mark – the so-called 'death zone' – where the body is acutely deprived of life-giving oxygen, consuming it faster than it can be replenished. No one at the time knew with any certainty how humans would cope at such altitudes and whether any strenuous activity would even be possible here.

But before any thoughts of attempting Everest's slopes could be entertained, as one of its soon-to-be famous pioneers, George Mallory, pointed out: 'It would be necessary in the first place to find the mountain.' To that end, the first reconnaissance mission to Everest was launched. It would prove to be one of the most challenging and inspiring of the seven expeditions undertaken before the outbreak of the Second World War. All seven were attempted from the north side via Tibet, and all were organised and led by the British climbing establishment.

It began with the setting up of a Mount Everest Committee (renamed the Joint Himalayan Committee in 1947) which was formed by the Alpine Club and the Royal Geographical Society. The club had the expertise required to ascend the mountain, while the society had the political clout necessary to secure permission to climb in Tibet. Together they would be responsible for coordinating and financing all such attempts.

The first British Reconnaissance Expedition of 1921 crossed into the country through the Chumbi Valley – the sliver of Tibetan territory between Sikkim and Bhutan which marked the traditional trade route between India and Tibet. Eventually, after trekking over virgin territory, the party found its way to Everest's northern slopes. Being of a reconnaissance nature, it had no thoughts of getting to the top; but by reaching the mountain's North

---

* From his article 'Mountain Medicine and Physiology: A Short History' in the *Alpine Journal* (1990).

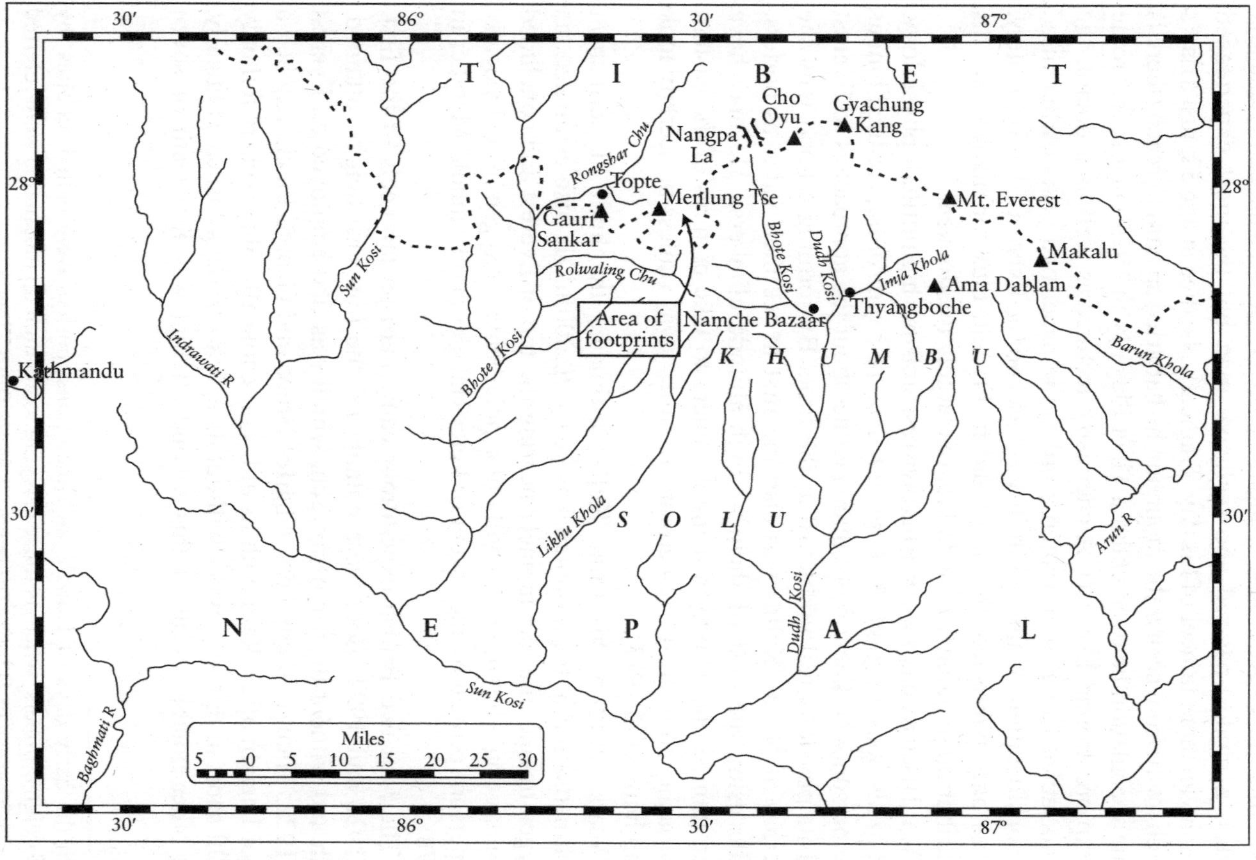


**Map 1. Mount Everest Region** (based on map in *The Ascent of Everest* by the RGS)

Col, where Mallory and Guy Bullock climbed to 23,000ft, they were able to mark out a feasible route towards the summit for future expeditions.

On this first expedition was another pioneer, the Scotsman Dr Alexander Kellas, a modest-natured and reclusive man but the most experienced Himalayan mountaineer of his day. Tragically, he died at age 52, just a day's march away from seeing the mountain he had tried so hard to reach (there is some speculation he even entered Tibet illegally in 1913 via a secret route to explore around Everest). A chemistry lecturer as well as a doctor, the bespectacled Kellas had written a milestone paper two years earlier titled 'A consideration of the possibility of ascending Everest'. Unfortunately, it was only published obscurely and in French, thus for many years his contribution to mountain medicine was largely overlooked.

Ward used Kellas's work in his own research into high altitude physiology, and in his book *Everest: A Thousand Years of Exploration*, credited him as 'the person who knew more than anyone about the approaches to Everest and its physiological problems' at the time. By forming a bond with the Sherpas of Nepal, Kellas was also the first to see their value as porters, while using the best of them as high-altitude climbers.[*] He may have even trained one or two in using a camera to take pictures of the eastern approaches to Everest from around 10 miles away (unless he secretly took them himself in 1913).

Years ahead of his time, Kellas estimated the limit of permanent acclimatisation in the mountains as being 20,000ft.[†] He also estimated the oxygen uptake of a mountaineer nearing the top of Everest and concluded the peak could be summited without supplementary oxygen by a physically fit person (proven by the ascent of Peter Habeler and Reinhold Messner in 1978).

The next two British expeditions came hard on the heels of the first, in 1922 and 1924. Both were notable for the immense heights attained, with and without the use of oxygen, which was first employed on Everest in 1922. Then, two climbers, Charles Bruce and George Finch, reached a record height of 27,400ft with its aid. This came after three others fell only 400ft short of this high mark without its use, a few days earlier. Tragically, the other notable event of this second attempt was the death of seven

---

[*] In the early days of Himalayan expeditions, porters were called 'coolies' by foreign climbers, whereas those carrying loads high up mountains were referred to as Sherpas or Bhotias (meaning 'people from Tibet').

[†] A later study confirmed his figure for those born and bred at altitude but set it 1,000ft lower for others.

Sherpas in an avalanche – the first of a number of mass tragedies on the mountain, which continue to this day.

Two years on, the altitude record was raised to 28,126ft by Edward Norton, with Howard Somerville accompanying him most of the way, neither aided by oxygen. Norton was later adamant he could have pushed all the way to the top but had turned back believing this would have meant almost certain death, as he could not have made it back to camp before dark.

It was the attempt made immediately afterwards, however, by George Mallory and 'Sandy' Irvine which has been permanently etched into the endless debate regarding the mountain's conquest. Both were using supplementary oxygen and were last spotted below a rock step leading to the top, yet they failed to return to camp. The rest of the party were devastated but, with the monsoon expected to break any day, a prolonged search was not possible and they were forced to retreat down the mountain. Back at Base Camp, they erected a stone memorial to the twelve dead from the first three expeditions: Mallory, Irvine and two porters in 1924, the seven Sherpas in 1922, and Kellas the year before. (As of 2025, the death toll stands at around 330.)

Mallory's body was found and retrieved in 1999 by an American research party following its possible discovery by a Chinese climber in 1975. (Ward was told of this find when he was in Beijing in 1980 but was unable to get any further details.) A badly broken leg and a snapped rope around Mallory's waist suggested a nasty fall had taken place. Some of Irvine's remains – a boot and sock embroidered with 'A.C. Irvine' – were located twenty-five years after Mallory's, in September 2024. But the camera they carried has never been found, which possibly could confirm whether either or both had, in fact, made the first ascent of Everest.

Ward, in his 2003 book *Everest*, gives three reasons why he believes they probably did not summit: their use of supplementary oxygen at too low a flowrate (2 litres per minute); they were likely suffering from severe dehydration; and the pair's clothing was inadequate and not windproof.* Nevertheless, in his earlier writing Michael put their effort in perspective: 'The courage, fortitude and determination of these early Everest climbers should make the modern Himalayan mountaineer, with his eiderdown

---

* Subsequently, Sale and Rodway in *Everest and Conquest in the Himalaya* have also pointed to weather data analysed in 2010 from daily measurements taken at Base Camp in 1924. This investigation revealed a dramatic drop in barometric pressure of 18 millibars on the day, thus adding over 350m (1,148ft) in equivalent altitude to their attempt, as well as indicating a major storm was brewing.

clothing, efficient oxygen supply and specially calculated diet feel very humble.'

Having surpassed 28,000ft during the third expedition and with less than 1,000ft to go, each of the next four British expeditions before the war had good reason to believe the prize of Everest was within their grasp. For varying reasons, however, including encountering the monsoon and atrocious weather conditions, none bettered the mark set by Norton – the 1930s turned out to be the decade of disillusionment.

The Tibetan government had closed its borders to further expeditions from 1924 to 1932, so it wasn't until this restriction was lifted the following year, after pleas for access by the India Office, that the remaining four prewar excursions were possible. A height of 28,000ft was gained on the next effort by three climbers, none aided by oxygen. Its use was still being hotly debated by the mountaineering community but was generally unpopular and seen by many as unsporting. However, others questioned why bottled oxygen had not been used when it had been available. There was much soul searching and recrimination, too, in the aftermath of yet another unsuccessful expedition, directed particularly at the organising committee, but Ward provided another perspective in *Everest*:

> [It] was not the organisation and leadership that had been at fault. The correct target was the failure to understand and investigate the medical/scientific problem of 'the last thousand feet' of Everest. That approach had to wait for another twenty years to be adopted.

The fifth expedition of 1935, due to its late start in terms of the monsoon's arrival, was reduced to reconnaissance and mapping in place of any summit attempt. Yet its leader Eric Shipton was involved in two encounters concerning future climbers which are worthy of note. Purely on a hunch, he hired a desperate 19-year-old named Tenzing Norgay as a porter for his first outing. He also formed a favourable view of mountaineers from New Zealand through one 'Dan' Bryant, already on his team – which would later lead directly to Ed Hillary joining his 1951 expedition, and thus being chosen in 1953.

The recruitment phase of the 1936 expedition, on the other hand, witnessed a Lieutenant John Hunt turned down by a medical board due to a heart murmur, despite a solid climbing record – he was advised to take care while ascending stairs in future!

The seventh and last expedition to set out before the Second World War in 1938 did reach a credible 27,400ft. This was first achieved by Eric

Shipton and Frank Smythe, without the use of supplementary oxygen, and then again by another pair. Importantly, this time one of the climbers, Peter Lloyd, used oxygen (at 2 litres per minute) while the other, Bill Tilman, did not. In effect this set up – in the actual environment itself – a controlled scientific experiment, albeit an approximate one as other factors were also at play. Nevertheless, as Ward pointed out, Lloyd was seen to move *faster* and with *significantly less* overall fatigue than Tilman, thus revealing the key that would unlock Everest's summit – one which he and other scientists would thoroughly research in the intervening years.

# 4

# Finding the Route Up

Returning to that Sunday morning when Ward chanced upon the newspaper report of a foreign party about to reconnoitre Everest, it would start a chain of events which would forever link his name with its history-making first ascent. Chris Bonington later commented on the 26-year old's next action:

> [His] imagination went much wider and farther than that of most young climbers or, for that matter, doctors. Even though he had never been to the Himalaya and had only experienced one Alpine season, he began planning a reconnaissance expedition to Mount Everest in 1951.*

Michael remembers his initial thoughts, and how it begged two simple questions: 'As I had so much spare time on my hands [at the RAMC] I decided to try to do something about it. But what? How could I get there?'

The newspaper article mentioned the foreigners intended approaching the mountain from the supposedly prohibited Nepalese side. This was itself something of a mystery, but made sense as the usual prewar route through Tibet was no longer accessible due to political reasons. The country had firmly closed its borders in 1950 after an invasion by Communist China forces. However, following a bloodless coup in 1949, Nepal had recently begun to allow foreigners in – fortuitously, just as one door had closed, another had possibly opened.

Ward concluded the logical place to start his investigation would be to first understand the southern approaches to Everest's summit, a task which he now began with great resolve. On examining the mountain's immediate geography by consulting books and maps, he noted the gigantic bowl formed by Everest and its neighbouring peaks, Lhotse and Nuptse. The only

---

* Quoted from his book *Kongur – China's Elusive Summit*.

feasible route seemed to be up the Khumbu Glacier, through its icefall, then along the Western Cwm, before ascending the South Col and its adjoining ridge to the top.* However, a more detailed study was clearly required to confirm whether this hypothesis was correct. It also made sense, as far as possible, to complete the bulk of the groundwork remotely, as this would be less costly and dangerous than trying to do so in the gigantic bowl itself.

To assist him, Michael contacted his old friend Bill Murray, who had just returned from climbing in the Himalayas and was experienced in organising expeditions. He also roped in another mountaineer who had been independently suggesting a reconnaissance of Everest, a Canadian named Campbell Secord working in London, whose flat soon became their base. He would also prove invaluable in their dealings with the Alpine Club and the Royal Geographical Society (RGS), two organisations crucial to mounting any expedition to Everest, by persuading them of Ward's competence and the need to take his plan seriously. On Secord's suggestion, Ward met with Larry Kirwen, Director of the RGS, to discuss his idea. Michael came away encouraged, noting 'he did not immediately start to produce difficulties; his attitude was more broadly based than that of a pure mountaineer'.

Ward began by researching what looked to be the first major hurdle, the Khumbu Icefall, but a search of books in the RGS's library uncovered little new information about this obstacle. Stretching for over a mile, it guards the entrance to the Western Cwm (see Map 2). The glacier in which it sits moves down the mountain approximately 3ft every day, resulting in massive blocks of ice calving and creating gaping crevasses within the icefall.

During the Reconnaissance Expedition of 1921, one of the few times an earlier party got close to this area, Mallory was able to get a partial view and take a photograph, but came away discouraged: 'We looked across into the West Cwm at last, terribly cold, and forbidding under the shadow of Everest … I do not much fancy [climbing] it would be possible, even could one get up the glacier.' The next year, his added comment that 'it revealed one of the most awful and utterly forbidding scenes ever observed by man' probably quashed any thoughts of this being a feasible route by most climbers.

Ward, however, was not daunted by Mallory's bleak assessment, taking heart from his own belief: 'Every other mountain seemed to have more than one climbable route on it, and there was no reason why Everest should be an exception.' To discover such a route, more photographs looking into the cwm were needed, but they proved hard to find and weren't in any of the books he consulted.

------

* *Cwm* is a Welsh word for 'valley' while *col* is French for a 'pass'.

Michael then remembered his old schoolmaster Kempson, who had been on the 1935 expedition, which had also limited its focus to reconnaissance. As it turned out, Kempson did have a snap which he had taken from a peak along the Nepal-Tibet watershed the following year, but it only revealed the top of the icefall. Later, Ward's team found another photograph which showed the whole icefall, resembling a chaotic mess of ice, and in this shot the view extended up the mountain and into the lower section of the Western Cwm. Unfortunately, none of these images disclosed what lay around the corner, into the upper reaches of the cwm and beyond it towards the South Col.

In 1933, the first flight over the peak had been made by the Houston–Mount Everest Expedition using two open-cockpit biplanes. Fortuitously, they had flown in from the Nepalese side as entering Tibetan air space was prohibited by that stage. Privately funded by Lady Houston, the crew took many photographs of the mountain and its surrounds, some of which were included in the expedition's publication *The Pilots' Book of Everest* (the same book Michael had won back at prep school). Ward and his partners eagerly examined these photographs, taken using a handheld camera, but found they contained insufficient detail of the gigantic bowl and its icefall. A second search, however, led to further images of the summit being uncovered which had not been made public. These included a helpful shot revealing the South Col lying below it, with a somewhat level snowfield that looked less daunting than the icefall.

Shortly afterwards, they found an *unpublished* map produced at some later stage from this aerial reconnaissance, which also incorporated findings from previous British expeditions up to 1935. This Houston map proved helpful as it laid out their target area and the mountain's individual components, but after examining it Murray cautioned: 'Its left hand half might be swept by avalanches coming off the South Face … It will indeed be a miracle if it goes. However it has *got* to be looked at by someone.'

Another map the trio consulted was a topographical one, produced by the Survey of India in 1930 to a quarter-inch scale (1:21,120). It showed approaches from the Nepalese side but no details of the mountain or its slopes which would be essential in planning a climb. What they desperately needed were close-ups of Everest itself.

In an article for his old college, printed in its *Peterhouse Annual Record 2001/2002* titled 'A Petrean on Everest 1951–53', Ward recalled how these images were finally discovered:

I searched the dank, filthy and uncatalogued archives of the R.G.S., examining each photo of the three to four thousand

> taken on the pre-World-War-II expeditions. After several weeks I was no further forward since all the photos were taken from Tibet. Towards the end of my marathon sessions I came across two buff unmarked envelopes. Inside were photographs taken on covert flights over Everest in the late 1940s. Though many were wrongly labelled as being Makalu … it was quite obvious that a reasonably easy route existed to the summit from Nepal … once the formidable Ice Fall guarding the entrance to the Western Cwm had been overcome.

The photographs had lain uncatalogued and unknown to staff in the RGS's archives, after being deposited there by flight officers years earlier. They proved to be crucial, especially a panorama from on high made up of three shots joined together. The images had been captured during unrecorded covert missions by the Royal Air Force in 1945 and 1947 from India and Nepal. Curiously, Ward makes no mention of finding them in his autobiography, only doing so in his later writing. Perhaps the clandestine nature in which the photographs were taken was still politically sensitive in 1972, whereas decades on this was no longer the case.

The last piece of information required by Ward's team fell into place soon afterwards, when he bumped into a geography student, Ian Mumford, working temporarily in the RGS's map room, as described in *Everest*:

> [He] told me that a hitherto unknown working drawing of both the north and south sides of Everest existed. It had been drawn by H F Milne, chief draughtsman of the RGS, and its existence was only known to one or two people. The drawing had been compiled with the help of A R Hinks, former Secretary of the RGS, from vertical and oblique photos taken during the [first] 'Flight over Everest' in 1933; they had combined these with the 1935 photogrammetric survey by Michael Spender on the north and south side of the mountain.

This remarkable map of the Everest region had been drawn circa 1937 to a scale of 1:50,000 and included numerous spot heights. It was clearly going to be of some importance but, although the staff knew of its existence, to begin with it could not be located, as Ward later commented: 'The irony of the vital Milne-Hinks Map is that by the time Nepal was opened to mountaineers it had been forgotten and "lost" by the R.G.S.' However, on his urging, the only copy in the map room was eventually found (later, it was lithographed and exhibited in 1952, but only a few copies exist today).

To Michael's delight, this map confirmed the route he had proposed working from aerial photographs: climbing the Khumbu Glacier and Western Cwm, then onto the South Col and finally its adjoining ridge to the summit, with the icefall at the base of Everest being the most dangerous obstacle.[*]

Armed with this information, Ward's team now approached the newly formed Joint Himalayan Committee, seeking funding and support to reconnoitre the slopes leading to the South Col and confirm whether an attempt would be possible via this route. To their frustration, they received a lukewarm reception as they found the committee deeply sceptical. The reason for this, Michael would learn later, stemmed from a report and photograph by a recently returned Anglo-American trekking party, which had included two vastly experienced mountaineers, Dr Charles Houston[†] and Bill Tilman.

These trekkers were the first Westerners permitted to explore Everest from the Nepalese side and had progressed a good way around the Khumbu Glacier during the winter of 1950. Climbing almost to the top of a small peak called Kala Pattar (meaning 'black rock'), from 6 miles away and a height of 18,000ft, Tilman took a snap of the mountain looking up the glacier. But he could not see around the corner into the Western Cwm and neither had the party entered and examined the icefall. In fact, they spent only six days near the mountain and were unable to make a useful reconnaissance.

Yet, soon after returning home, a statement from the trekkers published in *The New York Times* ended with: 'The south face may well be impossible and we could see no practicable climbing route.' Furthermore, Tilman's brief report in the *Alpine Journal* (1951) continued this pessimism by noting: 'Thus, although we cannot yet dismiss the south side, I think it is safe to say that there is no route comparable in ease and safety – at any rate up to 28,000ft – to that by the north-east.'

Even Sherpas at the time believed there was no viable route to Everest from their country. Three years earlier, Tenzing and a fellow Sherpa had accompanied a Canadian climber named Earl Denman on an ill-prepared and unsuccessful attempt, which they made after an unauthorised entry via Tibet. Later, in a letter dated 11 October 1949 which Tenzing had dictated to Denman, he stated:

---

[*] The key photographs and Milne-Hinks map were reproduced in an article by Ward & Clark in *The Geographic Journal (Vol. 158)*, 1992 (also included as an Appendix in Ward's *Everest*).

[†] No relation to Lady Houston who sponsored the flight over Everest.

> There is only one route to climb the Everest. That is the route
> from Tibet. But from Nepal creates many troubles. There is
> some route which is too stiff and narrow. It is impossible to
> reach the Everest from Nepal.[*]

As things stood, the Himalayan Committee was reluctant to support Ward's venture, seeing it as overly dangerous, particularly having to negotiate the icefall and being exposed to ferocious avalanches in the cwm. Ward disagreed with the committee and decided to proceed regardless, recalling: 'In the face of Tilman's adverse report I could see that trying to bring about this expedition was going to need a certain amount of aggression.'[†] Murray saw Michael's growing determination as a good thing, writing to him: 'It is quite amazing how you've spread enthusiasm – converting all and sundry … through what Plato would have called a divine madness coming over you. These are the sort of expeditions that are worth going on.'

But if the committee was not going to assist them, their group would need to raise its own funding, which amounted to at least £300 per member. This was a considerable sum in those days, and especially so for these young men who would also need up to four months leave from work. Despite this setback, by the spring of 1951 with Murray now installed as leader, they began looking for a few other young and competent mountaineers, able to pay their own way.

Their first choice was a climber already making his mark in the Alps, Tom Bourdillon, a tall and well-built physicist working on rockets. Unfortunately, he did not have any Himalayan experience. So, when to everyone's disappointment Cam Secord was unable to join them, they continued searching for another member who had previously climbed there.

Meanwhile, they were anxiously awaiting entry permits from Nepal, even as the preparation time for an autumn departure grew shorter. Murray did most of the organising, but the quandary he faced was whether to buy their gear and supplies beforehand. More so, because some foodstuff was still rationed post-war and required special permission before it could be purchased and sent overseas. In the end, he settled on buying all the necessary items immediately except for any perishables, on the assumption the Nepalese would agree to let them in. If they didn't, the goods would be stored for another attempt the following year or sold if they were refused

---

* When Tenzing eventually did summit Everest, he wore a woollen balaclava
  Denman had given him six years earlier.
† Later still, in an *Alpine Journal* (1993) article, Ward described the committee as
  'our bête noire' and its attitude as 'patronising and dismissive'.

permission altogether. Tom's father was also a mountaineer and a doctor, and he helped Michael put together the medical supplies list needed, including antibiotics to counter the infections they would almost certainly be exposed to in the Himalayas.

Around this time, Ward and his partners received some welcome news. Despite Tilman's pessimistic view and under continued pressure from Secord, the Himalayan Committee had finally acquiesced. 'The Mount Everest Reconnaissance Expedition 1951' was given its support in principle – although twenty years later, Ward learnt this was only because the committee had not expected the Nepalese to approve their application in the first place. Nevertheless, with its backing, he was able to secure leave of absence, but without pay, from the War Office. Having been recently posted to the Guards Depot at Caterham, Michael also managed to obtain some winter warfare equipment from its stores. This included warm clothing, and a twelve-man double-skinned dome tent designed for the Arctic which would prove most useful.

All this gear and supplies had to be packed away by mid-July and on the docks by the end of that month to make their scheduled sailing time. But two key items were yet to be resolved: there remained the all-important question of funding, and they still needed to find a fourth member.[*]

In terms of filling the last position, late though it was, things could not have worked out better. Eric Shipton unexpectedly returned home in mid-June from a posting in China where, as British Consul-General, he had been embroiled in a diplomatic struggle with the new communist regime. He relates what occurred next in his short book-cum-report[†] written soon after their return:

> After I had been in England for about ten days, I went to London and happened to call on Secord. He said, 'Oh, you're back, are you? What are you going to do now?' I told him that I had no plans, to which he replied, 'Well, you'd better lead this expedition.' I said, 'What expedition?' and he explained the position.
>
> At first, I did not take the suggestion very seriously, for it seemed that, owing to the recent political disturbances in

---

* Earlier, a Swiss named Alfred Tissières had been chosen but then had to withdraw for work reasons.

† *The Mount Everest Reconnaissance Expedition 1951.* Unless otherwise stated, all quotes by Shipton during this trip are taken from this book (which also contains many superb photographs).

> Nepal, it was unlikely that permission for an expedition would
> be forthcoming … It was [also] highly improbable that an
> alternative route [via Nepal] existed.

Then, contrary to Shipton's misgiving and everyone's amazement and relief, approval to enter and explore around Everest was received from Kathmandu. Yet even after Michael spoke with Eric, he seemed rather disinterested at first and put the chances of finding a southern route at thirty-to-one *against*. After weeks of deliberation, Shipton finally agreed to sign up, although driven primarily by his great desire to visit the homeland of his mountain friends, the Sherpas of Sola Khumbu.*

Murray graciously stepped down as leader in favour Shipton because, as he pointed out, 'no one alive knew Everest better than he', and brought much-needed credibility to their fledgling project. Eric also understood the workings of the Himalayan Committee and the people behind it, and insisted they become officially involved in what was, until then, a private venture.

For his part, Bill continued with all the organisation, while equipment and stores were being feverishly packed in Cam's garage. Fortunately, Michael was able to get most afternoons off from the RAMC to assist, but it was only with last-minute help from the Women's Voluntary Service that the packing was completed and transported to the docks in time.

As for funding the venture, which was estimated to cost £1,500 – this was finally resolved after the Himalayan Committee signed a contract for £5,000 with *The Times* (which later sold over 70,000 copies of a special supplement commemorating the reconnaissance). The committee now agreed to refund the climbers' expenses on production of receipts.

Looking back on their pioneering days, Murray noted: 'It is worth recording that this is the first instance where the members of an expedition to Everest have chosen themselves, chosen their leader, and initiated the expedition. It is unlikely to happen again.'

For Michael, it was all coming together. He would soon be in a different world exploring *the* mountain he had become obsessed with, recalling as they left London: 'Finally half-dead with fatigue Bill and I left Tilbury [Docks] on 2nd August. Tom and Eric were to follow by air. Against all odds we were off.'

---

* Today, Sola Khumbu lies in the Solukhumbu District. Sherpas reside predominantly in its northern Khumbu region.

# 5

# The 1951 Reconnaissance

Their ship sailed via the Suez, arriving two weeks and two days later in Bombay (today, Mumbai). Keen though he was to get started, Ward recalled: 'I was glad too that I was making this voyage by boat, it seemed a more fitting introduction to the medieval world of the Himalaya than an aeroplane flight.'

Unsurprisingly, India quickly proved the metaphorical assault on all five senses that it is for most Western travellers upon first landing there. His train journey with Murray was filled with wondrous sights, across a vast country only four years into wresting its independence from the British Empire. A day-and-a-half and a few train changes later on 22 August, with rain falling in sheets they stepped off into a quagmire of mud at the railhead in Jogbani, located on the Nepalese border.

The next day they met up with Shipton and Bourdillon, who had flown into Delhi and made their way to the border. Although the reunion was pleasant, the news they bought with them was not. Before leaving London, Shipton had managed to track down another set of photographs, reportedly taken by a pilot whose aircraft had drifted off course while ferrying supplies from India to China during the war. These images showed Everest from the south. One in particular had captured a view of the slopes leading up to the South Col which made them out to be impossibly steep. Michael remembered the feeling pervading the group:

> This was one of the lowest points of the expedition. Everything had worked till then and suddenly it seemed as though the cup was to be dashed from our lips almost before we had tasted the wine. Gloomily we speculated on the odds against us. There seemed little point in turning back when we had spent so much money and we told ourselves again and again that aerial photographs were known to give very wrong impressions especially with regard to the steepness of mountain sides.

36

After more discussion, no doubt taking heart from a photostat of the Milne-Hinks map they carried, the four reaffirmed their desire to push on to the mountain and see for themselves. This decided, the reconnaissance mission now truly got underway. And to complete their party, the four British climbers were soon joined by two other groups from vastly different nationalities.

The first was led by the best known Sherpa *sirdar* (head porter) at the time, Angtarkay (also spelt Angtharkay and Ang Tharkay). He brought twelve Sherpas with him for the march to Sola Khumbu, four of whom would be chosen to remain with the expedition for its duration. Angtarkay had already been on numerous trips into the Himalayas and Karakoram, including eight with Shipton before the war, and had carried loads over 27,000ft. An early recipient of the coveted Tiger Badge,[*] he was awarded the Legion d'Honneur for his efforts with a French team during the first ascent of Annapurna, the first 8,000m peak ever climbed.

Having previously heard so much about him, Michael was initially struck by his mild personality and diminutive stature, being barely 5ft tall and of average build. He would soon see firsthand not only the *sirdar*'s superb organisational capability, but also his forcefulness in getting them out of sticky situations. (Many years later, when no obituary of him appeared, Ward wrote one for the *Alpine Journal* in 1996 titled 'The Great Angtharkay: A Tribute', which he concluded by describing the *sirdar* as 'a legend in his own lifetime'.)

The second group to join the expedition a fortnight later was a pair of New Zealanders, Ed Hillary and Earle Riddiford. They arrived fresh from climbing in the Garhwal Himalayas with two fellow countrymen, one of whom was Ed's close friend George Lowe. As mentioned earlier, Shipton had previously climbed with another 'Kiwi', Dan Bryant, and had been impressed by both his ability and character. Just as he was about to fly out from London, he received a cable from the NZ Alpine Club requesting its members join them. 'In a moment of nostalgic recollection', without consulting his team, Shipton agreed to increase their party by two even though he knew nothing about these antipodeans, not even their names. And this, after having earlier turned down several strong British applicants on the basis of wanting to keep their party small. In the first instalment of his autobiography *That Untravelled World*, Shipton recalled:

> I soon began to regret this [decision] … I found it far from
> easy to explain my totally irrational actions to my companions.

---

[*] A Sherpa who climbed to high altitude was given the title 'Tiger' and a badge/medal by the Himalayan Club.

> They could not altogether hide their dismay, though they were
> too polite to express it … My momentary caprice was to have
> far reaching results.[*]

Interesting also in this regard was the revelation by Lowe, one of the two who missed out, which he made to Ward when they were on Everest two years later. He described how Shipton's limited invite to two New Zealanders had 'turned the four friends into a disharmonious quartet and gave lie to those naïve beliefs that only high motives and unselfish instincts flourish above the snow-line'.

Before the arrival of the two Kiwis, after a brief let up in the heavy monsoon, the four Brits with Angtarkay and rest of their porters drove out in a lorry from Jogbani on 26 August. But progress was slow, as they often had to stop and dig its wheels out of deep mud. Despite this, other than saving them many days of trekking, one advantage of using a lorry was the speed with which they crossed the jungle-covered plain known as the *terai*. It helped reduce the risk of contracting malaria which was rampant here, especially during the monsoon season.

Once the road ran out at the foothills 30 miles on, the lorry had to turn back and their difficulties really began, exacerbated by the heat and rain. According to Shipton: 'It was, in fact, the most arduous trek I have ever done through the inhabited regions of the Himalaya.' Yet it was one to remember for Michael: 'I was not particularly fit, but my spirits were high and I was excited by my first view of these hills which rise dramatically, without preamble, straight out of the plain.' Initially suffering badly from diarrhoea, he struggled up the steep paths while marvelling at the porters who looked to be 'weedy men with spindly legs and graveyard coughs'. Nevertheless, they hauled their heavy loads, up to 80lb each, with the help of their trademark headband and T-shaped stick – the latter used to rest on and relieve the weight off their backs after bursts of walking.

And walk they *all* did, as they slowly made their way towards Sola Khumbu. Often forced to take paths less trodden, they referred to their map drawn by the Survey of India to quarter-inch scale hoping to get bearings, but which they frequently found useless for lack of detail. At a town named Dhankuta, they called their first major halt to hire fresh porters but quickly found the locals reluctant to march during the rainy season. This led to a delay of four days, with Angtarkay having to follow later when others could be engaged. At all times, the *sirdar* had to keep a firm hand on his charges or risk facing rebellious behaviour. Once he hit a porter hard in the face

---

[*] Shipton also agreed to a Geological Survey of India officer, Dr Dutt, attaching himself to the expedition, although this appointment was uncontroversial.

before tying him up, leading Ward to observe: 'This quickened the rest as Angtarkay was a great deal smaller than they.'

When they reached the Arun River, from a nearby ridge Michael caught a glimpse of the Himalayas and Everest, still more than 100 miles away. Crossing the now-swollen river by ferry was another unforgettable experience. The 'ferry' turned out to be a simple hollowed-out canoe manned by two paddlers up front, and another who steered from the stern. Loading up to seven passengers at a time with their luggage, they cast off and paddled furiously, attempting to cross to with as little drift as possible. This manoeuvre was important because, after reaching the opposite bank some 100yds away, they had to physically haul their canoe back upriver before paddling downstream again to return to their starting point. The crew displayed their skill during the exercise, using a few deft strokes to avoid being swept downstream to the rapids below. Nevertheless, to ferry the entire party and their baggage took ten crossings and the best part of a day.

The waterways did provide some relief from the overbearing heat during the march, as the visitors would plunge in and sit soaking whenever they encountered a safe backwater. Even the porters, reluctant at first as they were inherently afraid of water, soon joined in. To keep cool while walking, the climbers stripped down to shorts and sandshoes, with each sheltering under an umbrella. Their minimal clothing also made it easier to spot any leeches attached to their skin. All the while they constantly battled diarrhoea, as sanitation among the locals was non-existent – the villages could be smelt long before they were seen.

After the British party had been on the trail for a fortnight, the New Zealanders caught up with them on 8 September at a small town named Dingla beyond the Arun River. They were fit and well acclimatised from their recent expedition to the Garhwal Himalayas. Still in disbelief at their good fortune, the pair were also in awe of Shipton and apprehensive about meeting the others. Hillary would recall this meeting in his first book *High Adventure*:

> As we climbed rapidly upwards, I couldn't help wondering what the four men we were meeting would be like … But these Englishmen – for all I knew they might shave every day; they might be sticklers for the right thing. We'd have to smarten up a bit and watch our language … My first feeling [on seeing them] was one of relief. I have rarely seen a more disreputable bunch, and my visions of changing for dinner faded away for ever.

As to Ed's first impression of Michael, he saw before him 'a well-built young chap with an easy impetuous manner'. Ward, who was finding the local food 'dull and hard to digest', was impressed by the southerners from a different perspective:

> From the way they bounded up the hill and the ease with which they wolfed down a horrid meal of boiled rice and indeterminate green vegetables they were both in training and used to the squalid aspects of Himalayan travel.

The full complement now pushed on together up the foothills heading towards Namche Bazaar, the main centre of Sola Khumbu and the last stop on the old trade route between Eastern Nepal and Tibet. The whole way there, Angtarkay managed to find them lodgings with locals at night. As Murray remarked: 'If there were any unfriendly people in Nepal we never met them.' This hospitality did lead to their sleeping bags often becoming infested with insects, but sharing a roof was much appreciated by the climbers. Their tents would not have coped with the full fury of the monsoon, although not all of the foreigners were discomfited to the same degree:

> Hillary retained vivid memories of one miserable night spent with Shipton under a flimsy bamboo shelter in pouring rain. The veteran explorer lay back in a damp sleeping bag, umbrella over his head to catch drips, smoking a pipe and reading a novel, as content as if he were reclining in an easy chair before a fire.*

Despite this being the worst part of the journey, the tropical forest teemed with beautiful birds and insects, their sound almost deafening at times. When they could, they caught magnificently coloured butterflies and beetles for the National History Museum in London. Finding a pathway through the jungle proved difficult, as the party often had to hack its way through dense undergrowth infested with bloodsucking leeches.† These were more than an irritant, latching onto the body and gorging themselves until wrenched away or burnt off by a cigarette stub, leaving behind sores which would not heal until they could dry out after the rains ended. When that happy day

---

* As related by Philip Temple in his book *The World at their Feet.*

† A leech releases an anaesthetic on attaching to the skin to prevent the host from sensing its presence, while its saliva contains a potent anticoagulant to ensure prolonged bleeding as the parasite continues to feed.

finally arrived on 20 September, Ward began the entry in his diary with: 'The end to the monsoon!'

Just two days before, the expedition had experienced its worst day of the march, and one which could have been fatal for some. They crossed a pass over 10,000ft high and arrived at a village only to learn the bridge across the swollen river below had recently washed away. A temporary one was being put up further downstream by a local man, by placing a few tree trunks lashed together with green bark onto rocks. It was built over a formidable cataract and held in place by pressure from the river itself, which was rising swiftly. After cutting a path through the thick undergrowth wide enough for the porters with their loads, the party descended the gorge to this rickety bridge. With no other alternative across, the climbers helped the porters before crossing over themselves; and only just in time as the structure was washed away moments after the last person, their leader Shipton, stepped onto the other side.

But the day's events weren't over yet. As the party zigzagged their way up the other side of the steep and overgrown gorge, someone accidentally disturbed a hornets' nest. Michael was painfully stung on the hand and shoulder, while some porters suffered worse with swollen faces and eyes which soon developed into acute fever. He quickly treated those affected, especially after being told that five stings could kill a man.

When the porters were stung, they dropped their loads and leapt off the track with one of their number disappearing altogether. After he didn't reappear, it was suspected he may have tumbled all the way to the riverbed. While Angtarkay was dispatched to seek help from a nearby village, the others searched frantically at the base of the cliff but found no sign of the battered corpse they expected recover. To everyone's relief, the porter was eventually discovered. As it turned out, he hadn't fallen over the edge but had retreated to a cave instead, suffering high fever.

With the hornets and leeches left behind, on 22 September the expedition marched into Namche Bazaar, two weeks later than planned due to the unrelenting monsoon. The only other mishap here involved another stinging insect. This time one of the party lost consciousness temporarily after eating local honey – it seems Nepalese honey is poisonous whenever its bees feed on rhododendrons.* And although it couldn't quite be counted as a 'mishap', all the climbers were worse for wear after partaking of the large quantities of *chang* (a type of beer) and *rakshi* (fermented *chang*). The

---

* Later, when Ward had to attend to Dr Dutt after he collapsed with a suspected
  heart attack, this also turned out to be a case of eating bad local honey.

drinks were pressed upon them by welcoming locals from the day they set foot in the Sherpas' homeland.

Michael thought *chang* looked 'a little like vomit' but once he acquired a taste for it, he found it refreshing. Over the next three days, while the team sorted out its stores and gear, he worked as a doctor among the villagers, armed with only a stethoscope and a small amount of medicines. He also made home visits to more distant families, who would otherwise rarely receive any medical attention. His fellow climbers, too, continued to need various levels of care: Tom was experiencing breathing difficulties and a sore throat; while the New Zealanders suffered from lingering dysentery – although this doesn't seem to have stopped the pair accepting their share of *chang*.

The village of Namche Bazaar, located over 12,000ft above sea level, was made up of around sixty houses at the time. Ward found it to be a 'disappointing place, unusually dirty and smelly even for this region' (unlike the town it is today, with modern facilities and a haven for trekkers). In contrast, he described the three-day walk to the base of the Khumbu Glacier as 'one of the most memorable experiences that I have ever had'. Their first stop, the remote Buddhist monastery at Thyangboche (or Tengboche), lived up to its hype: earlier mountaineers had described it as one of the most beautiful places on Earth.

From the monastery's grounds, they gazed up in awe at the stunning panoramic views of the high Himalayas, including the Everest group and, even closer almost overhanging the monastery, Ama Dablam (or Amadablam, 22,349ft). The latter is a spectacular peak with which, although Michael did not know it then, his name would be forever associated in years to come.

With sufficient supplies for two weeks reconnaissance and some handpicked Sherpas, the climbers approached the glacier and planned their next move; Ward recalls: 'I was overwhelmed by the scale which was unimaginably beyond anything I had experienced.' At this stage Shipton and others were still pessimistic, as noted in the expedition report he published on their return: 'If, as we expected, there proved to be no practicable route, we would undertake an extensive exploration of the main range, the southern side of which was almost entirely unknown.'

After setting up Base Camp around 18,000ft near the foot of the icefall, they split up into three groups. Two teams examined the sides of the Khumbu Glacier for a possible route up while the third climbed the side of a nearby mountain, Pumori (23,507ft), to study the icefall as a whole and see whether they could spot a way through. Neither Michael's group nor the other made much headway along either side of the glacier, but the two climbers on Pumori, Shipton and Hillary, struck gold. From a height of just

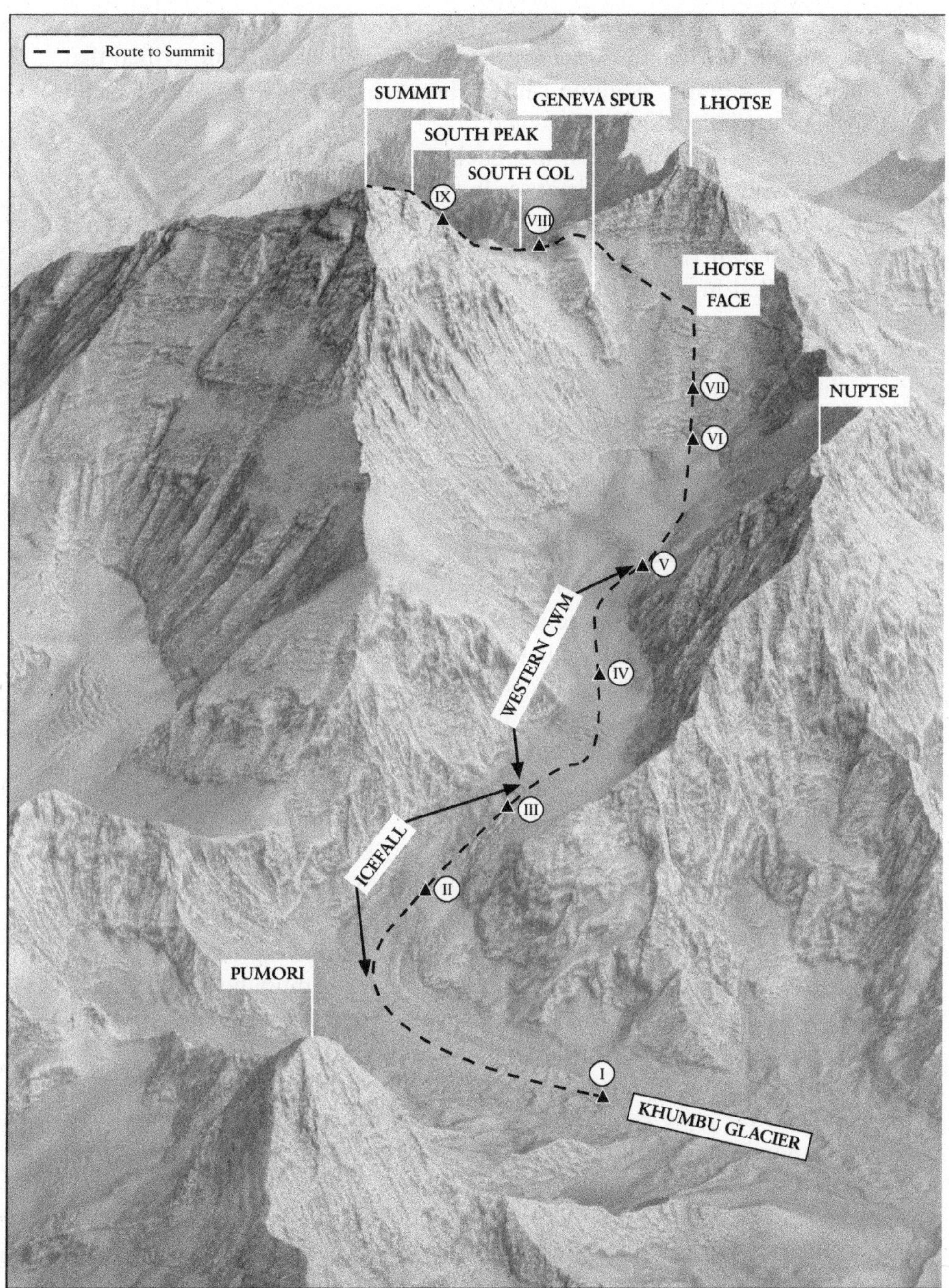


**Map 2. Reconnaissance and Ascent of Mount Everest 1951 and '53**
(based on 3D map created by Tom Patterson)

over 20,000ft, with powerful binoculars they were able to see up the icefall and along the full length of the Western Cwm. Hillary later described that moment in his book: 'Shipton said, "There's a route there!" And I could hear the note of disbelief in his voice.'

When they brought the news back to the others, Ward remembers thinking: 'Although we could not see the route above the South Col a serious attempt on Everest from this side was now possible, and all our doubts and fears vanished. It was a good feeling.' On a personal level, in *Everest*, he briefly recalled his own emotion: 'It was a great relief to me since I had cajoled this expedition into existence.' Shipton, too, was finally convinced, although with some qualms: 'The sudden discovery of a practicable route from the West Cwm to the South Col was most exciting. But we had come here to study the ice-fall, and this occupation soon sobered our spirits.'

They soon realised there was no way of bypassing the icefall by climbing around its steep sides. These were deemed too difficult and dangerous, leaving the party no option but to find a way through. Michael described what they faced: 'The lower part of the Khumbu glacier was a horrible maze of ice lumps and was covered in unstable stones. To carry loads up this way was to have a glimpse into purgatory.'

The climbers appreciated what was at stake in terms of risk, especially for their Sherpas. Unlike Alpine peaks, which can be ascended relatively quickly with small parties, back then a high Himalayan mountain was only attempted using heavily laden porters. These men had to retrace the route multiple times as they ferried essential supplies to camps fixed at increasing heights. The risk level, therefore, from recrossing a dangerous section such as an unstable icefall was magnified beyond comparison. The chance of losing many lives in the process was ever-present. Thus, the need to find a safe passage was imperative before the climbers could attempt the comparatively easier sections of the cwm and continue upwards.

Shipton's grave doubts about the icefall were compounded by the risk from avalanches which were likely to sweep through from the towering peaks above. In his report, he reminded future expeditions: 'The rules of mountaineering must be rigidly observed.' His caution stemmed from the mountaineering code established in prewar Britain which imposed strict limits on any level of risk taking. However, Ward's record of when the team came to discuss this aspect is interesting:

> Ed and Earle took a slightly different view and I think that probably the feelings of those members of the party who had not previously been to the Himalaya, was that we were perfectly prepared to 'give it a go'.

Over the next few days, despite determined attacks to penetrate the icefall, the climbers were defeated by bad weather and often hip-deep snow. On the fourth day, one group almost managed to get through, but close to the icefall's upper end the snow avalanched. Earle was only saved from being swept away because he was roped up to Shipton and a Sherpa named Pasang. Between them, they managed to halt his headlong plunge into a crevasse. Shaken by this near-disaster and the constant threat from avalanches, the team decided it wiser to retreat for now, despite getting to within 30ft of the top of the final wall. They would return in a fortnight, allowing the monsoon snow to stabilise in the meantime. They did at least walk away heartened by the solid progress made, having practically climbed the entire icefall in a single day.

Shipton planned to put their two-week hiatus to good use, as he felt some of the others needed to acclimatise further and get fitter. Ward was one of those feeling the effects of altitude, unlike the New Zealanders who had already spent three months in the Himalayas. The pair's overall skill and mature approach to climbing, gained in the mountains of their home country, had already made Shipton's impulsive decision seem an inspired one.

When the party split up this time, Shipton and Hillary explored south of Everest, while Ward, together with the three other climbers and six Sherpas, headed west. Their plan was to reconnoitre an adjoining glacier, the passes beyond it, and the flank of nearby Cho Oyu.* This was Michael's first opportunity at high mountain exploration and his excitement is evident:

> I think the uppermost feeling was an intense curiosity to see what the next bit of country looked like … The urge to go on and on, continually finding out what is round the corner, or over a pass, together with the pleasure of seeing it all fit into place, like a giant's jigsaw, became to me one of the most fascinating aspects of mountaineering and this was my first experience of it.

To complete this jigsaw, he started drawing simple maps freehand, taking bearings with a compass. It marked the beginning of his use of surveying techniques once employed by the Pundits. The information he gathered here would be incorporated into the first modern map of the Everest region published a decade later for the Royal Geographical Society.

---

* Cho Oyu, the world's sixth-highest mountain (26,864ft) lies 18 miles northwest of Everest. Its name in Tibetan means Goddess of Turquoise.

Following their period of acclimatisation, with Ward and the other Englishmen now markedly fitter, the climbers reassembled on 26 October determined to beat the icefall this time. Shipton and Hillary, having returned a week earlier than the others, had used the opportunity to re-establish Base Camp higher up at the foot of the icefall. They even hauled and set up the twelve-man Arctic tent Michael had begged from the Guards Depot, which the party found luxurious after their tiny tents. Upon entering the icefall, Eric and Ed discovered that within the last fortnight new crevasses had appeared in this constantly changing landscape. Even more worrying, they saw how over one area many ice towers and cliffs had collapsed, as if tumbled by an earthquake, as Shipton noted:

> It was impossible to avoid the sober reflection that if we had [previously] persisted with the establishment of a line of communication through the ice-fall and if a party had happened to be in the area at the time, it was doubtful whether any of them would have survived. Moreover, the same thing might happen on other parts of the ice-fall.[*]

This time, all the climbers went up Pumori to examine the jumble of shattered blocks with binoculars, before once again splitting up to maximise their chances of finding a way through. Eventually, with Bourdillon cutting steps up the perilous last stage, the whole team managed to force a pathway and finally stand above the icefall, on the lip of the Western Cwm.

Unfortunately, as Murray recounted, to their profound disappointment they were 'confronted by the biggest crevasse that we had ever seen … at the narrowest a hundred feet'. It stretched right across the cwm, and beyond it were indications of others, equally formidable. Without sufficient rope or time left in the day, short of moving Base Camp up and mounting a complex crossing over many days, there was little more they could do for now, as Ward wrote in *Everest*:

> Eventually we gave up. I felt frustrated by this decision, for here was a good piece of technical climbing which, as I was getting fitter, I would have liked to try. Bourdillon felt the same but both of our sirdars, Angtharkay and Pasang, were adamant that to ask Sherpas to carry loads through the icefall

---

[*] Of the four chapters comprising Shipton's report, one whole chapter was devoted to 'The Ice-Fall' and their battle to overcome it.

in such bad conditions would be asking too much; so, with deep reluctance, we descended.

The next day was 'decision day' for the team. Before it reconvened, Ward and Bourdillon scaled a nearby ridge looking for an alternative route while Shipton and Hillary revisited the ice barrier, but neither group was successful. Yet here was a golden opportunity to go even further, with the higher slopes of Everest tantalisingly close.* The decision to retreat, therefore, was a gut-wrenching one, but made by the team as a whole. Shipton ended his report on 'The Ice-Fall' saying: 'There was nothing for it but to submit, hoping that we would get another chance in spring.' An attempt then would probably be a better option, after winter snowfall had safely bridged many of the crevasses now exposed.

Ward also believed their decision 'was correct and sensible' at the time. Twenty years later, and with the benefit of hindsight, he had second thoughts:

> Looking back on it, with greater experience, there is no doubt that we should have continued. Subsequently I have made decisions to continue in much more dangerous circumstances – decisions which reflect both a change in my attitude towards mountaineering as well as a better understanding of conditions in the Himalaya. In modern mountaineering objective dangers are now accepted much more readily than in the past.

Although Michael was particularly disappointed 'not to be able to finish the job properly', the expedition he had initiated had achieved its overall objective: it confirmed by actual reconnaissance on Everest that the route discovered 'on paper' in England was feasible, and the dreaded icefall was not insurmountable.

---

* In *That Untravelled World* Shipton wrote that among Ward's initial team 'there was some talk of trying to reach the summit' but neither Michael nor anyone else mentions such a plan.

6

# Yeti Tracks and Tibetan Trouble

After the reconnaissance party returned to Namche Bazaar, the climbers prepared to make their way home by way of Kathmandu. They broke up into three pairs, each taking with them some of the Sherpas: Hillary and Riddiford headed home immediately, having already been away for six months; Bourdillon and Murray decided to go north first and explore Nangpa La, the high pass leading into Tibet; while Shipton and Ward set off northwest towards a large area marked 'Unexplored' on their map. But if Michael was expecting an uneventful trek back to complete his first Himalayan adventure, he was mistaken – there were two more noteworthy incidents waiting to play out, and for quite different reasons.

Earlier, he had observed how, beyond the snow line, exploration time was essentially determined by the weight one could carry in terms of food, fuel, and a tent. He had long discussions with Shipton, that great proponent of small expeditions, who believed such ventures to be inherently more flexible and thus more likely to succeed. This also meant sacrificing weight for speed, and Ward was told how two climbers and a porter, squeezing into a two-man tent at night, should be able to range widely for two weeks.

Shipton would now demonstrate his method to Ward, taking only one Sherpa with them and ten days' provisions. Sen Tensing had carried for Shipton previously, during a prewar Everest excursion when he earned the nickname Foreign Sportsman. This was because he wouldn't ever remove the mountain gear he had been issued, proudly wearing his foreign clothes even in hot weather. As Michael wryly observed about the resulting odour: '[It] seemed to be more pungent than in other Sherpas. After a few days I didn't notice it, and I am sure that we smelt as strong to him.'

By this stage Ward was in peak condition. From a medical perspective, he was experiencing firsthand the benefits of good acclimatisation, both physically and mentally, and described the difference as remarkable. He finally understood why the New Zealanders had fared so well at the start of the expedition compared to the rest, except for Shipton who acclimatised rapidly from years of experience.

From a lower peak beyond the village of Chule, Shipton and Ward were able to get another view of Cho Oyu, this time its western flank, and began to mark out a possible route up its slopes. (This quick reconnaissance turned out to be of more importance than they imagined, as Shipton would lead a full expedition to climb Cho Oyu the following year.)

The next day the trio headed west over two unnamed geographical features, a pass dominated by its striking mountain. These they named Menlung La and Menlung Tse (or Menlungtse, 23,570ft), after a nearby river, the Menlung Chu.* A few miles further west lay Gaurisankar (23,440ft), a mountain once thought to be the highest in the world, and still often mistaken for Everest because it stands almost directly before it when viewed from Kathmandu. During this time, Michael was making a Pundit-style route survey of the area; and one cartographical outcome of this expedition would be confirmation of the geographical positions of the Menlung Tse and its neighbour Gaurisankar.

Between the Menlung peak and its pass lay a glacier with a broad snowfield, which they descended late that afternoon. Here, at a height over 16,000ft, they stumbled across a line of large footprints (see Map 1), possibly made by two creatures which Ward recalls 'Sen Tensing declared without hesitation belonged to the yeti'. He promptly related how he and other fellow Sherpas had previously seen such an animal or half wild man – popularly known in the West as the Abominable Snowman. This incident had occurred at Thyangboche two years earlier, when one was spotted from a distance of around 25yds. Sen described the creature they had witnessed as being about 5½ft tall, covered in reddish brown hair with a pointed head. Now, he was visibly upset as they continued on, and his usual practice of reciting Buddhist prayers increased in both volume and frequency.

They followed the fresh tracks, probably not more than a day old, for a mile or so and Shipton photographed them before leaving the glacier. Two days later, when Bourdillon and Murray were returning from their trip north to rejoin them, they came across the same tracks. Tom also took photographs as the pair followed the prints for almost 2 miles.† Murray recorded this event in his diary and included it in an article he wrote soon

---

* In Tibetan, *la* means pass, *tse* denotes a peak and *chu* a stream or river.

† Although Ward stated: 'Bill and Tom ... had not seen the "footprints", which presumably had melted', Murray later clarified they had, but did not get an opportunity to mention it to the others.

afterwards for the *Alpine Journal* (1952), describing the reconnaissance expedition. Twenty years later, Ward wrote:

> The incident of the footprints did not appear to us to be of any great significance but our photographs have been debated ever since. They form the best set that have been taken of this 'mythical' animal's tracks and opened up controversy about the yeti which goes on spasmodically to this day.

Shipton took the four snaps that were made public on their return, noting: 'I have in the past found many sets of these curious footprints and have tried to follow them, but have always lost them on the moraine or rocks at the side of the glacier.' The last two pages of his expedition report each carried a full page photograph. The first image was a closeup with Ward's ice axe laid beside it for scale, below which a lengthy caption stated:

> Footprint of the 'Yeti' found on a glacier of the Menlung basin. In general the tracks were distorted and obviously enlarged by melting; but where, as in this case, the snow overlying the glacier was thin, the imprint was very well preserved and the form of the foot could be seen in detail. When the tracks crossed a crevasse we could see clearly how the creature, in jumping across, had dug its toes in to prevent itself from slipping back.

The second shot had the simpler caption: 'Ward standing beside the line of "Yeti" tracks.' One of the two unpublished photographs shows his boot next to a footprint. In *Everest*, Ward notes his shoe size as 42 (or 8½ British), from which he estimates 'the tracks were about 10–12 inches long, but broader than a normal 4½ inch wide boot'. (The following year, the Swiss spring party encountered tracks around the Khumbu Glacier with similar measurements, and in autumn one of their porters claimed to have been attacked by a yeti in the same area.)

When Shipton's report with these images was released, it caused an unholy stir, both among the public and the scientific community. His photographs were published in newspapers, science journals and popular magazines around the world, and their 'yeti story' often overshadowed the other outcomes and success of the expedition itself. This should not have come as a surprise, considering that among all mythical creatures the yeti has received the most attention in scientific journals, including top-tier publications.

Unfortunately, more light cannot be shed about the encounter in 1951 from Ward's expedition diary as it ends abruptly on 28 October, the day before the whole party decided to retreat from the icefall. Although some dates are listed after this period, the pages are curiously blank. It certainly raises the possibility that Michael may have made entries in another notebook – if so, this record has been lost.

Bill Murray, before he died in 1996, made a point of revisiting this incident in his autobiography.[*] He recalled when he and Tom met up with the others and discussed the tracks: '[We] found all three in a state of subdued excitement, recognisably genuine as they described the detail'. Bill also pointed out:

> I repeat this old story because in recent years it has been questioned and Shipton not alive to defend. In a *Sunday Times* article,[†] it was suggested that Shipton might have been a practical joker. I can refute that. Michael Ward and Sen Tensing were there too. [Tom Bourdillon had died in 1956.] Eric Shipton, like all of us, had a sense of humour, but we were not practical jokers or party to public deceit.

Murray may have also been responding after hearing of an interview given by Ed Hillary in 1984 to writer and mountaineer Jim Perrin, quoted again in his book *Shipton and Tilman*. During the interview, Ed – who had already left for home when the tracks were found – suggested the whole thing was an elaborate joke gone too far. The reignition of this controversy prompted Ward to quote Murray's denial above in his 2003 book *Everest*, to which he added the following comment:

> It is to be hoped that this account by Bill Murray, a universally accepted figure,[‡] will finally put an end to unworthy speculation that the story of the yeti tracks reflected some sort of tasteless joke conducted by Shipton, with a connivance of myself.

There had been another suggestion in that *Sunday Times Magazine* article that Shipton may have perpetuated the joke because he was still bitter about

---

* Published posthumously by his wife in 2002.
† By journalist Peter Gillman on 10 December 1989, who repeats his 'hoax' theory in an article for the *Alpine Journal* (2001).
‡ Murray had been described by some in the climbing fraternity as the 'Sir Galahad of the peaks'.

the leadership debacle leading up to the 1953 Everest expedition. However, as Ward previously pointed out in the *Alpine Journal* (1999), Shipton's account had been recorded the year *before* his dismissal, adding: 'This was no hoax and the events occurred exactly and precisely as described in Shipton's book on the Everest Reconnaissance and by myself in this article.'

It is not difficult to see how the discovery of these footprints in the snow had minds racing with the tantalising possibility that a half-human creature close to extinction – perhaps man's missing link with apes – was still walking the high Himalayas. In fact, similar tracks had also been found during expeditions to Everest from the Tibetan side, both in 1935 on the Rongbuk Glacier (again photographed by Shipton) and in 1921 on Lhakpa La. All these finds would trigger various 'yeti hunts' and arguments raging between the people of these mountains, the climbers, and the scientists. But more will be said later about the biggest of these hunts, led by Hillary and with Ward involved, albeit indirectly.

The day after seeing the footprints, before Ward and his two companions were joined by Bourdillon, Murray and their Sherpas, they went exploring south of Menlung Tse. Ward happened to look west across to a group of mountains he seemed to recognise, and then quizzed Shipton: 'Aren't they in Tibet, if they are the Lapche Kang?' To which he received the sobering answer: 'Yes, and if they are, we are.'

In his report, Shipton made no mention of this incursion into Tibet, probably for fear of not wanting to spark a diplomatic incident, particularly given his most recent assignment as consul-general in Communist China and his forced departure. Neither would he have wanted to create difficulties for future expeditions travelling into these border regions of what was now Chinese-occupied Tibet. But straying across the border did, in fact, expose his party to difficulty and danger. Years later, both Ward and Murray recalled this incident in their respective autobiographies – here's what happened:

Not being certain of their geographical position, as their map was practically useless here, they had to await the arrival of Angtarkay. He was familiar with a trail further on which was used as a minor trade route between Nepal and Tibet, running along the Rongshar Chu flowing roughly north-south. Since the Menlung Chu was its tributary river, by marching north along it they would arrive at this trail and could then turn back south towards Nepal. However, such a plan would mean having to first trespass even further into Tibet. The other alternative, of course, was to walk back towards Namche Bazaar, but this would add days to their journey and wasn't favoured by anyone.

While they waited for Angtarkay, Shipton and Ward decided to reconnoitre directly southwards, hoping to find a pathway to another river, the Rolwaling Chu, which flowed east-west and lay entirely within Nepal. It was along its valley that Hillary and Riddiford had previously returned to Kathmandu, so locating it would solve their dilemma. Climbing higher to look out over the surrounding cliffs and pine forests, they could just make out a shimmering line below, but to reach it would mean an almost vertical descent of some 7,000ft. After much discussion, taking into consideration the time required to find a way down and the uncertainty of this river being the Rolwaling Chu, they decided to return to camp. Here, they found Murray's group had arrived.

The next day the combined party debated their best course of action. Should they continue south and locate the Rolwaling Valley, or go north, deeper into forbidden Tibet and use the Rongshar Valley instead? Although the first option would be challenging due to the steep descent involved, Ward was keen to 'give it a go'. Shipton favoured the easier route but was worried about the risk of tangling with border guards and the consequences if they were apprehended.

As Murray recalled: 'When these fears were put to Ang Tharkay, he bristled, and angrily declared that we talked nonsense. Chinese power did not extend to such remote areas.' The other Sherpas could not understand the fears of the foreigners either, as they were used to moving and trading freely across this border. Yet Shipton was particularly reluctant, knowing he would be treated as a spy if caught due to his years of diplomatic work in China.* He was persuaded to do so partly because he thought they would probably be the first group of Westerners to pass through the Rongshar Valley.

They next day they set off for the Tibetan border, still 20 miles away. Initially, they marched north up the Menlung Valley, walking through stands of pine and rhododendrons as they passed between the twin towers of Menlung Tse and Gaurisankar. Upon reaching the Rongshar Chu around six o'clock, they hid in some woods waiting for darkness to fall, as the Topte *dzong* (meaning 'fort') stood just beyond the junction of the two

---

* In his book *Shipton and Tilman*, Jim Perrin goes even further, suggesting: '[Had] he fallen into Chinese revolutionary hands he would immediately have been perceived as a spy, and in all likelihood have been shot'.

rivers. It guarded the entrance to the twisting gorge they would need to pass through when they turned south for Nepal.

Later that day, when everyone was resting after a meal, some women gathering firewood chanced upon the group but didn't pay them much attention. Once it was dark, they slowly crept along the narrow track using whatever moonlight filtered onto the floor of the deep gorge. Crossing an old cantilever bridge and skirting a small village, they managed to pass undetected despite the loud barking of dogs. By two o'clock the next morning, they were all exhausted after nearly sixteen hours of trekking, the last few over uneven ground in near-darkness. They were staying upright almost by instinct alone and desperately needed a few hours of sleep. After putting the last village behind them, they managed to convince Shipton of this, even though he preferred continuing to the border under the cover of darkness.

When the party awoke, it was clear they had overslept, as the sun was up and any advantage lost. Hurrying on, they hoped to reach the frontier before anyone discovered their presence but soon heard shouts behind them. Quickly they were overtaken by seven Tibetan militiamen brandishing swords and ancient firearms. Apparently, the commander of the fort had been alerted by the women after their encounter in the woods, and the climbers' bootprints in the snow at dawn had confirmed their intrusion. Unable to produce any paperwork, the militiamen demanded the whole party return with them. And not just to Topte either, but to the larger *dzong* in Tingri located 60 miles inside Tibet for interrogation by Chinese troops. This was an altogether more daunting prospect, and the incident was fast turning into a nightmare – Murray described what occurred next:

> We asked Ang Tharkay to try bribery. We had only a thousand
> rupees left in the expedition's kitty (£75), and feared that this
> would not be nearly enough to buy our freedom. Ang Tharkay
> took firm charge. To our near-dismay, he opened the bidding
> at 5 rupees. The Tibetans' leader could not contain his anger.

A long and fierce argument erupted, which the climbers watched with growing trepidation from a short distance. When he finally came back to consult with them, Angtarkay said the guards were demanding ten rupees per foreigner before they would release them. Then, as suggested by the *sirdar*, the guards would go back and inform their commander the intruders had already escaped across the border. Although this seemed a perfectly acceptable solution to the climbers, for Angtarkay this was far too large a sum and he balked at paying it. This time when he returned to continue negotiating, both sides seemed to be on the verge of exchanging blows when suddenly, after a few more words from him, there was silence followed by smiles all round. The guards had agreed to split the difference and accept seven rupees each.

Soon afterward, the party walked across the frontier bridge into Nepal and eight days later were in Kathmandu. Michael's first Himalayan expedition – three glorious months of exploration and climbing – was over. The future, too, couldn't be brighter as far as attempting Everest was concerned. There was every expectation the route which their reconnaissance had confirmed would, with improved snow conditions next spring, lead a team from Britain to the top. However, as he would soon realise: 'A nasty shock was waiting for us.'

# 7

# Preparation for 1953

lying back to London, Ward was stunned to learn someone else had stolen the march on British hopes of being the first to attain the 'Third Pole'. He later described his first reaction to this news: 'I was incandescent with rage to find the Swiss had obtained permission to attempt Everest in 1952.' However, he went on to add: 'But this turned to our advantage.'*

The story of how this advantage was gained recalls the pioneering developments in the field of high altitude medicine and physiology. Tied up with this history is Ward's own involvement in finding the solution to a challenge which came to be known as 'the last thousand feet' – a glass ceiling of sorts on Everest that had stubbornly resisted being broken thus far. Earlier, even as he was preparing to go there in 1951, Michael was thinking beyond this reconnaissance to the ultimate goal itself:

> There were two obvious obstacles: first a new route from Nepal had to be found and the second was medical. This was evidenced by the total failure of each expedition mounted by the Himalayan Committee to solve the medical and physiological problem of 'the last thousand feet'.

To tackle the latter problem, he contacted staff at the Medical Research Council (MRC) in London. Convinced that supplementary oxygen would be essential, Ward was searching for the medical proof necessary to convince the mountaineering fraternity.

Since the early British expeditions of the 1920s, a fierce debate had been raging in mountaineering circles about the use of oxygen to succeed on Everest. Disagreement centred on whether this aid was in keeping with the spirit of climbing, and the prickly issue of what constituted 'sportsmanship'.

---

* From *A Petrean on Everest 1951–53*, as is his next quote explaining the 'two obvious obstacles'.

Many well-respected mountaineers at the time had spoken out against its use. Frank Smythe had summed up their feeling on this subject when he said:

> I would prefer to fail on that mountain without oxygen than I would to climb it with oxygen, for to my mind the whole charm of mountaineering lies in the employment of skill and energy with the minimum of artificial aid. It is the climbing, not the getting up that matters most in mountaineering.

Other climbers, especially those who understood the impact of extreme altitude on the human body, thought otherwise, as Ward noted in *Everest*:

> In all, there had been fifteen deaths on Everest expeditions [before 1953] an unacceptable mortality rate of five percent. It was decided [by the Himalayan Committee], therefore, that all attempts on the summit should be made with adequate supplementary oxygen. There was no evidence that contemporary mountaineers were fit enough to climb the peak relying on acclimatisation alone. That achievement [by Habeler and Messner] had to wait for 25 years until 1978.

Ward fervently believed that other than finding a feasible route, only by overcoming the medical and physiological problems beyond 28,000ft could the groundwork be laid for a successful summit attempt.

The previous year, during frantic preparations a month before departure, he had met Tom's father Dr Robert Bourdillon, who was involved in medical research. As well as assisting him to prepare the expedition's medical supplies list, as mentioned earlier, he introduced Michael to staff at the laboratories of the MRC. Here, two scientists would soon prove invaluable: Dr Griffith Pugh and his boss Professor Otto Edholm, who headed up the recently established Division of Human Physiology.

Ward made an appointment to visit Pugh late in 1950, taking his research documents along with his collection of photographs of Everest. He found him lying in an ice-cooled water bath in his cluttered laboratory, conducting experiments on himself studying the effects of hypothermia. Griff, who was notoriously absentminded, had forgotten all about their meeting and was in a state of near-collapse when roused. Later, in his equally messy office, the two viewed images of Michael's proposed route up Everest. Ward was somewhat taken aback when Pugh declared matter-of-factly that barring the icefall, since he (once an Olympic skier) could ski down this route, mountaineers should be able to climb up it.

Although Ward's first impression of Pugh was of a rather shambolic scientist, they got on well together during their many subsequent meetings. Standing over 6ft tall, with light blue eyes and startling red hair, he summed up Griff's physical appearance as being: 'In all an arresting sight.' A mountaineer himself, Pugh was *never* one to suffer fools.

He was immediately impressed by Ward's grasp of high altitude physiology, while Michael appreciated not being talked down to by someone who was clearly an expert in this field and sixteen years his senior. Although now a clinical physiologist rather than a practising doctor, Pugh used similar methods to physicians in diagnosing and treating ailments associated with excessive cold and altitude. Ward also noted his approach was clearly innovative but well tested out in the field.

With the benefit of Pugh's expertise and undivided attention, Ward was able to discuss the many medical problems to be faced on Everest, ranging from a variety of lesser illnesses to those which could be life-threatening. Griff was already familiar with these conditions through first-hand experience during his wartime service in the RAMC, when he became an expert in mountain survival. The pair carefully examined a table Michael had been preparing describing the symptoms of altitude such as fatigue and frostbite. Investigating the problems that caused these symptoms, then finding solutions to prevent them, would sum up the vital work Pugh would undertake in the lead up to Everest.

The overriding challenge was one of reduced oxygen level, which is roughly halved by the time a person goes from sea level to 18,000ft, and drops by two-thirds in the thin air on Everest's summit. This causes climbers to pant harder as they gasp for oxygen, which in itself becomes increasingly tiring. Coupled with the physical demand posed by steep slopes, it forces them to stop more frequently as they gain height, but such rest periods slow down their rate of ascent dramatically.

Edward Norton, for example, after attaining his record 28,126ft, described the experience: 'The trouble was that one went so miserably slowly uphill … I only mounted something under 100ft and progressed horizontally about 200yds in my last hour'.

The critical question for climbers nearing Everest's summit as they invariably slowed down, was whether they could reach the top in sufficient time to return to their last camp before nightfall. The stark alternative was being caught out in the open, exposed to intense cold, often fierce winds, and almost certain death.

On the face of it, the use of supplementary oxygen should greatly assist climbers in preventing this chain of events as they approached the top. Ward's big questions revolved around: why then, even with its aid, had the best of them failed to summit on previous expeditions? Was it giving them the boost expected; and if not, why not? And why had most complained afterwards of the extra effort required to carry their oxygen sets? Pugh wondered whether the weight of the sets was the problem. By way of a straightforward yet clever experiment, he provided the answer, as Ward described in *Everest*:

> A simple series of tests on a bicycle ergometer, with myself as a subject carrying weights of up to 40lbs (equivalent to the weight of an oxygen set), showed conclusively that a higher flow rate of oxygen was needed both to compensate for the weight of the set and to increase climbing rate.

Ward went on to note: 'The increased flow rate transformed climbing performance on Everest and was the main reason for our success in 1953.'

With a good start made on the scientific aspects of overcoming 'the last thousand feet', Ward had departed for Nepal on the 1951 Reconnaissance with the intention of confirming his proposed route, although finding a solution to the last thousand feet was never far from his mind. It would require a holistic approach, going beyond the use of supplementary oxygen and dealing with other medical issues such as diet and dehydration.

During the reconnaissance, with his doctor's hat on, he had carefully observed all the climbers, keeping track of their general health in his diary; for example, noting how their individual weights altered over time. He now began formulating some basic concepts around how the human body coped at altitude. First, it was clear that one's fitness improved with acclimatisation. Furthermore, he observed that at greater heights general wellbeing became more important when undertaking hard physical or mental labour, whereas at lower altitudes one seemed to get by. On any summit attempt of Everest, contrary to the prevailing view, he believed the technical climbing difficulty was going to be relatively minor compared to three other factors: combatting the extreme cold, wind, and altitude.

In his long talks with Shipton, Michael had been amused by 'Eric's maxim that the real danger of a Himalayan expedition was of getting bedsores rather than having an accident'. The veteran maintained this was because a Himalayan day amounted to five hours, while the rest of the time was spent in one's sleeping bag. His old partner Tilman thought much the same, suggesting a box of books was a mountaineer's most cherished load and bed sores his occupational disease.

Although he physically enjoyed their type of extended exploration, Ward was beginning to form his own views about the time he was devoting to mountaineering: 'I always felt subconsciously that something was missing. This missing element was undoubtedly an intellectual stimulus and it is difficult to pinpoint the exact reason for such a need.' Fulfilling this need would soon lead him not only towards writing about the mountains, which he unreservedly loved, but also deeper into the embryonic area of mountain medicine.

Since this was a new field of study, there were no textbooks available to consult, so Ward resorted to scouring reports from early climbers and other first-hand sources. On his return from the Himalayas in 1951, he wrote a short paper titled 'In Eastern Nepal', describing the many illnesses, diseases and epidemics he had witnessed among the locals there. It was accepted by a prestigious medical journal, *The Lancet* (1952), the first of many papers he would publish in various journals over the coming years.

By this stage, Michael felt he was 'temperamentally unsuited' for general medical practice and was determined to specialise and become a surgeon instead, reasoning: 'Perhaps surgery appealed more to my sense of the dramatic, and because I enjoyed a practical skill with determinate results.' This was an ambitious career goal, and over the next two years he would need to devote a great deal of time to further study. Consequently, he would have to put aside his newfound passion for the Himalayas if he was to pass the exacting examination process required to become a surgeon.

Meanwhile, the British climbing establishment, which had monopolised expeditions to Everest until now and misguidedly viewed the mountain as its own preserve, was recovering from the news of the Swiss coup. It soon became apparent that the Nepalese had also given its rival exclusive permission to climb both in spring and autumn – unbeknown to the Brits, they had actually applied in May 1951. In terms of technical mountaineering ability, the newcomers, with professional Alpine guides in their party, were more experienced than any British party to date. All the more reason the Brits were fearful that Swiss success on their first attempt would make them look rather foolish after their long string of failures beginning in the 1920s.

The Swiss, for their part, went out of their way to be accommodating. As in fact did Shipton, visiting them and sharing his findings and photographs from the recent reconnaissance. Since the British had already marked out a feasible route to the top, the Swiss generously proposed both countries combine resources and mount an attempt together. But to the dismay of Shipton and his fellow climbers, the Himalayan Committee declined their offer in the belief that joint leadership and mixed nationalities would be unworkable on such a large and demanding expedition. Perhaps this was wise but, given the size of the prize, nationalism no doubt played a role in the committee's stance.

Instead, it was decided to send a British team that year to another nearby peak, Cho Oyu, in preparation for its own bid the following year (*if* the Swiss were unsuccessful in their two attempts). Cho Oyu was an ideal choice, not least because Shipton and Ward had spotted a possible route towards its summit from the Nepalese side during their excursion there. At almost 27,000ft, it was certain to test the ability of members to acclimatise and climb to higher altitudes. Just as importantly, other than test the mechanics of the oxygen sets, they were to confirm the laboratory finding of Pugh and Ward: that increasing the flowrate would compensate for the extra weight of these sets and deliver the boost in performance needed.

The climbers chosen for Cho Oyu were obviously going to be frontrunners for the Everest team. So it was with great reluctance that Ward declined the place offered to him by Shipton, who was appointed to lead both expeditions. Although this decision risked his place for the bid next year, Michael had two other pressing priorities which he could not overlook. The first required him to complete two years of National Service, and the other was to advance his medical career towards becoming a surgeon.

Although the first imperative, serving in the Royal Army Medical Corps, was a straightforward matter, the second was not. It meant achieving primary fellowship, initially by passing two demanding exams, the first covering anatomy and the other physiology and pathology. The degree of difficulty involved meant extra study was required by candidates, many of whom took unpaid time off work to prepare. These assessments were a prerequisite before one could, after years of on-the-job training, attempt the third and final exam in clinical surgery to attain the coveted Fellowship of the Royal College of Surgeons. By choosing not to defer his examinations in favour of a place on the Cho Oyu team, Michael signalled his determination to become a surgeon.

On rejoining the RAMC, he returned to the Royal Herbert. Later, he was posted to another hospital in Folkestone on the south coast of England, before completing his National Service in October 1952.

Meanwhile, the Shipton-led party prepared to leave for Cho Oyu with nine climbers including Tom Bourdillon and Cam Secord, and this time three from New Zealand: Ed Hillary, George Lowe and Earle Riddiford. In addition, Griff Pugh had been selected to spearhead the research programme as part of the MRC's unwavering support for British efforts to succeed on Everest. Other than putting to bed the oxygen issue, Pugh was tasked with finding answers to the other physiological problems experienced high on the mountain. This was the first expedition of its kind, since it would combine mountaineering with medical research and conduct field experiments at high altitude.

Arriving at the base of Cho Oyu, to their immense disappointment the climbers soon realised the intended route up its southern face was too steep and simply not feasible. The only alternative was to attempt the peak from the north, but this would mean crossing over into Tibet, which they did not have permission for. They debated whether to do so anyway and take a calculated risk they would not be apprehended by border guards, even though these sentries probably already knew of the climbers' presence there.

Shipton was reluctant to take this risk, particularly after his experience the previous year when with Ward and others they had bribed their way out. The other consideration was, if they weren't as fortunate this time, a border incident might jeopardise British access to Everest the following year. The lengthy discussion that ensued over the next two days was exasperating for all concerned and often acrimonious.

In the end, the party decided not to risk venturing into Tibet and thus gave up any thoughts of ascending Cho Oyu – a frustrated Hillary would later admit: 'Afterwards I had a terrible sense of shame that we had given up so easily.' To salvage what they could, the expedition now split up into three groups to explore the surrounding region and climb a few lower peaks (except for Riddiford, who decided to return home).

Leading the third group, Pugh set up his physiological camp at 20,000ft on the Menlung La, which Ward had previously noted as a possible site for a scientific camp, close to where he and Shipton had encountered the suspected yeti footprints. Bourdillon and two other climbers assisted Pugh, faithfully undertaking his tests. He monitored all four of them as they ascended a steep snow track, first without oxygen and then at three different flowrates using open-circuit sets. This led Pugh to discover that by *doubling* the flow used by prewar expeditions – from 2 litres per minute to 4 – the expected improvement in performance was indeed delivered. The main effect of this boost would be to enable climbers to ascend above 25,000ft continuously rather than intermittently (as Hillary and Tenzing would do on Everest).

Returning home, Pugh detailed his findings in a seminal report titled *British Himalayan Expedition to Cho Oyu, 1952*, which Ward described in *Everest* as 'one of the most important in the history of scientific, high-altitude exploration'. He also noted in the *Alpine Journal* (1990): 'It is no coincidence that by 1960 every 8,000m peak had been climbed following the precepts of this report.'

In his other journal articles, too, Ward gave enormous credit to Pugh as the architect for finding solutions to the major problems caused by extreme altitude: oxygen lack (hypoxia), dehydration, hunger, mental and physical deterioration, and cold injury (hypothermia). As Michael pointed out in the *Alpine Journal* (1995): 'Unless each and every one of these factors is combated, as they were on Everest in 1953 with the scientific work, but *not* by the Swiss in 1952, then the odds against success are considerably lengthened.'

As well as discovering the optimum flowrate for using supplementary oxygen near the summit, Pugh went further still. He determined that a lower rate of 1 litre per minute would help climbers get a good night's sleep, which they otherwise found particularly difficult at extreme altitude, thus adding to their overall deterioration. (All this increased oxygen usage would be possible by filling more into alloy cylinders made from higher strength and lighter materials, which had been developed during the war by the RAF.)

On his party's return to Britain, Shipton was criticised for his leadership and the expedition to Cho Oyu considered a failure by most in the climbing establishment. But, as Ward stated in the same article above: 'In fact, nothing could have been further from the truth.' In saying this, he was referring to outcomes of the physiological programme, noting *In This Short Span*: 'Their results were of unprecedented value, for the first time the problems posed by high altitude were defined in the field. This was the decisive advantage that we in 1953 were to have over all who had gone before us.'

The debacle surrounding the change of leadership from Eric Shipton to the 'outsider' Colonel John Hunt, just months before the 1953 Everest Expedition got underway, has already been covered by most of the players involved at the time and many writers afterwards, so need not be revisited here. That Shipton's 'dumping' in favour of Hunt left a bitter aftertaste among almost everyone concerned is undoubtable. The rights and wrongs of the outcome arrived at by the Himalayan Committee, as well as the decision-making process itself, depends on one's point of view – influenced, no doubt, by the eventual success of the expedition. More so because, with the Swiss failing on both their attempts, the French gaining permission for 1954, and the Swiss again in 1955, British prestige – and not just mountaineering prestige – was at stake.

The Swiss had assembled the strongest and most experienced team to date when they arrived on Everest in the spring of 1952. On their first attempt ever, they managed to climb higher than any British expedition had done previously. Despite coming tantalisingly close, they were defeated on the final assault for two main reasons according to Ward. First, their oxygen sets were ineffective and unable to provide the summit pair, Raymond Lambert and Tenzing Norgay, the boost required. Second, the Swiss were grossly dehydrated as their stoves were unable to melt sufficient snow for drinking water, while the summit pair only had an empty tin and candle to melt a fragment of ice.* A few months later, the second Swiss attempt in autumn also failed; this time primarily due to encountering overwhelming cold and wind, as Lambert noted in his diary on that fateful day: 'It was impossible to go on in such conditions and at such a height.'

While the Swiss and Cho Oyu efforts were underway, Ward participated on some climbs around Zermatt in the Alps with four other British mountaineers over a two-week period. Shipton had organised this excursion through Alfred Gregory with the objective of identifying other potential 'Everesters' for the following year (only Gregory and Ward would eventually go). Although they experienced atrocious weather, the team managed to climb four peaks but then had to abandon a fifth, due to massive snowfall and the consequent danger from avalanches.

Michael, having developed a close relationship with Eric, was as shocked as his fellow climbers when the sudden change in Everest leadership was revealed that September. He largely stayed out of the controversy which erupted, but later pointedly stated in *Everest* that the scientific contribution by the MRC was far more important to the success of the expedition than the replacement of its leader. Ward was obviously keen to be part of the 1953 attempt. Other than being one of Britain's foremost climbers at the time, and with recent Himalayan experience, here was the opportunity to validate the reconnaissance he had initiated two years earlier.

In accepting Hunt's offer to join as Expedition Doctor, however, he made it clear he also wanted to be considered for any summit team. Perhaps

---

* In the *Alpine Journal* (1971) Ward noted: 'A good rule is to drink too much, enough to allay thirst is insufficient, as the sensation of thirst is blunted due to oxygen lack – as is the sensation of appetite. It is most important that adequate fuel must be taken to melt snow for water.'

Hunt chose not to say anymore then, for the minutes of the Himalayan Committee's meeting on 28 October record:

> Dr Ward, whom Colonel Hunt was not prepared to accept solely on his merits as a climber ... [was] invited to join the expedition as Medical Officer, it being made quite clear that he was not a member of the climbing party. Dr Ward could assist the expedition physiologist, and it was hoped that this solution would satisfy the Medical Research Council who had again asked for the inclusion of a second physiologist.

Interestingly, neither Ed Hillary nor George Lowe, both of whom would soon acquit themselves with distinction on Everest, were originally selected by Hunt as they were based in New Zealand and unable to be interviewed. Fortunately, other senior members persuaded him to include the two. This was a true reflection of the pair's ability, as the prevailing attitude in the Alpine Club at the time was that only public school 'gentlemen', who were further educated at Oxford, Cambridge or Sandhurst – as were the rest of the team – could be considered suitable for selection.

Although like Ward, Hunt was an old boy of Marlborough College and taught to climb by their housemaster Kempson, at the time Michael knew little about his new leader:

> My first impression of John was of some disturbing quality that I sensed but could not define. Later I understood this to be the intense emotional background to his character, by no means obvious, and yet an undercurrent came through ... In fact, John proved to be thoroughly agreeable in the field and although he has his quasi-religious approach to mountaineering he does not try unduly to impose it on his companions.

In the lead up to the Everest expedition, as well as studying for his primary fellowship, Ward spent considerable time with Pugh at the MRC in Hampstead. They worked together on testing protocols in his laboratory and went for long walks across the heath discussing the problems the climbers would face, how to test for these, and ways to combat them. A few years after returning from Everest, they would jointly publish two articles which appeared in *The Lancet* (1956) and the *Alpine Journal* (1957) both titled 'Some Effects of High Altitude on Man'.

As medical officer, it would be Ward's responsibility to prepare for all possible emergencies, and he sought advice from various professionals beforehand; his biggest worry being how to treat a possible case of acute appendicitis. The other was to be called on to act as dentist in an emergency. This, he dealt with by imploring individuals to visit their own dentist before leaving home, warning: 'I *can* pull teeth – but I'm not good at it.'

Ward's investigation into previous Himalayan expeditions revealed how many parties had been decimated by various maladies contracted in the field. From recent first-hand experience, he believed *prevention* of illness during the trek to Base Camp was the biggest medical challenge they would face. Even at lower altitudes, he saw significant opportunity to improve physical performance on the march in, and during their acclimatisation period. Conversely, he knew poor health during the early stages would undermine acclimatisation and eventual performance on the mountain itself.

Pugh, who was also chosen for the Everest team as its physiologist, was of the same view. He had monitored the health of climbers and porters trekking to Cho Oyu and came away critical of the party's rudimentary approach to hygiene and sanitation. The pair now agreed that simple preventative measures, if rigorously enforced, could stop the needless outbreak of maladies such as diarrhoea and respiratory issues. Although rarely life-threatening, these were often debilitating and could sap the energy of those afflicted for long periods.

Their preventative measures would include purifying drinking water, taking anti-malarial drugs, and not eating or sleeping in local dwellings to reduce the risk of contracting diseases. The Swiss had taken similar precautions on Everest, and Ward noted how in the first few weeks at altitude their mountaineers were approximately 80 per cent fit. In contrast, the fitness of the British party on Cho Oyu was a paltry 20 per cent.

For Michael, the time leading up to departure for Everest was incredibly busy and tiring. After completing his National Service in October, even while making his own preparations as a climber and Expedition Doctor, he spent months on a course studying for his primary fellowship examination. Something had to give, and despite his sacrifice in foregoing Cho Oyu, in his autobiography the disappointing result of this exam was noted in four words: 'Not surprisingly, I failed.'

Another prize, however, awaited him; one that in all probability could not be attempted again, and which represented a once-in-a-lifetime opportunity.

# 8

# Acclimatisation

W ard sailed for India on 12 February with the main party of the 1953 British Expedition to Mount Everest and their baggage. As well as getting to know his companions better, the voyage was a welcome opportunity to recover from his exhausted state and a dented morale after his exam result.

From Bombay, the members made their way by train and lorry to the Nepalese border at Raxaul, the railhead lying south of the capital. All the time, as the party changed between various transports, they kept a watchful eye over their 500-odd packages, especially on the final leg when an overhead ropeway was used to sling loads from ridges across the valleys into Kathmandu.

Here, Michael met another important companion, a Sherpa named Nawang Gompu (or Gombu). He had been assigned as his personal aide, just as other Sherpas were customarily paired up with each of the other 'sahibs'. Ward described him as 'small but fat and rounded', with a shy, somewhat bewildered look. He was Tenzing's young nephew, and this would be the 17-year-old's first outing. He was also, until recently, a novice monk at the Rongbuk Monastery in Tibet but, on hearing of his uncle going with the sahibs to Everest, had run away to join the expedition. During the march in, Michael recalled how Gompu caught everyone's attention as 'the only Sherpa to ask his Sahib to walk a little more slowly as he was finding the pace too fast!' Yet this belied his ability on mountains: he would be the youngest of them to reach South Col (and in 1965, became the first climber to summit Everest twice – a record not equalled for fifteen years).

Tenzing also joined the party in the capital, having arrived from Darjeeling with Gompu and eighteen others, all engaged as high-altitude Sherpas and he as the expedition's *sirdar*. After describing Tenzing and his soon-to-be-famous 'charming smile', Ward would note: 'Unusually he wanted to get to the top of Everest, an ambition extremely uncommon among Sherpas [then], although they possessed the physical capacity.'

After meeting their sahibs in Darjeeling, however, the Sherpas' first night resulted in one of the most controversial incidents of the expedition off the mountain, and one to which Ward might have inadvertently contributed. Upon medically examining the whole group, Michael disqualified one of their best, Gyalsen, having detected a potentially serious heart problem. Later that day, the Sherpas were shown their accommodation at the British Embassy. It turned out to be a shed that was once the stable, now converted into a garage, without any toilet facilities and where twenty other porters were already billeted.

Tenzing's group were elite Sherpas and included several 'Tigers' with formidable records, who felt humiliated at being shown such shabby quarters when the Westerners were allocated rooms in the embassy building. Their outrage was probably fuelled by Gyalsen, who was still moping around after's Ward's medical assessment and faced an uncertain future, probably never being able to work at high altitude again.

The next morning the embassy staff found many of those lodged in the garage had used its front as a toilet, urinating on the road. As Tenzing recalled in his autobiography:[*] 'This made the Embassy staff really angry, and they were given a lecture; but I don't think anyone was listening very hard.' This incident was not reported in the official expedition account but nevertheless underscored, not for the last time, the cultural divide between the sahibs and their Sherpas.

The remaining members who hadn't sailed from Britain with Ward and the advance party came together in Kathmandu. On 10 March the expedition headed for Sola Khumbu; the whole party now comprising thirteen foreigners and over 350 porters. This seemingly large number was not dissimilar to what the Swiss had estimated the previous year, as René Dittert noted in their expedition book *Forerunners to Everest*:

> To put a party of four men in fighting condition above 26,000
> feet requires three hundred men at the start in Kathmandu.
> More or less the proportions of war … Who was it who said
> that war, in the final analysis, is only a question of transport?

Hunt, of course, thoroughly understood this equation and the importance of getting logistics right. He now split his expedition into two groups for the long march in. While the first had a relaxing and carefree trek, Ward and Pugh, who followed a day later in the second group, were kept busy with

---

[*] As told to James Ullman (Tenzing was illiterate) in *Man of Everest*.

medical and physiological work. Unfortunately, this division of the team meant Michael did not get an opportunity to spend much time with his leader and build a closer relationship, as he had with Shipton. Hunt later expressed his regret about this missed opportunity, and it could have helped the pair understand each other better on Everest, when the pressure would mount.

Ward and Pugh were accompanied by 200 porters and one other climber, Charles Wylie, an officer from the Gurkha Rifles. He could speak fluent Nepalese and was an indispensable link between climbers and porters, with previous first-hand experience turning these hillmen into the finest of soldiers. Their fearlessness was well known, and Michael was called upon once to attend to injuries following a fight between a Sherpa and a porter after kukris (curved Nepalese knives) were drawn.

The expedition marched across the grain of the country, crossing many streams and rivers as the waterways in Nepal flow southwards whereas Everest lay due east from Kathmandu. As they passed through inhabited areas, Ward studied the numerous medical challenges faced by locals in these foothills. Many suffered from serious ailments including malaria and chronic dysentery, while the infant mortality rate was high as he noted in *Everest*: 'Only the fit survived in Nepal at that time.'

Arriving at villages along the way, Michael would hold clinics and treat locals as best he could; Gompu becoming expert at identifying those in genuine need while weeding out others who came out of curiosity or fun. Sometimes their ailments could be deadly serious, as in the case of a severely anaemic pregnant woman he examined. Her 8-month-old unborn baby was in breech position and probably dead. A Caesarean section in a modern hospital could have at least saved the mother's life but Ward could do little here (he learnt afterwards she did indeed die).

Pugh had an exhaustive testing regime planned out, performing experiments on himself and Ward to confirm or reject his various hypotheses. One such question was whether at high altitude, a mountaineer with the ability to breathe faster than another of comparable build should be able to climb higher and better? To answer this, they measured their oxygen uptake during exercise, which involved repeatedly charging up sloping tracks over a defined distance and height. Their exhaled air samples, after being analysed back home, would confirm this to generally be the case.* Furthermore, it showed that climbers at rest on Everest's summit would

---

* Exhaled air was collected in a Douglas bag made of polythene, specifically used for such sampling.

need to breathe at maximum rates just to maintain consciousness, unless they used supplementary oxygen.

Fortunately, these early days weren't only taken up with medical work, and the natural beauty of the region often overwhelmed Michael, whose writing again shines through in retelling his experience:

> The mist-covered ranges of the foothills led the eye up to the main peaks, which after a while became covered in cloud. I shall never forget these few hours of sheer delight … The mountains were elegantly defined and etched white against blue. A massive barrier that seemed to me to be a fitting place for gods to live. All morning I walked with their physical presence beside me. In the afternoon the path left the ridge and plunged through pink and red rhododendrons …

The weather wasn't always fine though, and could sometimes turn nasty, as once when they encountered a ferocious hailstorm with stones the size of golf balls. All the while, clouds surged across the mountains and valleys, revealing glimpses of enticing peaks in the distance, and the nights could be bitterly cold.

Within a fortnight of starting out, they crossed over high passes to enter Sola Khumbu, the homeland of the Sherpas, who had originally migrated from Tibet and brought their Buddhist beliefs and customs with them. Michael saw prayer wheels and flags everywhere. He also regularly heard the hoarse blowing of horns and chanting by monks living in the many monasteries dotting the region.

Arriving in Namche Bazaar, they camped a distance away from the main village, as this was one of the health measures Ward and Pugh insisted upon. Such precautions largely prevented gastrointestinal and respiratory issues across the party, and the overall level of illness experienced was negligible compared to the Everest expeditions of the 1920s and '30s.

Finally, they pushed on to the monastery of Thyangboche whose beauty, enhanced by the backdrop of towering mountains, never fails to impress visitors. Here, they were reunited with the first group, who had set up camp in nearby meadows and begun opening the many loads to sort through their gear. All the porters were paid off at this point and they promptly headed home, leaving behind the twenty high-altitude Sherpas with their sahibs.

From their campsite, the mountaineers could see snow being blown by high winds off the peaks above, indicating that, at least for the moment, they were too early to attempt Everest. Instead, they used this time as their acclimatisation period, climbing peaks up to 20,000ft to improve fitness levels. Importantly, this was also the opportunity to gain familiarity with their oxygen sets, which needed to be tested thoroughly.

Most of the climbers, though certainly not all, shared Pugh and Ward's view that supplementary oxygen would be critical high on the mountain; although from a purist's viewpoint, everyone would have preferred to climb without it. Since this was unlikely, it was obvious that the uninterrupted delivery of oxygen from their pressurised cylinders, when required and at the correct flowrate, was going to be vital.

Oxygen delivery apparatus had been developed initially for airmen flying at high altitude and further refined during the post-war period. Two types now existed for mountaineers, an open and a closed-circuit system. Both involved carrying bottled oxygen on a metal frame which was connected to a reservoir bag and then to a face mask. Beyond these similarities there were significant differences between the two:

In the open-circuit, on inhaling, a climber's mask allowed surrounding air to be enriched with oxygen, but most of this mixture went to waste when exhaling. The portion absorbed by the body had the effect of reducing the climber's apparent altitude to around 20,000ft, thus delivering a boost in performance above this height. However, since the wasted oxygen amounted to 90 per cent of the bottles' contents, it seemed an inefficient way to use a precious resource which had been shipped from England and then hauled up by porters.

The closed-circuit system, although heavier, avoided this waste by recycling the exhaled air, passing it through a canister of soda lime to remove the unwanted carbon dioxide. In this case, a tight-fitting mask excluded all outside air; and breathing pure oxygen meant the mountaineer was effectively moving at sea level which gave an even bigger boost.* On the face of it then, this seemed a significantly better system. But during trials it had proved troublesome to operate and caused climbers to overheat and feel suffocated when breathing rapidly. Worse still, if the set happened to fail high on the mountain, the user would effectively be transported from sea level to his actual altitude in an instant, which could cause him to black out, become comatose, or even die. This meant climbers using this type of set needed to be adept at spotting and repairing faults as they arose.

Although the closed-circuit system was in an advanced stage of development, it was nonetheless still experimental. In contrast, the open-

______

* During 1953, the climbing rate under comparable conditions using closed-circuit sets was 933ft/hr versus 430ft/hr for open-circuit. In contrast, without using oxygen the previous year, Lambert and Tenzing achieved only 233ft/hr.

circuit set had already been widely used by aviators and was readily adaptable to mountaineering due to its simplicity and reliability. Both systems had been used on previous Everest expeditions, and each had their champions and detractors.

Even before the expedition left Britain's shores, there was intense debate about the relative merits of each system among scientists and mountaineers. This was highlighted the previous year with the Swiss, as Ward summarised: 'In the spring Lambert and Tenzing failed to reach the summit by about 600ft, because of malfunctioning oxygen sets not tested rigorously enough at sea-level – an elementary mistake which cost them the summit.'[*]

The Swiss had chosen the closed-circuit design based on mine rescue apparatus. In describing their missed opportunity due to the various problems encountered, Chris Bonington explained:

> [But,] most of all, it was because the oxygen sets used by Lambert and Tenzing were ineffective, feeding them insufficient oxygen to compensate for the weight of the cylinders they were carrying. The sets were so primitive that they could be used only while resting, which meant the men had to carry the extra load of oxygen bottles without getting any benefit from them while actually climbing.[†]

Determined not to make the same mistake, the British invested much time and effort into these oxygen sets, hedging their bets by developing and taking both types, twenty sets in all. They also carried almost 200,000 litres of oxygen, ten times more than the Swiss.

During their acclimatisation period, the climbers and their Sherpas needed to test both systems at altitude. It was imperative they all become comfortable donning the sets and breathing in what the Sherpas called 'English air' and which they used with almost childish delight. The party split into three groups over two separate periods, ascending lesser peaks around Everest for almost three weeks.

During the first period, Ward was in a group led by Ed Hillary together with the Gurkha officer Charles Wylie and Wilfrid Noyce. As mentioned earlier, when Michael was a schoolboy he had heard of Wilf's bad fall and how he had cheated death by the quick action of his partner, Menlove Edwards. Noyce had suffered two other serious accidents since then, leading Ward and other contemporaries to believe he was accident prone,

---

* Quoted from his preface to *Everest, Chomolungma, Sagarmatha*.
† Quoted from his book *Quest for Adventure*.

possibly because he was missing 'some vital protective instinct'.* Other than being a fine mountaineer, Noyce was also a linguist and author. Ward found him to be a thoroughly interesting companion, noting in *Everest*: 'It was one of my greatest regrets that I did not ask him to join the 1951 Everest reconnaissance expedition.' Wilf, giving a firsthand account of the 1953 expedition in his classic book *South Col*, would recall: 'Mike was the easiest and pleasantest companion, aware that his post as doctor limited his activity, yet not perturbed by this limitation.'

On 30 March, Ward's group set out to explore west of the Khumbu Glacier around Chola Khola (a *khola* being a stream in a deep valley). Two years earlier, during the reconnaissance he had passed through this area ringed by mountains and was now keen to understand it better in terms of its topography. They climbed two peaks around 20,000ft, both being first ascents, allowing them to test their oxygen sets and other gear. From these summits Ward was able to view the jigsaw of mountains, valleys, and glaciers that lay before them. This episode reinforced his growing love for exploring and mapping remote mountainous regions: 'I felt that two peaks and filling in a blank on the map was good enough for ten days.'†

For his second acclimatisation period, Ward joined a group led by Hunt, together with Noyce and Tom Bourdillon; their main objective being to thoroughly test the oxygen sets. Tom and his father Dr Robert Bourdillon were stalwarts of the closed-circuit apparatus, having invested enormous effort researching and improving this system. Hunt, wanting to test this set himself, used it to climb a lesser peak next to Ama Dablam with Bourdillon, while Ward and Noyce tested the open-circuit system over an extended five-hour period. All the climbers found their performance improved with the sets used.

Worryingly, Hunt began experiencing difficulty with his breathing over the next few days, as mentioned in his book *The Ascent of Everest*: 'This trouble was later diagnosed by Ward to be incipient pleurisy. Thanks to his prompt and skilful care, I had fully recovered from this a few days later.' While he rested, Michael and the others ascended another peak around 19,000ft, further improving their fitness levels.

However, when he returned to Base Camp, which had already been established by another group, Ward was furious to find it located on the same spot the Swiss had occupied the previous year. Little regard had been

---

* Noyce and his climbing partner, Robin Smith, were later killed in 1962, after falling 4,000ft while descending Pik Garmo in the Soviet Pamirs.

† That autumn Charles Evans completed a detailed photo-survey of the area, which would be incorporated into a map of the Everest region, published in 1961.

paid to sanitation, mounds of human excreta were everywhere, and the hygiene in the kitchen area was deplorable. Three of the climbers, Mike Westmacott and both the Georges (Band and Lowe), were already down with severe diarrhoea, which would soon become near-chronic.

Ward had the camp resited with clearly marked latrines. He also made frequent unannounced visits to check the cleanliness of both the cooking facilities and the cooks. But this lapse in hygiene standards would prove particularly costly for Westmacott and Band. Although they were superb mountaineers, it debilitated them for a period and meant neither was able to get high on Everest. Ward did his best to help them recover as quickly as possible, but this incident served as a salient reminder that much could go wrong, including from a medical perspective, and even before they set foot on an unforgiving mountain. To achieve their goal would demand constant vigilance, every day and in every aspect, not just during the ascent itself.

**9**

# The Ascent

◈◈◈◈◈◈◈◈◈◈◈◈◈◈◈◈◈◈◈◈◈◈◈◈◈◈◈◈◈◈◈◈◈◈◈◈◈◈◈◈◈◈◈◈◈◈◈◈◈◈◈

The whole party now moved up to tackle their foremost challenge, finding a route through the Khumbu Icefall, which Ward described as 'easily the most dangerous part of the whole ascent'. Since it would be used by everyone over the coming weeks, often daily, it was imperative it be made as safe as possible. Hillary's group, after setting up Base Camp at 17,900ft on 12 April, had made an early start on the first portion of the icefall as part of their second acclimatisation phase. When Michael arrived here a few days later, he climbed up the shoulder of Pumori again and looked up the Western Cwm with mixed emotions:

> The last time I had been here had been our first view of the southern route; and I remembered the relief that I had felt when I had seen that there was a possible route here. I could not help feeling very cocky that my opinion had been better than that of the more experienced Alpinists in London. I could not help feeling sad, too, that only Ed, Tom and I, of the 1951 Reconnaissance, were here this time.

The climbers again found the icefall demanding and stiflingly hot as ever. Due to the constant downward movement of the glacier, its surface had changed in the last two years but still remained chaotic. Massive 100ft pillars tottered threateningly all around them as they threaded their way through boulders of ice, over cliffs and across crevasses. The latter were bridged where possible with lengths of aluminium ladder, bamboo poles and even small tree trunks which they had brought with them in anticipation of securing a safe trail. But 'safe' was a relative word, as Michael noted:

> It was surprising how fatalistic we became: the danger we accepted, and the altitude helped dull the sharper pangs of apprehension. However, the Ice-fall was a very dangerous place and most of us had a number of near misses.

They were especially concerned for the Sherpas who would spend the most time here, repeatedly crossing the area while hauling the bulk of their supplies and gear higher up the slopes. Camp II (19,400ft) was established halfway up the icefall, but few slept or lingered there because of the threat level. Everyone was relieved when Camp III (20,200ft) was set up at the start of the Western Cwm, before Camp IV was established at its head 1,000ft higher as Advanced Base Camp on the first day of May.

As well as assisting where he could to mark out a feasible path, Ward helped Sherpas carry loads to the various camps, all the way up to Camp V sited at 22,000ft. Having passed the 20,000ft mark, supplementary oxygen could be used in the push to establish higher camps, allowing the climbers to further test and gain familiarity with both types of breathing apparatus. The sets were heavy, making up 35 of Michael's 50lb load. They could be troublesome too, as he experienced first-hand. Once, while struggling to keep up with the others over a number of hours, he was beginning to have real doubts about his stamina until he discovered his set was delivering only half-a-litre of oxygen per minute. Charles Wylie also had nasty experiences with his set when he nearly fell off an ice slope, after his apparatus suddenly cut out on two occasions.

At Camp V Ward took samples of exhaled breath from the climbers and collected blood from finger pricks, which would be used to continue their study into the process of acclimatisation. He was constantly monitoring the party's overall health as they pushed higher. Hillary, for example, who had been leading the charge through the icefall and had spent four nights at 20,000ft, was beginning to struggle with sleep and appetite, indicating he needed further acclimatisation. Later, in his article for the *National Geographic* (1954), Hunt would relate how Ward helped add humour during their assault by dispensing his two pet prescriptions: 'You'll feel better when you get lower down'; and 'Here, try these; they're no good'.

Michael wasn't immune to acute mountain sickness either, experiencing blinding headaches and nausea at this camp, with nightmares that kept waking him up, gasping for breath. He felt only 60 per cent fit and was frustrated at being unable to overcome a rundown feeling. Using oxygen while sleeping would have made a difference, but it was in short supply and reserved for those getting to South Col and beyond. Only after going back down to Base Camp, was he able to fully recover. Here, he met up with Hunt again who, as usual, had been pushing himself too hard. Michael thought he looked dreadful and had 'grave doubts about his ability to function efficiently high on the mountain even with oxygen'.

The deleterious effect of high altitude was impacting all the climbers by this stage to varying degrees. In terms of overall fitness, Ward's medical assessment was that four of them – Gregory, Hillary, Lowe, and Noyce – were in the best shape. He found it harder, however, to evaluate two others – Bourdillon and Evans – who had been using the closed-circuit system, but they seemed to be coping well (none of the others used these sets on Everest).

Soon afterwards, the open-circuit set was put through its paces over an extended period by Hillary and Tenzing, who climbed from Base Camp all the way to Camp IV. They returned the same day to report their sets had functioned well and provided the boost expected at a flowrate of 4 litres per minute.

Around this time, as the party steadily advanced, there was much anticipation building among the climbers. Finally, on 7 May they gathered in the mess tent for their leader to announce his assault plan. The group now included the *Times* correspondent James (later Jan) Morris, who had recently joined them in anticipation of reporting the expedition's outcome. He later wrote in his book *Coronation Everest*: 'Men would be made famous by this conference, and legends given birth.' (He was not wrong.)

Hunt first explained his rationale for wanting to use two teams and both types of oxygen sets. Then he named the climbers and teams that would make a bid for the top, together with the support personnel involved, as Ward recorded in his diary:

> 1st party closed circuit Tom B and Charles Evans. To South Peak from South Col (!!) and then see if they can go on – if not turn back.
>
> 2nd [party] Ed and Tenzing on open circuit. Stop night at Ridge Camp which had been put there by John and Greg with 7 special Sherpas …
>
> Myself – Reserve – an honourable part – but the best for me as a doctor I think.[*]

Naturally, Michael would have been disappointed not being chosen as one of the summit four, but this had been made clear to him from the start. In his autobiography *Life is Meeting*, Hunt noted:

> Michael Ward, who had accepted to join the expedition as our medical officer, was an outstanding climber … it was particularly hard for him to be asked to make his climbing

---

[*] Ward's handwriting for the words 'honourable part' is barely legible.

> contribution to the Assault Plan below the level of South Col, in the case of illness or accidents to other members of the party. I was in no doubt about his chagrin at the time.

Whether this disappointment at 'missing out' clouded Michael's comments immediately after John finished talking and sought comments is difficult to say. The discussion was heated by all accounts, and the merits and weaknesses of Hunt's controversial plan continue to be debated to this day, particularly its impact on the first assault team and their chances of success.

Ward was vocal for two separate reasons as he explained in his own autobiography. Firstly, speaking in his capacity as the medical officer, he suggested Hunt not include himself in the party that would establish the final Ridge Camp (IX, 27,900ft):

> I did not think that he would be fit enough and my conclusion was based on his age and his performance to date … I told him this in no uncertain terms as the role of the ridge party was vital; especially so, as there was to be only one assault from a high camp. He was somewhat taken aback by the vehemence of my comments, and naturally disagreed with me.

Morris captured this incident and the exchange of words in his book:

> Had anyone any questions or observations? Hunt asked, looking benignly round the tent with a soldierly air, as if he were about to order his company commanders to synchronize their watches. 'Yes', said Michael Ward, with a vehemence that nearly knocked me off my packing-case. 'I certainly have. I think it's a great mistake that you're going so high yourself. It's a great mistake. You've done too much already. You shouldn't go with that support team. I feel this very strongly.'

Ward's second observation was made not only as a mountaineer who had researched previous summit bids, but also as a physician who understood the role of oxygen and the limitations of their sets:

> I thought, as did others, that this was an odd plan. All the old Everesters had told us again and again to make the last camp high enough – and common sense dictated that there should be two assaults. Yet Tom and Charles were asked to climb from 26,000 feet to 29,000 feet in one day and return, using

a relatively untried apparatus that, on its performance on the Lhotse face, seemed no better than the open circuit at four litres per minute.

Other than believing the first pair's chances were being unnecessarily compromised by not having a higher camp to start out from, Ward was acutely concerned about their exposure should the closed-circuit system develop problems, as he explained in *Everest*:

> In case of failure, or partial failure, of their oxygen sets, which they had already experienced, they would be at grave risk, it seemed to me, of being at one moment at the equivalent of sea level and the next at 28,000 feet. This could result in unconsciousness and coma, with no place of relative safety – a tent – within reasonable reach to provide shelter.

He then suggested an obvious improvement to Hunt's plan: Make the final Ridge Camp available for the first pair also, rather than erecting it only for the second team a day or so later. However, as Ward went on to record:

> The change in the plan would be negligible, but despite strong representation from myself, and also from Alf Gregory who insisted that the first assault had no prospect of success and would serve no useful purpose, Hunt felt it was not possible to make this change.

It is not clear why their leader chose not to, and Hunt was not forthcoming in his book published soon afterwards. Whereas he fully explained his plan in terms of the makeup of the two teams, their order, and the sets they were to use. Perhaps with his military background and senior rank, he was not used to having his plan questioned, at least not in the strident manner Ward had. Certainly, his desire to personally ensure the establishment of the vital Ridge Camp was the role of a good commander leading from the front, and there is no doubt his leadership qualities were admired by the entire party.

This disagreement, however, probably clouded his relationship with Ward forever, and the pair would differ again on an even more important issue after the expedition. Morris had this to say about Michael's outspokenness at the time:

> Ward himself was a distinguished climber as well as a physician, and in a way, of all those present in the tent, he was

the best qualified to offer an opinion on the plan; for if it had
not been for his vision, we would have not been on Everest
at all.

As the party progressed higher up the mountain, Ward, often with Pugh's
assistance, was having to diagnose and treat the various ailments affecting
the men with increasing frequency. For example, heavy breathing in this
low humidity atmosphere led to painfully dry throats, made worse by
coughing; while panting let in the sun's rays, resulting in the roof of the
mouth becoming sunburnt and sore.

At one stage, Michael had to go back down the mountain to attend to
the expedition's cameraman Tom Stobart, who was thought to have come
down with pneumonia. Although he recovered quickly, it meant he could
not ascend higher than 20,000ft. On their return, desperate for some good
'action footage', Stobart pleaded with Ward to be caught on camera making
his way through the dangerous icefall while fixing guide ropes for the
Sherpas. This scene would soon be viewed by audiences across the world,
on release of the resulting documentary *The Conquest of Everest*.[*]

Long before Hunt's Ridge Camp (IX) could be considered, somewhere
below South Peak, Camps VI and VII had to be established. These would
be on the imposing face of Lhotse towering in front of them, as Michael
described: '[Lhotse's] true scale could be appreciated when parties were
climbing there. The black dots were tiny and moved infinitesimally over
the hours.'

The mammoth task to prepare this slope, which involved cutting a
staircase of steps and fixing guide ropes, was given to George Lowe with
four Sherpas assisting, and who were later joined by Wilfrid Noyce. After
a few days, when Noyce was reassigned duties in readiness for leading
Sherpas higher up the mountain, Ward went up to Camp VII (24,000ft) on
17 May to replace him. But Michael found himself struggling to gain this
extra height, and it took all his strength and willpower to get there.

Here, he heard of Lowe's experience the previous night with insomnia,
brought on by high altitude. Despite usually being a sound sleeper, after five
days there he was struggling and so had resorted to taking a sleeping pill,
with dramatic effect. Waking up with a start after twelve hours, he fell asleep
again for an hour while kneeling to light a primus as he prepared breakfast,
and would have fallen onto the stove but for Noyce's intervention. Later that
morning, as the pair climbed higher, Wilf opened a can of sardines to perk

---

[*] George Lowe, who was also an amateur photographer, shot all the high footage
for Stobart and later directed the documentary.

George up, but he dozed off yet again, this time with a sardine hanging out of his mouth. With difficulty, Noyce eventually managed to bring him staggering back down to camp, where he promptly fell asleep once more until dawn, while Hunt fretted down at Advanced Base Camp on their lack of progress.

Ward wondered whether taking such pills could pose a similar risk to other climbers, in which case he would have to ban their use at high altitude. He was concerned enough to take the same dose as Lowe that night but, contrary to expectation, found he hardly slept at all, instead experiencing vivid dreams of being suffocated.

The next day he set out with George to mark out a route further up the Lhotse face but began feeling terribly cold and progressively weaker. Just below 25,000ft he found he could not go any further, forcing the pair to return to camp. They tried again the next day, but after gaining only a few hundred feet Michael was again beaten, his legs were almost uncontrollable and he felt weaker than ever. Had he reached his 'altitude ceiling' beyond which his body simply could not cope – not ever? He must have wondered this at the time:

> Obviously I was disappointed at my failure, but the effect was misted and dulled by altitude. We descended very slowly to Advanced Base Camp in the afternoon. On the way down I tried as hard as I could to think of a reason for my poor condition, for I was going much worse than George all the time over 23,000 feet. I could think of none.

On their arrival there, the pair met their anxious leader, who was becoming increasingly frustrated that the Lhotse face remained an obstacle. He had allocated four days for this task, but it was now already day ten and the expedition was in real danger of grinding to a halt. Hunt was less than understanding of Lowe being unable to complete the job he had been assigned, as Ward again wrote *In This Short Span*:

> John, who was naturally extremely strung up by the continued failure, was as my diary primly records '*excessively rude*' to George who had been striving for ten days on the Lhotse Face.

> 'Flectere, si nequeo superos, Acheronta movebo.'
> ('If I cannot bend the gods, I will let hell loose.')

By all accounts, Lowe's effort on Lhotse was Herculean, and Hunt did himself no credit with his outburst – which, it must be said, was uncharacteristic of him. George made no mention of this incident in his book *Because it is There*, and neither did Hunt in his account other than to praise Lowe's effort during those critical days 'which will go down in the annals of mountaineering as an epic achievement of tenacity and skill'.

In the final chapter, Hunt reflected: 'It is a remarkable fact that throughout the four months that we were together, often in trying circumstances, I never heard an impatient or angry word passed between any members of the party.' This statement was obviously stretching the truth, and the same could be said in a few other instances. Understandably, given this was the official account, Hunt was trying to portray 'his' historic expedition in the most favourable light.

It should come as no surprise that cracks were appearing in this large team, struggling under enormous stress in freezing conditions with most, including Ward, at the limit of their endurance. For the record, in his diary entry of 20 May the two italicised words above were both capitalised and double-underlined, indicating how angry he was at the time witnessing Lowe's rough treatment.* Michael also wrote that George had been 'working damned well. Quite ashamed to have him [John] in the party which has been very friendly so far.' Although Ward did not publish this last remark, only the 'excessively rude' comment followed by his cryptic line in Latin by Virgil, it would not have helped his deteriorating relationship with Hunt (noting that Ward's autobiography was released years after the event, in 1972).

The next day, to Hunt's immense relief, Wilfrid Noyce and Annalu, following the trail blazed by Lowe, were able to push past the Lhotse face, over the Geneva Spur and onto South Col (26,000ft). The assault of the summit was finally on!

After Camp VIII was established there, on the same site the Swiss had used the previous year, Tom Bourdillon and Charles Evans made the first bid for the top. They went out heavily loaded. In addition to carrying all their gear, their closed-circuit sets weighed around 12lb more than the open-circuit type – a significant difference at that altitude. Ward was at Advanced Base Camp (IV) at the time, helping Pugh with physiological work, where he learnt of their departure via radio with mixed emotion:

> I felt immeasurably sad and annoyed that they were not being
> given a proper chance. It seemed such a useless waste to start
> from the South Col – an attempt doomed to failure – when all
> that was needed was a night at a high camp.

---

* In 2013, when Lowe published his *Letters from Everest*, the one dated 22 May 1953 revealed how he felt back then: 'I had a bad night as the general feeling, although unsaid, was that I had failed somewhat.'

Despite this handicap, the pair made a promising start and climbed an unprecedented 1,500ft in about an hour-and-a-half. It demonstrated yet again the superior boost delivered by the closed-circuit system, which Tom believed would overcome not having the use of a high camp. But in the end they failed to summit, primarily because the mechanics of these sets proved unreliable. Without a high camp available, there was no shelter where Tom could repair their sets or recover overnight. After managing to reach South Peak, 300ft short of the top, they realised they were running low on oxygen. There simply wasn't enough left in their tanks to make the summit and return safely back to camp, although Ward later commented: 'I know that if Charles's set had been working properly they would have gone on and risked the sets running out of oxygen on the way down.'

Michael knew how hard Tom (and his father) had worked from the beginning to develop the best possible apparatus for the whole expedition, and thus felt his disappointment keenly. Tom, for his part, never stopped believing that had things gone a little differently, he could have been the first to summit Everest. (In his book *Quest for Adventure* Bonington agreed, writing: 'Had Bourdillon and Evans been granted that top camp, in all probability they would have been the first men on top of Everest.')*

Meanwhile Hunt, against the explicit advice given to him by Ward, his expedition doctor, had arrived at South Col with two Sherpas to help establish Ridge Camp for the second assault team. His fitness had been deteriorating over the last few days, as Michael observed:

> John looked absolutely whacked; his face grey and tired, and his voice that of an old man. But his powers of recovery were quite remarkable and each morning he seemed his energetic and usual self. I felt, however, that this could not go on for too long.

On the day John returned to Advanced Base Camp, Ward recorded in his diary that Hunt suffered 'a partial mental and physical collapse'. For now, Hunt made a final contribution to the expedition's success by carrying loads up with Da Namgyal to a dump about 1,400ft beyond South Col. Here, the loads were picked up by another support team comprising Gregory, Lowe and Ang Nyima as they continued up with Hillary and Tenzing, all using open-circuit sets. The five established Ridge Camp (IX) at 27,900ft on 28 May, before the three support climbers returned to South Col.

---

* Tom Bourdillon died three years later in a climbing accident in the Swiss Alps.

The next day, as Hillary famously described in his chapter titled 'The Summit' in Hunt's *The Ascent of Everest*, he and Tenzing became the first climbers to stand on top of the world.

Meanwhile, Ward had climbed back to Camp VII on 26 May, convincing Noyce to accompany him. He wanted to take more lung air (alveolar gas) samples, stored into glass ampoules, to further his research. He was also itching to become more involved and get higher up the mountain. While there, they could provide support to the first returning assault team.

Although Michael experienced no problem acclimatising to the increased height on this occasion, it was too late now for him to go any higher, onto South Col itself. One can understand his dejection in this regard when he later revealed: 'Besides treating the occasional sore throat, basically I had nothing to do.' But the pair's presence at Camp VII did turn out to be fortuitous: When Hunt and Ang Temba shepherded the exhausted Bourdillon and Evans back down, just before camp the Sherpa fell into a crevasse. The other three had not the strength left to pull him out, and it was left to Noyce to rescue him.

Three days later, Ward was with Hunt and the others back at Advanced Base Camp (IV) when they first saw Hillary and Tenzing coming back down the mountain led by Lowe, who, unable to contain himself, gave the soon-to-be-famous thumbs up. In his autobiography, Ward simply recalls: 'We ran breathlessly to congratulate them'; while the documentary footage shows him among the first to rush up and shake their hands.

Although he had not taken any further part in either assault, nevertheless this was a hectic time for Michael as he made certain history was captured from a medical and scientific perspective, and as accurately as possible. This meant interviewing climbers soon after their return, as he explained in *Everest*: 'If we delayed, they would tend to favour their own performance in many subtle and different ways. Having taken clinical histories from tens of thousands of patients over 40 years, I can vouch for this.' (The Swiss Foundation for Alpine Research had also advised interviews be conducted on the spot for this same reason.)

In fact, after two brief entries on 21 and 22 May, the remaining half of his handwritten diary is taken up by medical observations. On returning home, he rewrote these notes into a more readable form, had them typed up, then made a few minor corrections in ink while proofreading the pages.

The final twenty-page document begins with the following statement (the heights given in square brackets are also his):

> Notes taken by Michael Ward from each member of the expedition who went up to the South Col [26,000 ft] and then beyond to the summit.
>
> All notes were taken at Camps 4–7 [21–24,000 ft] within 24–48 hours of the individuals return, and sometimes within an hour. They are the most detailed and accurate available and are akin to a clinical history.*

Michael recorded all their pertinent details, including for any Sherpa attaining South Col. His notes show their food and fluid intake, rest and sleeping times, the loads each carried, as well as their general health and any ailments suffered. Importantly, he also recorded their use of supplementary oxygen and the impact this had on individual performances, knowing this would form the basis of future study.

Ward especially took careful notes from both assault parties – a facsimile of his typed up notes for Hillary and Tenzing, including the time they spent on the summit, is shown in the Appendix. Incidentally, in terms of that irrelevant question from the public and media which later refused to go away, Ward's notes confirm what the successful pair were eventually forced to tell the world: 'From South Peak to Summit Hillary led all the way.'†

In his clinical notes for Tom Bourdillon, while transcribing from his diary Ward inserted a bracketed paragraph – with one word underlined – in which he revisited his plea for a high camp for the first assault pair:

> If Hunt had allowed a camp to be put up as Camp 9 – which Hillary and Tensing used – at 27,800 ft, Evans and Bourdillon could have used this overnight as Hillary & Tenzing did and gone on to summit next day. This was suggested to Hunt in planning meeting earlier in West Cwm by myself backed by others, but he refused to change his plans. In effect this meant that Evans and Bourdillon had to climb 3,000 ft from South

---

* A summary can be found in Ward's article 'Everest 1953, First Ascent: A Clinical Record' published in *High Altitude Medicine & Biology* (2003). Because of language difficulties, histories from Sherpas were generally not taken. However, everyone concerned underwent a physical examination; the results of which were jointly published by Pugh and Ward in *The Lancet* (1956).

† See entry for 29/5 in the Appendix.

Col to Summit using oxygen sets that were known not to be fully reliable. If the sets had broken down – being at one moment at sea-level in the depths of their lungs – the next moment they would be at 28,000 ft, with the risk of coma and death. A tent at 27,000 ft would have been life-saving. Yet Hunt refused to change. It is abundantly clear that Hunt <u>never</u> clearly understood the central basic problem of Everest and how it was overcome – though he was told often enough.

With his overriding focus on capturing clinical history, Ward did not record any details of the ascent itself in his diary, nor his thoughts upon hearing how the last thousand feet was finally overcome. In the anticlimax that followed, he makes no mention of their descent from the mountain either, or the long trek back to Kathmandu; although Hunt recorded in *The Ascent of Everest*: 'Temporarily, the party divided. Charles Wylie and Michael Ward undertook the hardest job, that of escorting our baggage by road and rail to Lucknow …'

The great adventure was over. Ward could justly claim to have contributed as much to the success of the expedition as any other man on Everest's slopes that day. In terms of his unique contribution, not only did he discover a viable route up the mountain, but he also instigated the reconnaissance which confirmed it. Like all the others there, he too would be profoundly affected by the events of 29 May 1953 for the rest of his life.

## 10

# The Big Debate

Recalling the day Everest was finally summited, after the first rush of emotion and overriding relief, Ward wrote: 'I remember that no member of the party was particularly elated and our initial mood was one more of satisfaction than delirium.' For the British public this was not the case, as euphoria swept through the nation following the coded telegram sent by Morris to his newspaper. *The Times* broke the story as crowds were gathering on the streets of London for the coronation of their new monarch, who was woken up the night before to receive the news.* And this news was a *big* deal, as the article made clear:

> Seldom since Francis Drake brought the Golden Hind to anchor in Plymouth Sound has a British explorer offered to his Sovereign such a tribute of glory as Colonel John Hunt and his men were able to lay at the feet of Queen Elizabeth for her Coronation Day.

Michael Ward was one of *those* men. On his return home, he would have felt immense pride reading the flood of messages from well-wishers and cuttings from newspapers. The *News Chronicle*, for example, ran with the headline 'All This and Everest Too'. Talk of their accomplishment filled the streets, yet in true British tradition, particularly of that era, Ward said little about how he felt. But Morris's description of that day years later is worth recalling:

> The moment aroused a whole orchestra of rich emotions among the British – pride, patriotism, nostalgia for the lost past of the war and derring do, hope for a rejuvenated future … People of a certain age remember vividly to this day the moment when,

---

* Following his scoop, Morris's book describing the first ascent was aptly titled *Coronation Everest*.

> as they waited on a drizzly June morning for the Coronation
> procession to pass by in London, they heard the magical news
> that the summit of the world was, so to speak, theirs.

The people of Nepal and India were just as elated that one of their own had stood on Everest, and Hillary's iconic photograph of Tenzing holding their flags high plastered their newspapers. For the Sherpas of Sola Khumbu, more than any other people, their homeland and lives would be forever altered by this singular event.

For Ward, the success of the expedition and the role he had played began to sink in with the first of many receptions he would attend with the others as soon as they were off the mountain. Some were conducted on a grand scale, beginning with one hosted by Prime Minister Nehru in Delhi, although neither Michael nor the other climbers were suitably attired for the occasion, understandably not having packed dinner jackets with their gear for the Himalayas.

While in India, and using only an oxygen apparatus as a prop, Ward also gave the first of many lectures he would deliver. This one, surprisingly, was to the Institute of Nuclear Physics and came about following an invitation by an English professor lecturing there, who had been to Everest on an earlier expedition.

Arriving back in London, invitations to 'the conquering heroes' continued unabated, beginning with a dinner attended by Queen Elizabeth II, which Ward simply described as a 'high spot'. Soon afterwards, at Buckingham Palace he stood in line to be congratulated and watched as she knighted Hunt and Hillary, and pinned the George Medal on Tenzing, recalling: 'This was an extraordinarily relaxed occasion which surprised me.' Michael found the same atmosphere prevailed at many of the other receptions, leading him to comment: 'Perhaps our hosts found it a change to talk to people who were not overtly connected with politics or power.' There were many such hosts to talk with and engagements to attend in the heady days that followed, as the British public could not get enough of its Everesters.

Later that year, Ward met his queen again when the royal family attended the opening night of *The Conquest of Everest*, a seventy-eight-minute documentary which went on to win a British Academy Award and was nominated for an Oscar. He featured prominently in the film, appearing in multiple scenes battling the mountain. When Hunt released his official account of the expedition soon after returning, Ward was an integral part of that too and had prepared one of the appendices with Pugh titled 'Physiology and Medicine'. (*The Ascent of Everest* quickly became a best seller and has been translated into some thirty languages.)

The seemingly endless round of receptions kept many of the Everest party well occupied, but Ward had little time 'for the adulatory cheer of audiences'. The post-Everest lecture circuit was also proving to be lucrative for some members of the party, but Michael decided to focus full time on his studies instead, having fallen a year behind his fellow students. However, as he was essentially unemployed during this period, he did give the odd lecture, often teaming up with two or three others, each member being paid £25 plus travel expenses per lecture.

The experience gained from this public speaking would help Ward in his career. He learnt early on to overcome any initial apprehension by memorising the first few lines of his address before continuing in a more relaxed manner, letting his knowledge of the subject matter take over. Together with Charles Evans, who was also a doctor, they delivered a Hunterian Lecture at the Royal College of Surgeons the following year. Soon, as he put it: 'I learnt to appreciate the addictive thrill that actors and politicians may enjoy on the right occasions.'

To make ends meet, Ward also earned a little from occasional locum work, recalling: 'By living very frugally indeed I kept just solvent. Penury was a great spur to success.' Difficult and grinding though it was, Michael persevered with the extra study essential to resitting his primary exams, not least because it had a failure rate of over 80 per cent. His persistence paid off when, six months after returning home, he passed. Now he could begin the practical work necessary to becoming a surgeon.

With Everest finally 'conquered', there now arose an obvious question in the minds of mountaineers, scientists and a curious public: After a string of failed attempts by equally competent climbers and well-equipped expeditions, what was the primary reason for this success? The answer to this question would divide the mountaineering community, and its search watched with avid interest by the scientists who had assisted them along the way. Regrettably, over the years, it would put Ward in conflict with some members of his team, and especially their leader John Hunt.

The experience of the 1953 expedition, as well as the Swiss the previous year, meant the debate around the use of supplementary oxygen had largely 'moved on', except for the purists. Initially, the often-heated discussion had centred on whether oxygen was even necessary at high altitude and, separately, if its use was in keeping with the spirit of climbing. Having seen the crucial difference bottled oxygen had made nearing the summit, it now begged the question: was it *the* primary success factor? Ward and Pugh had predicted from the outset it would be, but a number of their fellow climbers on Everest thought otherwise.

There was also the question of the role scientists had played during the expedition's preparation. How significant was their contribution in terms of understanding human physiology at high altitude, which had led to improved food, fluid and oxygen intake? And what of their work in developing better climbing gear? These questions would mark the start of a big debate: science versus stamina and skill. Hunt's official account left no doubt as to his view, as his book's opening paragraph set out:

> This is the story of how, on 29th May, 1953, two men, both endowed with outstanding stamina and skill, inspired by unflinching resolve, reached the top of Everest and came back unscathed to rejoin their comrades.

Hunt was a staunch believer in the power of the human spirt to overcome the odds. Furthermore, he held onto an old fashioned and romantic view of mountaineering that bordered on the religious, and one which had far less room for the contribution of science. His final chapter, titled 'Reflections', began with:

> What were the reasons for our success? How was it that we succeeded in getting to the top when so many others before us had failed to do so? I am adding the second question only to give what, in my mind, is the one reason transcending all others which explains the first. For I wish once again to pay tribute to the work of earlier expeditions.

He then went on to describe how each effort had built a 'pyramid of experience' based on their predecessors' efforts – this being the critical success factor – until the summit was finally attained. This was Hunt at his noble best, giving other expeditions due credit. In terms of the highest point reached, however, this pyramid analogy was not entirely correct. After the third British attempt of 1924, the next *four* had been unable to better the mark of 28,126ft set by Edward Norton.

In order of importance, Hunt's second reason for success was 'sound, thorough, meticulously detailed planning'. This, of course, was his strength, acquired through years of service as an officer in the army. It was the main reason he was chosen to lead the expedition ahead of Shipton, which he had then proceeded to run as a military campaign to great effect.

Finally, Hunt paid tribute to the excellence of their equipment, the firms that produced them, and those who gave financial support, before going on to note:

> Among the numerous items in our inventory, I would single out oxygen for special mention. Many of our material aids were of great importance; only this, in my opinion, was vital to success … But for oxygen, without the much-improved equipment which we were given, we certainly would not have got to the top.

As discussed earlier, before the expedition had set out, one of the key discoveries Pugh made was that an oxygen flowrate of 4 litres per minute was required to counter the weight of the heavy oxygen sets and deliver the boost in performance needed. But oxygen wasn't the only factor that an application of science had positively influenced. After the Cho Oyu expedition the previous year, Pugh had found solutions to other problems faced at high altitude, such as dehydration, hunger, mental and physical deterioration, and cold injury.

Ward believed the scientific contribution to their success on Everest had not been sufficiently acknowledged, nor Pugh's work in particular – he said so publicly, and to his dying day. It is important to bear in mind that Ward's view of the role science played came from years of research and experience in mountaineering. He was a key member of the Himalayan Scientific and Mountaineering Expedition of 1960–61 (to be discussed later), and the thesis produced from his work here and in Bhutan earned him a Doctor of Medicine qualification. Over the years, Ward also wrote around ninety articles for various medical and mountaineering journals, as well as the first textbook on the subject, *Mountain Medicine*.

Mountaineer and author Eric Vola, writing the foreword to the second edition of Ward's *Everest: A Thousand Years of Exploration* in 2013, eight years after Michael died, described how some of the acrimony surrounding this big debate played out:

> The controversy really took off when Michael Ward published his mountain memoir *In This Short Span* in 1972, in which he wrote of his disagreement with John Hunt's assault plan and the scientific work which had been key to the climb's success …
> The controversy became fierce in 1973 for the 20th anniversary

of the first ascent. Michael made a speech in the presence of the Duke of Edinburgh developing his scientific thesis and rightly attributing all the merit to Griffith Pugh. Soon after his speech, John Hunt, furious, shouted at him, 'No one wants to hear about that science,' and to Michael's ironic silence he added, 'I hate scientists' then turned to another member of the expedition saying, 'Someone should shut Ward up!'

Michael, however, would not be quieted. His sense of fair play would not let history be distorted in this way. A fellow expedition member, Westmacott, once observed: 'Mike was a strong character, with strong views which he did not hesitate to express.' Hunt's stance always troubled Ward – in a letter to another Everester in 2004, he recalled: 'He sometimes lost his temper and told me how much he hated science and scientists.'

During the 40th anniversary celebration of the first ascent, when Queen Elizabeth and members of the Royal Family hosted a reception, Ward spoke up again, recalling the role science had played in their success and firmly shining the spotlight on Pugh (who died the following year). One of their colleagues, James Milledge, would later write: 'There is no doubt that through his writing and lecturing he helped establish Pugh's reputation.' However, in his recent biography of Ed Hillary, author Michael Gill has viewed Ward's action as self-serving and had this to say about the issue:

> The other revisionist proposition was that Griffith Pugh was the individual who made the 1953 expedition successful. This suggestion came from Mike Ward, who had already earned a special place in the history of Everest through his launch of the 1951 reconnaissance. Without him the British might well have missed out on their 1953 place. He has his own claim to be 'the man who made it possible'… Ward was troubled by the thought that the scientist Griffith Pugh, and by association his companion Mike Ward, had received less than the recognition due to them.

Gill was with Pugh, Ward and Milledge during the Himalayan Scientific and Mountaineering Expedition and got to know them well. His comment about Ward, however, is misplaced and cannot go unanswered. In none of Michael's writing, including his unpublished autobiography, is there an indication he sought more glory, or that he was disenchanted with the recognition he did receive. He unreservedly credited Pugh and his colleagues at the MRC for many of the technical advances made in summiting Everest. His trait of ensuring credit was given where due is evident in other instances too, for example: his articles about the Pundits who were overlooked by their British officers; his acknowledgement of Dr Alexander Kellas's pioneering contribution to mountain medicine; his obituary of Sherpa Angtarkay when no one else wrote one; and together with a colleague, he wrote Pugh's obituary.

Returning to that day of Everest's 40th anniversary celebration with the queen, as it turned out, Pugh's daughter Harriet Tuckey was also in the audience. She was stunned to hear of her father's invaluable contribution, of which she knew little because, as she has readily admitted, for most of her life she disliked him intensely. But Ward's address inspired her into many years of research delving into his life and work, in the process finding new respect for a parent from whom she had been estranged for much of her life.

Michael had urged Harriet to write her father's biography, which was eventually published on the 60th anniversary, titled *Everest: The First Ascent*. Towards the end of it, she wrote:

> Of all those who sought to ensure that Pugh's achievements were recognised, the man who tried hardest was Michael Ward whose tireless campaign to force Sir John Hunt to acknowledge Pugh's contribution to the success on Everest made him unpopular with his fellow expedition members, who all felt great loyalty for their former leader.

This controversy also affected Ward's family. His son Mark posted on his website that same year: 'At home my father remained remarkably sanguine about all of this.' When verbally attacked, Michael would maintain his 'ironic silence … ah, how well I remember the futility of arguing with those silences'. Despite not letting 'all of this' affect him, Mark recalled: 'However, up to his death, my father, like Griffith Pugh, continued to suffer the scorn and cold shoulder of the leader of the '53 expedition, John Hunt, and his acolytes.'

Mark also chose to post a poignant picture of the Everesters taken during a reunion in Snowdonia in front of the Pen-Y-Gwryd Hotel. It shows his father standing apart, looking on at rest of the group. (Another snap signed by everyone and mounted in the hotel's bar, shows him standing with the others, but on the extreme left and still somewhat apart.)

Michael would not let the frustration from this ongoing controversy spill over into his writing, nor get into a war of words with his detractors. But he did continue to stand up for what he believed. In his book *Everest*, in the chapter titled 'Science and Success' dealing with the outcome of this expedition, he closed with:

> For the first time, detailed and comprehensive scientific methods were applied to the problems of Everest. This marked out our party as different in its approach from all the previous Everest expeditions, each of which had been well organised but without this extra dimension. It was good science, applied by everyone who took part, that got us to the summit.

There were, of course, other factors involved which Ward has omitted, some of which were beyond human control. These included the timing of the monsoon and weather conditions high on the mountain itself; and – never to be discounted – good old lady luck. One cannot help wondering, however, at least from Ward's perspective, whether much of this debate and the acrimony with Hunt could have been avoided in the first place, had his leader given science and the scientists involved their fair share of credit.

# 11

# From Doctor to Surgeon

The years between returning from Everest and his next big Himalayan expedition starting in 1960 were somewhat anti-climactic for Ward in terms of mountaineering but nevertheless busy ones. And important too, marking the period when he steadily worked towards, and then realised, his other significant goal – becoming a surgeon.

Having recently passed his primary exams, the last hurdle involved years of supervised work to gain the necessary experience. Then, he would have to satisfy a group of examiners during his final assessment, including a theoretical aspect that would require more study. His immediate need, however, was to find employment again. By good fortune, he was able to secure a position as a Junior Lecturer in the Academic Surgical Unit of the London Hospital. It was the largest in terms of teaching in the capital, and one of the busiest hospitals in Europe.

Here, he examined and treated an endless stream of outpatients from many nationalities. Michael also spent a lot of time assisting with operations, which he quickly realised was the only way to learn practical surgery. To begin with, he was given the task of sewing up incisions, recalling: 'I was told that to survive as a surgeon I had to enjoy every stitch and every knot I tied. Perfection was the only aim.'

To gain broad experience, Ward worked in various roles over the next seven years at the London and two other hospitals nearby. Since he wasn't fully qualified yet, tenures only lasted between six months and two years, which created difficulties: 'I was constantly on tenterhooks, looking for another job, studying for an exam, and working at my present job.' The latter was demanding, as he and two other doctors in the casualty ward often saw over a hundred cases a day. Moreover, they had to be on call every third night, which meant sleeping in the hospital overnight, and during any 'spare' time were allowed to assist with emergency operations. Michael would later reflect on the prerequisites for becoming a surgeon as involving 'a vast knowledge, a thick skin, manual dexterity and the ability to go without sleep'.

The day of his final assessment in clinical surgery eventually arrived. It involved both written papers and the diagnosis of several patients over a few days in front of a panel of stony-faced examiners. Although this assessment had a failure rate of around 70 per cent, Ward managed to convince them he was competent and ready to practice. Soon afterwards, at the ceremony to confer his Fellowship of the Royal College of Surgeons in 1960, one of the examiners cheerfully told him 'it now starts to become really difficult' – years after his retirement, Michael noted 'he was quite right'.

Ward began by taking on roles in London hospitals as a registrar. Rather than specialise, he wanted to become a general surgeon and work towards securing a senior registrar's post at a teaching hospital. His ultimate goal was to become a consultant surgeon, but realised from the outset this would not be easy and the competition intense.

The work could be described similarly, and Michael later wrote about this intensity during his longest rotation lasting almost two years. He was then based in the London Hospital's cardiothoracic unit, which undertook lifesaving procedures on vital organs in the chest cavity:

> Because of the type of work, which was on the borders of the
> possible and sometimes beyond it, the effect that it had on the
> fragile temperament of some of those involved turned out to
> be one of the most demanding of the many different types of
> surgery I did.

Despite the inherent tension and drama, Ward could be philosophical about the medical profession, as he explained once to his fellow mountaineers: 'There are only two kinds of illness, one you recover from and one you die from. Our role is purely peripheral.'[*]

During this time, Michael was climbing whenever his busy work schedule allowed. In 1952, he also joined the Club Alpin Français after being nominated by two of France's premier climbers, Bernard Pierre (whom he also climbed with in Wales) and Gaston Rébuffat.

Back at home that same year, he was a founding member of the breakaway Alpine Climbing Group (ACG), formed to encourage young and ambitious British mountaineers seeking to raise their standards to the highest order. To ensure members remained active and were attempting the hardest of routes, they were subject to scrutiny every two years, and an age limit was set with automatic expulsion after forty years. Tom Bourdillon was chosen as its

---

[*] Said during an expedition to Mount Kongur in 1981, as retold by cameraman Jim Curran.

first president and the group included a few Everesters. Notably, the best young climbers were invited to join the ACG irrespective of their social standing, which raised many an eyebrow in a still class-conscious society, and women were allowed to join for the first time. (The ACG later merged with the Alpine Club but still remains active today; the latter refused to admit women until 1974.)

Although Ward may have become a first-class mountaineer, writing later, Bonington would put his ambition into perspective: '[He] was in the traditional mould of prewar climbers – essentially amateur, knowing that however great his enthusiasm for climbing, his career in medicine would always take priority.'

Before long, Ward was in his thirties, and at age thirty-two married Jane Ewbank, who was in her early twenties. She had been working in fashion and public relations, with little interest in either mountains or medicine which, as Michael pointed out, 'provided a balancing factor to two such obsessional occupations and this perfectly suited us'. They had been married only six months when he seized an opportunity to work at the Royal Victoria Hospital in Montreal, Quebec, as part of an exchange programme lasting one year. A few months before leaving home, sculptor and medical researcher Dr Mary Catterall created a likeness of Ward's head. As with all her work, this was done from memory only, without sittings or photographs. (She also made a bust of John Hunt.)

In Montreal, Jane was able to find well-paying work as a copywriter in the fashion trade. This was just as well, since Michael's paltry salary as a young doctor was insufficient for their upkeep, not even covering the rent, and was a source of ongoing frustration. The culture of money there could not have helped either, as Jane mentioned in a letter home: 'It seems that either you are rich or you might as well crawl under a stone.'

Unable to afford a flat – or a car – they found lodgings in a boarding house close to the hospital, next to Mount Royal where they lived during their stay in Canada. In winter they bought cheap wooden skis and had fun learning the rudiments of the sport, whizzing down its slopes. To improve their skills, they travelled south across the border into New York State to a ski centre in Lake Placid, then graduated onto the slopes of neighbouring Whiteface Mountain.

This was an exciting time for the young couple, living in a beautiful French-speaking city across the other side of the Atlantic. Despite being short of money, they made most of the opportunity, visiting some of America's big cities while Michael attended medical conventions and visited hospitals; although he was appalled at the way patients were assessed financially before treatment was considered.

During their time away, between them, they wrote regularly to Michael's parents, often on a weekly basis. In one of those letters, Jane attached a newspaper clipping from the *Montreal Star* with the headline 'Everest Veteran Tests Laurentians'. It followed a talk Michael had given as guest of honour at the annual meeting of the Alpine Club of Canada's branch in Montreal. The lengthy article was accompanied by two action shots of him ascending a rocky needle of one of the Laurentian peaks around Val David.

Ward climbed whenever he could and on both sides of the border, such as when he went rock climbing with friends on Noonmark Mountain in upstate New York. He finished his stint in Canada by travelling west across the country to British Columbia to climb in the Bugaboos, a mountain range in the Canadian Rockies rising to 11,000ft with spectacular spires. While Jane visited Vancouver with her father (her mother had died the previous year), Michael spent three weeks rock climbing there in July with some Canadian friends.

They completed a first ascent of the South Face of Marmolada; the face itself being somewhere between 800 to 900ft high. In an article for the *Alpine Journal* (1960), he reckoned the degree of difficulty 'fell nowhere below Very Severe', and described how they managed to summit after spending seven hours on the face. He rated the East Ridge of Bugaboo spire as 'one of the finest pure rock ridges' he had climbed; this one being a second ascent.

Canada was an eye-opening time for the young couple with easy access to many of the glamorous cities of North America. It raised questions in their minds whether this could be the place to make their future home – their decision reveals something about the pair:

> Jane and I have nostalgic feelings; but we were glad to return
> to England. It had become clear to us that we were essentially
> Europeans and whatever the difficulties we would be unwise
> to uproot ourselves on any permanent basis.

Soon after returning home, in a letter to his parents at the end of November 1959, Michael announced: 'The most important news really is that Jane is going to have a baby in April' (their only child, Mark William).

Ward resumed his career in the recently established National Health Service (NHS). Initially, he worked as a senior registrar over a four-year period at various hospitals, including the Poplar Hospital (later absorbed into the NHS) which served the area around the old East India Docks. In his unpublished biographical notes, Michael recalled an incident here when his drive for efficiency was not appreciated:

I kept the hospital as full as possible all the time and because the waiting lists were so long, I managed to cut them down by doing extra operations over the holidays, except for Christmas; arguing that as the medical staff had to be in the hospital anyway, they might as well use their time profitably rather than hanging around getting bored. Naturally, no one got paid extra for this, but the cancer of bureaucracy did not like it at all as it was outside their imagination, and so they stopped me doing it.

As an adult, his son Mark recalled another such incident: 'On one memorable occasion, when the umpteenth strike closed down his operating room, he called up a fleet of taxis to pick up his patients and drive them through the picket lines to another hospital so he could continue his scheduled operations without interruption.' Lives often hung in the balance on his operating table, but Ward would reflect:

Hope is the key; patients should never be deprived of this. Beside it, Faith and Charity are quite irrelevant ... Surgeons are often accused of being clinically detached, uncaring, ruthless even; but we have to survive too in order to perform to the best of our ability. Surgery is not a game of football.

Michael continued working for the NHS even after attaining his goal of becoming a consultant surgeon in 1964, and would remain in it for thirty years.* He chose not to seek the lucrative rewards of a Harley Street private practice as many London specialists did, not even on a part-time basis. Instead, he worked to ensure medical care was accessible to all – an ideal he passionately believed in. Years after his death, Jan Morris, by now a famous writer, and no doubt remembering his outburst to Hunt on Everest, would describe Ward as 'a fiery English surgeon who was to dedicate all his later life to the public health service'.

---

* As a consultant, Ward worked at Poplar Hospital (1964–75), St Andrew's, Bow (1964–93), and Newham (1983–93). He also lectured clinical surgery at the London (1975–93).

# 12

# The Silver Hut

During the winter of 1960 and into the spring of the following year, Ward took part in the Himalayan Scientific and Mountaineering Expedition 1960–61 led by Ed Hillary, with Griff Pugh as scientific leader. It became better known as the Silver Hut Expedition after the Sherpas named it so, due to the distinctive silver paintwork of the main hut-cum-laboratory.

From a scientific perspective, its groundbreaking research would not only improve safety for mountaineers but ultimately benefit large numbers of people living in mountainous regions all over the world.[*] For this reason, it was a far more important undertaking than climbing a difficult mountain or, for that matter, the first ascent of Everest. This is not to understate the mountaineering aspects of the Silver Hut Expedition: a remarkable first ascent of Ama Dablam followed by an attempt to summit the fifth highest mountain in the world, Makalu (both to be discussed later).

Although this expedition was Pugh's brainchild, Ward did have a hand in its conception.[†] He recalled on the trek to Everest in 1953, while sheltering inside a tent with Pugh during a violent downpour:

> During the two hours of the storm, which lasted almost until dark, we talked about Griffith's work on the Menlung La in 1952, and how really the only efficient way to study man at high altitude was on the spot rather than in a laboratory. I remember saying that transporting a laboratory to high altitude and keeping it equipped would cost a great deal of money. Thus the seeds of the high altitude programme, in which we both took part seven years later, were planted.

---

[*] In an article titled 'Man and the Mountain Environment' in the *Alpine Journal* (1969), Ward noted: 'About ten million people live at altitudes exceeding 12,000ft mainly in South America, but about one-fifth in Central Asia.'

[†] Alexander Kellas first mooted setting up a high altitude laboratory in 1917.

The expedition became more than just an idea directly from the efforts of Pugh and Hillary; one focused exclusively on science while the other on mountaineering and, as it turned out, a hunt for the elusive yeti.

As well as being together on Cho Oyu in 1952, the pair had met up again during the Commonwealth Trans-Antarctic Expedition 1955–58 led by British scientist and explorer Dr Vivian Fuchs. His mission was to make the first land crossing of Antarctica, a distance of over 2,000 miles starting from Shackleton Base on the shores of the Weddell Sea. Fuchs's team planned to travel in a convoy of six vehicles, including three specially built Sno-Cats, crossing the continent via the South Pole before arriving at a newly constructed Scott Base at McMurdo Sound on the Ross Sea. Coinciding with the International Geophysical Year, the team would undertake important research along the way. It also set out with every expectation of being the first overland party to reach the South Pole since the famous race of 1911–12 between Roald Amundsen and Robert Falcon Scott.

Fuchs had recruited Hillary, now a world celebrity, to lead the New Zealand component and secure his government's involvement and funding. Yet these two men were vastly different in personality as Ed admitted: 'I felt that Fuchs and I had little in common – he was far more serious and dogged than I could ever be and he spent so much time emphasising the scientific worth of the journey and playing down the sheer adventure of it.'

Ed's preference for adventure over science was understandable for someone of his makeup and love for the outdoors, especially bagging peaks. One of his oft-used 'quotable quotes' maintained: 'Nobody climbs mountains for scientific reasons. Science is used to raise money for the expeditions, but you really climb for the hell of it.' His mind-set would lead to difficulties, however, around the setting of priorities at Silver Hut which, even more than the Trans-Antarctic Expedition, was conceived as a scientific venture.

In Antarctica, Hillary's primary roles were two-fold: build a base at McMurdo Sound for housing the New Zealand research team; then lead a support group laying food and fuel supply depots for the second half of Fuchs's planned route. But Ed was not expected to go to the Pole itself. As it turned out, once Scott Base was operational, he and three others, unencumbered by having to undertake any research, made better progress across the desolate continent than Fuchs's twelve-man party. After laying the depots, Hillary then controversially led his group, driving three converted farm tractors, all the way to the South Pole, to the chagrin of his usurped leader.

There was outrage from sections of the British public too, who somehow saw the Pole as theirs, just as they had Mount Everest. Moreover, they had been encouraged by the press into picturing opposing teams led by Fuchs and Hillary competing in a second 'race for the Pole'. Interestingly, Ward had a different view to most of his fellow Englishmen about what transpired: 'To ask anyone to stop short of the Pole, let alone Ed, who was temperamentally hardly suited to such a supporting role, was asking too much.'

Still, at times it had been a trying expedition for Hillary, as his biographer Michael Gill described: 'Over the years one never heard Ed talk much about his dash to the Pole. It became part of his mythology, taking farm tractors across the ice, but there were some sore spots there that were best left alone.' In his autobiography *Nothing Venture, Nothing Win* Hillary explained:

> The press had a field day on the pros and cons of our journey but for me the decision had been relatively straightforward. I would have despised myself if I hadn't continued – it was as simple as that – I just had to go on.

While they were together at Scott Base, Hillary and Pugh first discussed the possibility of taking a party to the Himalayas with both scientific and mountaineering goals. Although they talked about the idea further over the next few years, it was clear that securing funding for such a project would be a major hurdle. This was solved when Hillary convinced an American company, publishers of *World Book Encyclopedia*, to become their primary sponsor to the tune of $200,000 by including a third objective: a search for the yeti. The world remained impatient to see this supposed creature whose line of footprints Ward had been photographed standing next to.

In the autumn of 1959, Hillary and Pugh caught up with Ward in his flat in Kensington to sound him out about joining their expedition. It would be made up of three parties: a group to construct the hut, Pugh's team of scientists who would occupy it, and Hillary's team searching for the yeti. Although he was immediately interested, Michael was sceptical about any media-driven search for the Abominable Snowman, telling Ed: 'If this is going to be a stunt, I've had it.' He also had concerns about the priority research work would be given, knowing Hillary did not have a scientific bent nor the patience for it. Moreover, he had learnt from Pugh that Ed's handling of the scientists at Scott Base had not always been tactful.

Nevertheless, Ward was keen to join them as it married his two great interests, mountain medicine and climbing. Their plan to also attempt one of the major Himalayan peaks was more than an added attraction too. And he was heartened to know Pugh would be the scientific leader as Michael had full confidence in Griff's ability and capacity for work.

Besides which, Hillary was planning to be away on his yeti hunt while the research programme got underway, which led Ward to muse: 'Perhaps the thought of spending a winter with a lot of scientists depressed him!' In fairness to Ed, this may have been due to his experience on Cho Oyu, when Pugh had measured his blood count as being ridiculously low. It led him to write in *High Adventure*: 'There and then my faith in science and scientists disappeared for ever.'

This time, their endeavour would depend upon setting up the highest laboratory ever established at 19,000ft. They planned to staff it with scientists who would spend many months there studying the long-term effects on humans living at high altitude. The height of the lab was chosen for two main reasons. The first was to build on research already completed on populations living around 15,000ft in South America. The other was to ascertain whether, as was suspected, 17,500ft represented the maximum height for permanent habitation.* Another important decision the trio made during their meeting was to build the hut in autumn, soon after the monsoon had dissipated. This would allow research to be conducted over winter when the weather was better, despite the cold.

The culmination of the scientific programme was to be an attempt of Makalu (27,825ft) in spring. It had only been climbed once before, by a large French team in 1955 using open-circuit oxygen apparatus. This time, however, the attempt was to be made without oxygen by some of the scientists and mountaineers, based on the reasonable hypothesis it should be possible as they would be thoroughly acclimatised by this stage. They would also be joined by a few newly arrived climbers and the two groups would undergo clinical observation to allow comparison of their performances and the impact of acclimatisation. (In the final count, twenty-one members were involved at various times during the entire expedition as scientists, climbers, and yeti hunters, with many having multiple roles.)

Before Hillary and Pugh left Ward's flat, they discussed where to site the all-important laboratory – soon to be dubbed the Silver Hut. They agreed to locate it on the upper Mingbo Glacier which lay south of Everest, just below Ama Dablam with Makalu rising some 13 miles to the east. The hut was to be prefabricated and shipped to Bombay, before making an arduous journey via Kathmandu to its final site – the last leg from Namche Bazaar would be on the backs of many porters. Before its shipment, Michael was

---

* The study would establish that, due to inevitable weight loss (1–3lb per week), the maximum altitude lowlanders can permanently live is 16,500–18,000ft.

involved in a test run putting the hut together in London and came away impressed at how well its panels fitted together to form a tubular structure.

The hut measured around 12ft in diameter and 22ft in length, looking much like the fuselage of an aeroplane, and was to be mounted on adjustable legs to ensure a level floor. There were more than a hundred panels involved, all painted silver. Made from sandwiches of marine plywood covering 3in of insulating plastic foam, the thick panels would protect the occupants and their gear from the high winds and freezing temperatures. No piece was made more than 4½ft long and each weighed under 20lb. This would allow porters to carry bundles of up to three panels at a time, as they wound their way up tracks and across mountain streams for nearly 200 miles.

Meanwhile, as scientific leader Pugh put much thought into choosing the other four members of his group, all specialists in their fields. Each would have their own programme to complete and, on returning home, was expected to write up and publish their findings. Just as importantly, they would have to work harmoniously while cooped up in a small hut for many months, a long way from anywhere. Another considerable task that fell to Pugh was organising the laboratory equipment and spares, since everything required had to be carefully itemised and shipped out well before they left England.

Ward had been working as a senior surgical registrar when first approached by Pugh and Hillary. After securing leave of absence from his hospital, he signed up to go but, although his salary was to be paid by the expedition, he still had some misgiving: 'My feelings were very mixed – I was leaving Jane for seven months, with a seven-month-old baby, and whilst I was quite confident of the safety of our programme it was difficult to convince people of this.' *

Ward flew out from London on 19 October 1960 with another scientist, Dr John West, to Delhi, where they changed to a smaller Dakota aircraft to land in Kathmandu. Here, as the first page of his expedition diary records, given the paucity of doctors in that country, Michael was immediately dragged off to the nearby United Mission Hospital to assist its staff with a

---

* During a conversation with Jane in April 2025, when I asked whether her husband's long absences were a problem, she replied: 'Michael was away a lot. I didn't mind and didn't stop him; I supported him. This was part of his person.'

medical emergency. Little did he suspect then, they would soon be returning the favour.

He and West had brought two Lloyd-Haldane Gas Analysers with them, which were vital for the laboratory work planned.* Pugh, who had travelled to Sola Khumbu a little earlier discovered, to his distress, that the mercury-filled glass tubes in the first pair shipped out had arrived broken. Without these instruments, at least three of the most important projects could not be carried out. Luckily, he had managed to alert Ward and West in time to bring replacements, which they carried on their backs across Nepal, despite entreaties from the Sherpas to relieve the sahibs of their loads.

Days after leaving the capital in mid-December, they trekked past Thyangboche monastery to Mingbo village, an idyllic yak pasture with stone-walled enclosures. It sat 15,000ft up and was where Base Camp had been established. The pair began their work here while acclimatising over ten days, before moving into Silver Hut with the other scientists. Ward's main focus was to clinically examine the physiological condition of each of the hut's inhabitants, particularly through blood and urine analysis. He would need them to act as his 'guinea pigs', just as the other scientists would carry out various tests on each other throughout their stay.

Michael's other interest was to better understand the different afflictions occurring at altitude which had been historically lumped together under the general label 'mountain sickness'.† He would also study the deterioration which sick climbers at high altitude experienced. Since living conditions experienced by such mountaineers were invariably poor, it was impossible to differentiate how much of this decline was due to oxygen lack versus surviving in cramped tents, often sleep-deprived, and with inadequate food and fluid intake. A high-altitude laboratory would, for the first time, remove poor living conditions as a variable, thus isolating the impact of altitude on the human body. Ward would be able to evaluate the severity of any deterioration by measuring variables such as physical fitness, mental awareness, weight loss and blood values. Like the other scientists, he had a big programme of work planned which he was keen to complete.

In Mingbo, Ward caught up with Pugh to hear what had occurred since the expedition had arrived in Kathmandu and engaged hundreds of porters

---

* This analyser measures the percentage of carbon dioxide and oxygen in air.

† In 1968, Peter Crew's *Encyclopaedic Dictionary of Mountaineering* described *mountain sickness* as: 'A malady comparable with sea and air sickness which affects people not accustomed to high altitudes, and caused by insufficient acclimatisation, mild forms of sunstroke, exposure to the glare of sun and snow, etc.'

to haul gear up to Base Camp. Hillary's group had arrived there first and marched directly from the capital to the remote Rolwaling Valley. It lay just south of the Menlung basin, where Ward and Shipton had encountered those footprints. At the time, this region in northeast Nepal was considered the most likely home of the yeti. Three other expeditions had visited here previously hoping to find evidence of its existence, but none were successful. (Reinhold Messner also searched for many years and over a much wider area across the Himalayas, including Bhutan and Tibet, as detailed in his 1998 book translated from German, *My Quest for the Yeti.*)

Hillary's ten-man yeti party included a pair of animal experts from America, a biologist, and the director of a zoo in Chicago. Splitting into two teams, they spent six weeks scouring the high slopes around the Rolwaling Valley. Using telescopes, cameras activated by trip wires, and 'yeti whistles', the team attempted to make whatever contact they could with their prey. They also went armed with tranquilliser guns in case they came across one. But the hunters found nothing to shoot at nor any real evidence of its presence, although they did manage to capture two live pandas.

Eventually, Hillary did secure what locals claimed was a yeti scalp from a monastery in Khumjung village near Namche Bazaar, and he was also able to examine two similar ones. Since their shape belonged to no known animal, these scalps generated much excitement among the hunt party. Patchily covered with bristles and resembling a conical helmet, the one from Khumjung was said to be 240 years old. Following lengthy negotiations, the villagers finally agreed to its release for a six-week period, but only after a donation of 8,000 rupees was made for renovations to the monastery and a promise to build a school in the area.

Then, with a village elder to chaperon the revered object, together with an interpreter and the expedition zoologist in tow, Ed made a dash for Chicago, then Paris, and finally onto London. At each stop, the scalp was examined by experts. Their overall conclusion was that it was a fake and had somehow been moulded from the hide of a serow, a goat-antelope. Likewise, the three fur skins that locals had assured Hillary were from yetis all proved to be from the rare blue bear which lives in eastern Tibet. In the expedition's book *High in the Thin Cold Air*, Ed stated:

> Pleasant though we felt it would be to believe in the existence
> of the Yeti, when faced with the universal collapse of the

main evidence in support of this creature the members of my expedition – doctor, scientists, zoologists, and mountaineers alike – could not in all conscience view it as more than a fascinating fairy tale, born of the rare and frightening view of strange animals, moulded by superstition, and enthusiastically nurtured by Western expeditions.

What then of the footprints Ward had stood next to in 1951? Earlier, hunting on a glacier with partially shaded slopes, one of Hillary's teams had come across a set of well-defined tracks in the snow thought to be made by a fox. On examination, they found sections of the tracks directly exposed to the sun had melted to closely resemble those photographed by Shipton. Moreover, Hillary and others had found similar tracks. This convinced his experts that the probable origin of such footprints was wandering animals such as foxes, snow leopards and bears. As Ed wrote in his book:

> Wherever we found them, and they had by now become commonplace, it was the same story – tracks the Sherpas swore to be authentic Snowman were quite obviously those of some small unsuspecting quadrupeds promoted by sun and local imagination into the realm of Himalayan fantasy. But this still did not preclude Yetis, too, from making Yeti tracks.

Understandably, his last sentence tried to keep the door ajar 'just in case', but Ed was no longer convinced. Perhaps it was the failure of not finding any evidence after a long and expensive search that prompted Hillary to dismiss the whole affair. But in the process of distancing himself from it, he dragged Ward's name back into the story.

In recalling those four photographs, he said: 'Knowing what a cynic Shipton could be I had a feeling he might have tidied up that track a little, just for a laugh! I told him so many times, but he always denied it.' A decade on, in the 1984 interview mentioned earlier for Jim Perrin's book, he went much further:

> What you've got to understand is that Eric was a joker. He was forever pulling practical jokes, fooling around in his quiet way. This footprint, see, he's gone around it with his knuckles, shaped the toe, pressed in the middle. There's no animal could walk with a foot like that! He made it up, and of course he was with Sen Tenzing who was as big a joker as Eric was. They pulled the trick, and Mike Ward just had to keep quiet and go

> along with it. We all knew, apart from Bill Murray maybe, but
> none of us could say, and Eric let it run and run. He just loved
> to wind people up that way.

If Hillary had believed this to be the case from the outset, it is difficult to understand why he would have made the yeti hunt a primary objective of this expedition – unless as a way to secure funding from *World Book Encyclopedia*. Of course, whatever Shipton did or didn't do, it does not preclude the existence of such creatures as Ed had rightly pointed out, but his later comments seem inconsistent with his earlier actions.

During an interview in France *before* they got underway, he was enthusiastic, saying: 'You will come with me on the greatest adventure of my life, the *chasse à l'abominable homme des neiges dans l'Himalaya.* Yes, the Yeti exists and I am going to prove it to you.' A year on, *after* his hunt, in a newspaper report his stance had changed: 'Nothing called Yeti exists in flesh and bone, only in stories. Any further expedition in search of it would be sheer waste of money.'* Furthermore, his article titled 'Epitaph to the Elusive Abominable Snowman' for *Life* magazine (13 January 1961) concluded by saying: 'Of course, the yeti still remains a very real part of the mythology and tradition of the Himalayan peoples – and it is undoubtedly in the field of mythology that the yeti rightly belongs.'

As far as Ward was concerned, that should have been the end of the matter, as he had viewed Ed's yeti hunt as a distraction from their research programme at Silver Hut. However, Ed's interview with Perrin had named Michael as being a party to this so-called joke. To add to the controversy, in his book Perrin went on to relate another incident which occurred in 1993. While he was belaying Ward, now 68 years old, on a rock climb in Wales, according to Jim, Michael hinted he had always known of Shipton's alleged hoax:

> I spotted him tussling with a particularly recalcitrant section
> of vertical crack coated with green slime, and yelled down:
> 'So, Michael, about that photograph of the Yeti footprint …?'
> As I did so, I paid out six inches of slack on a rope which
> hitherto I'd kept snug and tight. His eyebrows disappeared
> under the rim of his helmet. 'Take in, you bastard,' he gasped,
> face ruckling into a smile. It told me everything.

---

* Both preceding quotes are from his biography *Edmund Hillary* by Michael Gill.

Unfortunately, Perrin chose to read far more into a smile than was intended because, as pointed out earlier, Ward rejected any suggestion he had ever played along with 'the trick', as explicitly stated in his book *Everest*. Jokes aside, he would have surely told Hillary the truth – *if* this was the case – to prevent Ed's yeti party spending six weeks on what proved to be a rather pointless exercise, especially when there was so much scientific work at stake.

After he put the failed hunt behind him, Hillary pushed on to Silver Hut, to participate in the expedition's two original objectives, research and mountaineering.

Meanwhile, as Pugh walked up with Ward towards their new winter home, Griff told him of the difficulties he had encountered dealing with their leader, particularly in getting Ed to acknowledge him as the scientific leader and act accordingly. Although Pugh's frustrations had boiled over at one point (Hillary likened it to a 'tongue lashing'), with help of two other members Griff and Ed had managed to patch over their differences and the pair's relationship had since improved.

Arriving at Silver Hut, Michael was overwhelmed by 'the spectacular views down the Mingbo Glacier across many peaks that disappeared into a haze of cloud'. And even more so when he looked up at the tooth-like face of Ama Dablam, which towered overhead. The hut's location provided the occupants 'an inside view on a number of storms', and in the *Alpine Journal* (1961) he described what else was on display:

> Behind these great peaks the sun would set touching them with all the many colours of the spectrum. On stormy evenings it was as if an immense smith's furnace had been lit and great flames appeared to shoot upwards colouring the mountain slopes black, orange, red and gold. These great shafts of colour appeared to pierce the clouds before fading into a cold, greenish-blue sky.

In the face of peaks surrounding it, the Silver Hut seemed miniscule and vulnerable. The main building was tied down by guy wires embedded into the glacier and designed to withstand winds of 100 miles per hour. (Fortunately, the weather and temperature during that winter turned out to be far less severe than expected.)

Inside, the hut was comfortable. Its insulated shell and triple-glazed windows could counter outside temperatures down to −50°C, allowing the scientists to work in shirt sleeves. It contained eight sleeping bunks and a laboratory area which took up the last third of the floor area. A specially fabricated kerosene stove warmed the open-plan room. The kitchen, however, was moved to a large dome tent outside, after it was discovered the primus stoves were giving off high levels of poisonous carbon monoxide. Smaller tents were also pitched nearby to be used for storage together with one of two ice-caves, while the other served as the toilet.

The facility was powered by an external wind generator hooked up to batteries stored under the floor. This system provided adequate lighting for writing up their work in the evenings. Much of their spare time at night was spent reading, playing chess, listening to the radio, or even talking to 'ham operators' around the world.

The hut's prefabricated panels had been assembled in a single day by a team led by structural engineer and mountaineer Norman Hardie from New Zealand.* His four-man construction party included another of his countrymen, Wally Romanes, an expert builder. Romanes also erected a smaller wooden hut 1,000ft below Silver Hut to act as a staging post and additional sleeping quarters. Fitted with four bunks, it became known as the Green Hut due to the brightly coloured canvas he used for its outer covering. Both huts quickly proved more comfortable than Base Camp in Mingbo, so even the lab work which could be carried out at lower levels was relocated up to Silver Hut.

Ward soon met up with the rest of Pugh's multi-national team: Other than Dr John West, an Australian physiologist working in London, there was Dr James Milledge, an Englishman, and Dr Sukhamay Lahiri from India. There were four others who would make up the wintering party and assist with scientific work. The first two were Captain Motwani from the Indian Army,† and an American named Barry Bishop who was a glaciologist and surveyor working for *National Geographic*.‡ The other two were New Zealanders: Michael Gill, a final year medical student, and Wally Romanes, the only non-scientist and described by Ward as 'the most practical and

---

* Hardie was with the 1955 British expedition to Kangchenjunga (28,169ft), the world's third-highest mountain, during its first ascent when he also summited.

† Motwani was studying the effects of high altitude on troops stationed at Himalayan border posts.

‡ Bishop's long article 'Wintering in the High Himalayas' later appeared in this journal (1962, Vol. 122).

useful person on the party'. Years later, Jim Milledge recalled how Michael Ward had lightened his interaction with them:

> [Mike] was senior to most of us in both years and certainly in mountaineering experience. I think, to the New Zealanders and Americans, playing the part of 'rough Colonials', his background of public school and Cambridge and his accent suggested that he belonged to the aristocracy. Mike played up to this role and I remember him addressing them as, 'My dear chap', much to their amusement.

Although the scientists would have to work in cramped conditions with their gear often stowed helter-skelter, the group got along surprisingly well with few disagreements overheard, as Ward observed: 'Perhaps the altitude helped to keep our tempers – it is really too exhausting to have a good argument at high altitude.' Lack of space could also lead to other issues as Bishop noted:

> Occasionally mercury was spilled from the physiologists' equipment. Then we *had* to clean up, for mercury can poison the air in a restricted area. On such occasions we crawled around on hands and knees, chasing quicksilver around the floor and into paper cups to put back into bottles.

Pugh had mandated a minimum of six hours of work and two hours of exercise daily, although at times the two activities were inseparable, such as when measuring an individual's maximum work capacity. This assessment, involving a bicycle ergometer, was one in which they all participated. It took up more time and effort than any other test and was particularly exhausting. A stationary cycle's back wheel was attached to a band that was gradually tightened to increase resistance as the 'guinea pig' pedalled away madly. He did this while keeping pace with a metronome and exhaling into a Douglas bag to collect his lung air samples.

This test measured the maximum amount of oxygen a person could take in over a set period of time. It would hopefully show the scientists whether a mountaineer with a greater maximum intake would perform better at high-altitude climbing than one with a lower intake. During the test, the subject was hooked up with electrodes connected to an electrocardiogram (ECG) machine measuring his heartrate. At the end of a session lasting a few minutes, a blood sample was taken. After a short break, the process was restarted but with the work rate increased and the cycling continued.

So exhausting was this process at altitude that only one test could be completed by an individual on any given day, and often he had to be held onto the bicycle by others towards the end. The whole experiment was carefully repeated every month to track the physiological change occurring in each person. Setting up and using the bicycle, however, made the laboratory area even more congested for the other scientists.

Ward reckoned 'it was an exercise in obsession and machismo to complete a successful maximum work test', but their competitive spirit soon kicked in as individuals tried to outdo each other. Unfortunately, Hillary, who had shown outstanding strength on Everest, had returned to New Zealand over winter so couldn't be benchmarked against (Ed would join them again for the attempt on Makalu). Nevertheless, the members of the wintering party each took their turn on the ergometer, mostly without complaint, although Michael recalled: 'How I grew to loathe and detest this machine as, day after day, I cycled for miles, getting nowhere, and becoming more and more tired.'

At the end of a tiring day, or when they got sick of the confined space, he and the others would don their skis and head down the slopes of the glacier for some welcome relief. His previous training in Canada stood him in good stead now, as they timed themselves whizzing down a makeshift slalom course marked out with bamboo poles. Griff, being an Olympic-class skier, was easily the best, but Michael found his own skill improving steadily during what was only his second season. At 19,000ft, they had exclusive use of the highest ski field in the world. Flying down its slopes to the icefall, there was the odd crevasse to watch out for. Of course, this ski field came without a chairlift, so after an eight-to-ten-minute downhill run there was no escaping the thirty-minute slog back up.

All this frenetic work and exercise helped them rest well at night. But Michael found the stove warmed the hut too much, so he chose instead to sleep in an ice-cave he dug out. Although the temperature inside was always below freezing, lying on an insulating mat in two sleeping bags, he found it sufficiently warm. In fact, even during the fiercest of storms in the dead of winter, his dugout was comfortable, except that his breath froze on his nose and lips overnight.

Ward's resistance to cold was put to shame soon after New Year, however, when a remarkable stranger arrived without warning at Base Camp. He was an unassuming Nepalese pilgrim in his mid-thirties who went by the name of Man Bahadur. He told them, on hearing that a group of Europeans was making a pilgrimage to the holy mountain of Everest, he had decided to join them. Man Bahadur had marched eight days from his village in the lowlands, dressed only in comparatively light clothing and a turban, without gloves or footwear. During the night in Mingbo, in sub-zero temperatures, he would simply sleep out in the open in the lee of a rock without any other covering.

The scientists were intrigued by him, not least because he would munch on their glass pipettes and test tubes. They convinced the mystic to be subjected to various tests, so they could determine the reason for his extraordinary resilience to cold. They even watched over him in relays throughout the night to ensure he was not somehow cheating. Their bank of tests included measuring his core body temperature and keeping a record of his food intake.

Eventually, the scientists concluded Man Bahadur avoided hypothermia because his metabolism adjusted better to cold, producing more heat from food than normal people. By shivering economically, his body was also able to generate additional heat. He did not suffer frostbite on his bare hands or feet, despite the air temperature falling at times to around −15°C, because his body somehow controlled blood circulation to his extremities and kept the skin temperature of his feet above 10°C.

Man Bahadur's visit made a big impression on Ward and got him rethinking the footprints Shipton had photographed. It eventually led him to write an article for a medical journal titled 'Everest 1951: the footprints attributed to the Yeti – myth and reality'.[*] He included a photograph he had taken of a Nepalese highlander with deformed toes sticking out at almost right angles from both feet, making it impossible for him to wear shoes. Ward reasoned such a person with 'club foot' deformity walking barefoot in snow could have made those tracks, while the claw marks observed on the prints may have resulted from deformed toenails known as rams horn nail.

But could a local in the Himalayas walk barefoot in snow over long periods without suffering severe frostbite? Man Bahadur was living proof this was possible, and Michael later saw other natives in the Bhutan highlands able to do the same. Ward's intention here was to raise the possibility of another explanation which hadn't been considered. Not only could such prints be made by animals as Hillary's party suggested, but also by a human with abnormally-shaped feet. Perhaps not wanting to reopen this debate, Ward's conclusion was ambivalent and ended with the statement: 'It is doubtful if this puzzle will ever be solved.'

Solving the 'puzzle' of human acclimatisation at high altitude was a different matter altogether – it was the *raison d'être* of the Silver Hut Expedition. Each member would return home to publish the results from

---

* See *Wilderness and Environmental Medicine* (1997). Ward published a similar article titled 'The Yeti: Myth and Reality' in the *Alpine Journal* (1999).

their own experiments and research in various books and journals. Their work would cover not only human physiology, but also the study of glaciers and weather in the Himalayas.

Some presented their findings soon afterwards to many of the world's leading experts at the prestigious J. S. Haldane Centenary Symposium held at the Oxford School of Physiology in 1961. The final tally in terms of their scientific output, according to Milledge, was twenty papers in peer-reviewed journals, plus another sixteen papers, articles and books. Thirty years later, he could still report: 'Many of the findings were not repeated for many years, and none have been refuted.' He later went on to add: 'For most of us scientists it turned out to be a career-changing experience in a most positive way.'

# 13

# First on Ama Dablam

By the middle of February, Ward had completed much of his research work whereas Pugh and a few others had fallen behind schedule, particularly with an onerous set of tests that measured cardiac output. To catch up, Griff and the other scientists involved required exclusive use of the lab area for two weeks. This meant Michael and the others unexpectedly found they had a good deal of spare time on their hands. He would seize this opportunity to record his finest accomplishment as a mountaineer.

Ward's focus turned towards a peak he had often contemplated, not least because it dominated the skyline looking out from Silver Hut. He was awestruck by Ama Dablam, as is probably every other mountaineer who has stood in its presence, often described as the Matterhorn of the Himalayas. On first seeing it, he wrote: 'This was without question the most staggering of all the peaks that I had ever seen.' Gazing up its tall neck, the gleaming ice patches which appear to resemble a necklace around its bosom, and its long ridges that form outstretched arms, it is not hard to see how the peak got its name: *Ama* meaning mother in Sherpa language and *dablam* being the traditional locket worn on a chain by their women.

At 22,349ft, the mountain is lower than some of its neighbours but this belies the degree of difficulty involved in climbing it – at the time, it was considered one of the hardest routes in the Himalayas. On seeing it for the first time, John Hunt described this 'giant fang' in *The Ascent of Everest* as appearing 'utterly inaccessible, outrivalling the most sensational aspects of the Matterhorn', while George Lowe simply believed 'that peak will never be climbed'.

Until then only two serious attempts had been made to reach its top. In 1958 a member from Alf Gregory's team, John Cunningham, had been defeated by a rock overhang at around 19,500ft. A year later, two of Britain's finest mountaineers, Mike Harris and George Fraser, were last seen at 21,000ft on the mountain's north ridge but never returned to tell their companions whether they had attained the summit. Both these attempts had been made during warmer weather, unlike the window of opportunity now

115

available; as Ward later recalled: '[To] climb it *en passant* [without much preparation] as it were, in winter, seemed ludicrous'. From his workbench, he had ample opportunity to critically study the mountain and search for a route up via its southern approaches.

A few weeks earlier, Ward asked Gill to assist him with an experiment which involved ascending a nearby peak, Rakpa, named after a lively Tibetan pup that been presented to the expedition. Michael wanted to count the number of cells in their blood before and after a one-day strenuous climb. This would help him better understand the function of the adrenal gland when stressed, as part of his research into high altitude deterioration. Although Rakpa stands almost 3,000ft below Ama Dablam, it is significantly steeper with sides covered in 'flutings' (channels formed in snow and ice by meltwater). These run the length of the mountainside, making its upper slopes look impossibly steep. None of the expedition team had prior experience climbing ice-flutings at this altitude, and whether the slopes would avalanche when stepped on was another big unknown. In fact, Ward would later class this ascent as technically more demanding than Ama Dablam.

After taking blood samples at six o'clock in the morning, he and Gill managed to summit Rakpa by half-past four that afternoon. They were back at Silver Hut to collect more samples by eight o'clock that same evening, highlighting how fit and well acclimatised the pair now were. This rapid ascent had included scaling icy slopes at angles up to sixty degrees (without the use of modern ice gear). Their success suggested to Ward the upper flutings on Ama Dablam could also be climbed at a speed fast enough for an alpine-style final push, without supplementary oxygen (as opposed to the slower siege-style climb with oxygen used on Everest).

In preparation for the attempt, Wally Romanes and a Sherpa named Gumen Dorji first reconnoitred Ama Dablam on 19 February from Silver Hut, which now constituted Base Camp. They established Camp 1 around 18,500ft at the foot of its south ridge, from where the serious climbing would begin. The next day they went further up to the foot of a steep tower of yellow rock which had stopped Cunningham back in 1958, where they found the remnants of the fixed rope he had left behind. On their return, Wally described the challenge posed by this Yellow Tower and suggested it might take a long time but then added 'she'd be a good climb in New Zealand'. Ward, in his *Alpine Journal* (1961) article, wrote: 'As he is not given to over-statement, I was not at all optimistic.'

Michael was directly involved in the next stage. Together with Barry Bishop, Gumen Dorji and Pemba Tensing, they climbed up to the first camp carrying 40lb loads. Just prior to arriving there, on the exposed slope

*Right*: **A young Michael Ward.** (All photos on this page from Ward Family Collection)

*Below left*: **Michael Ward rock climbing in north Wales, c. 1944.**

*Below right*: **Michael and Jane's wedding, 1957.**

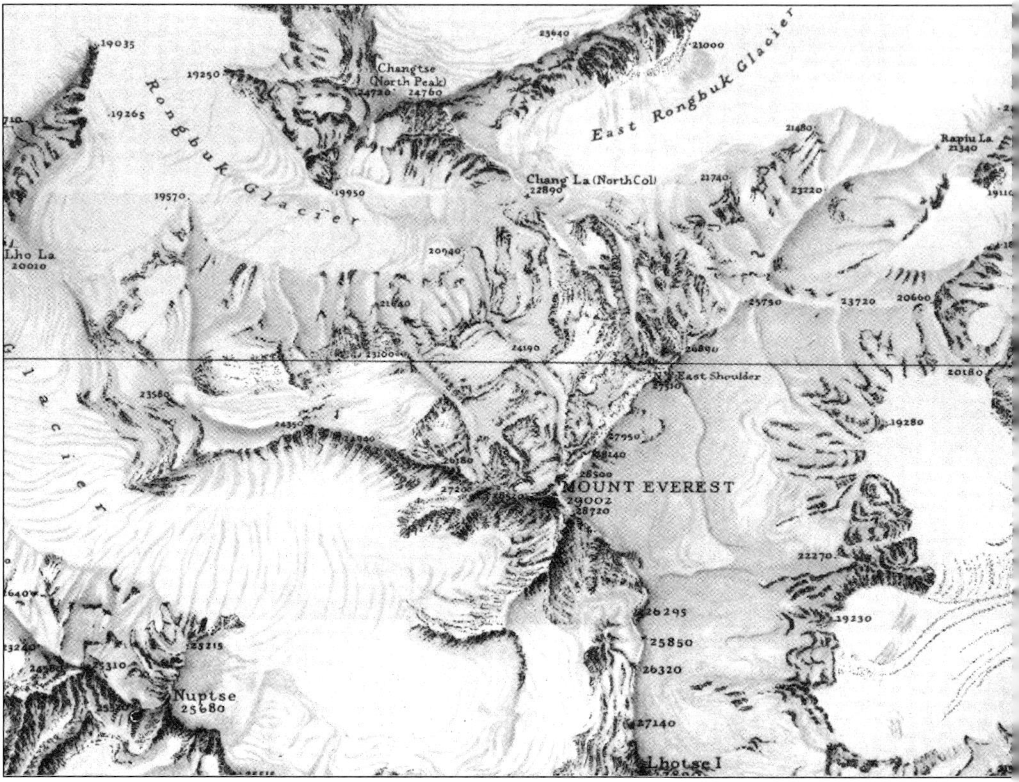

*Above*: **Extract from Milne-Hinks map, c. 1937.**

*Below left*: **Bill Murray.** (Photo from Ward Family Collection)

*Below right*: **One of the Pundits: Kishen Singh, 1905.**

*Above*: **The 1951 Everest Reconnaissance team.** (Photos on this page from Royal Geographical Society Collection, Getty Images) *Left to right, sitting: Ward and Hillary; standing: Shipton, Murray, Bourdillon and Riddiford.*

*Right*: **Michael Ward standing beside line of 'yeti' tracks, 1951.** (Photo by Eric Shipton)

**The 1953 Mount Everest team.** (Photo from Alamy) *Ward standing in centre, to right of Tenzing.*

**Triumphant Everesters at London airport.**
(Photo from Mirrorpix, Alamy) *Ward standing to right of Tenzing.*

**Everesters' reunion
in Snowdonia.**
(Photo from Ward
Family Collection)
*As posted on Mark
Ward's website; his
father stands apart
from the group.*

**Everesters with Queen Elizabeth II, 1993.**
(Photo by Martin Keene, from Alamy) *Ward standing to right of Gombu, his Sherpa from 1953; Pugh in wheelchair.*

**The Silver Hut, 1960.**
(Photo by Mike Gill)

*Right*: **Ama Dablam.**
(Photo from Ward Family
Collection)

*Below*: **Sketch map
by Michael Ward of
mountains in Bhutan,
1964.**

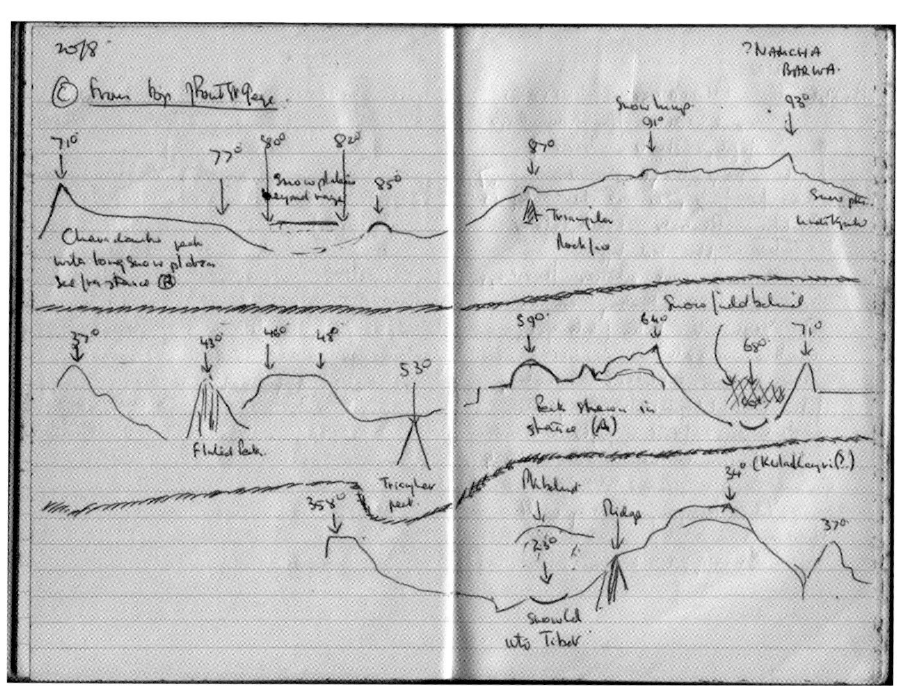

**Mt Kongur Reconnaissance Team in London, 1980.**
(Photo from Ward Family Collection) *Left to right: Rouse, Ward and Bonington.*

**Mt Kongur Base Camp Team (excludes Climbers), 1981.**
(Photo by Chris Bonington) *Left to right: Williams, Wilson, Ward, Clarke, Milledge and Curran.*

the party were hit by a white-out coupled with vicious wind. It was strong enough to blow the terrified group over and fling stones at them; Ward recalls: 'Pride, I am certain, was the only emotion that kept me going, also it was too late to turn back.' Exhausted after pitching their tents, with only a cup of soup for nourishment, they found it hard to stay warm at night. By this stage the Sherpas were done in so the next morning, with difficulty, Ward pushed on with Bishop: 'Once again we hoped that we would soon find some bit of the ridge that was so obviously impossible that we could, with a clear conscience, turn back.'

After negotiating a few narrow ridges and fixing ropes on several pitches, they arrived at the base of the Yellow Tower. Here they devoured sardines and biscuits while pondering how to overcome the cliff face that rose between 100 to 150ft ahead of them. The pair eventually decided on a frontal assault up a 'bloody awkward' groove-chimney, before taking on the rock overhang which had defeated Cunningham. Although battling it for the rest of the day, they could not get past this barrier and, as light began to fade, were forced to retreat for the night.

Next morning, they carried their tents up to a small glacier at the foot of the tower and renewed the attack. On 26 February, after some deft climbing and with the help of *étriers* (short ladders), they finally managed to clamber over. Hillary commented on their efforts in *High in the Thin Cold Air*:

> The ascent of this section was a considerable feat on the part of Ward and Bishop. For a day and a half, with the help of some twenty *pitons* [steel spikes], they fought their way up the slender cracks and smooth slabs. Artificial climbing, using 'hardware', is an exhausting procedure at this altitude where a powerful muscular effort cannot be sustained for long before one is brought to a panting halt by acute respiratory distress.

The pair were at least thankful this part of the ascent, the most trying so far, had been possible in the warmth of the sun, without being exposed to the ferocious wind. To their relief the next rise, which they named Red Tower, turned out to be 'an easy scramble' in comparison and by late afternoon the south ridge had been overcome.

Now the mountain proper stood in front of them as they peered up a notch towards two rocky steps that rose almost vertically and looked imposing. Before night overtook them, they fixed a 50ft wire ladder down from the top of the Yellow Tower and used it to return to camp, where they found Romanes and two other Sherpas had arrived.

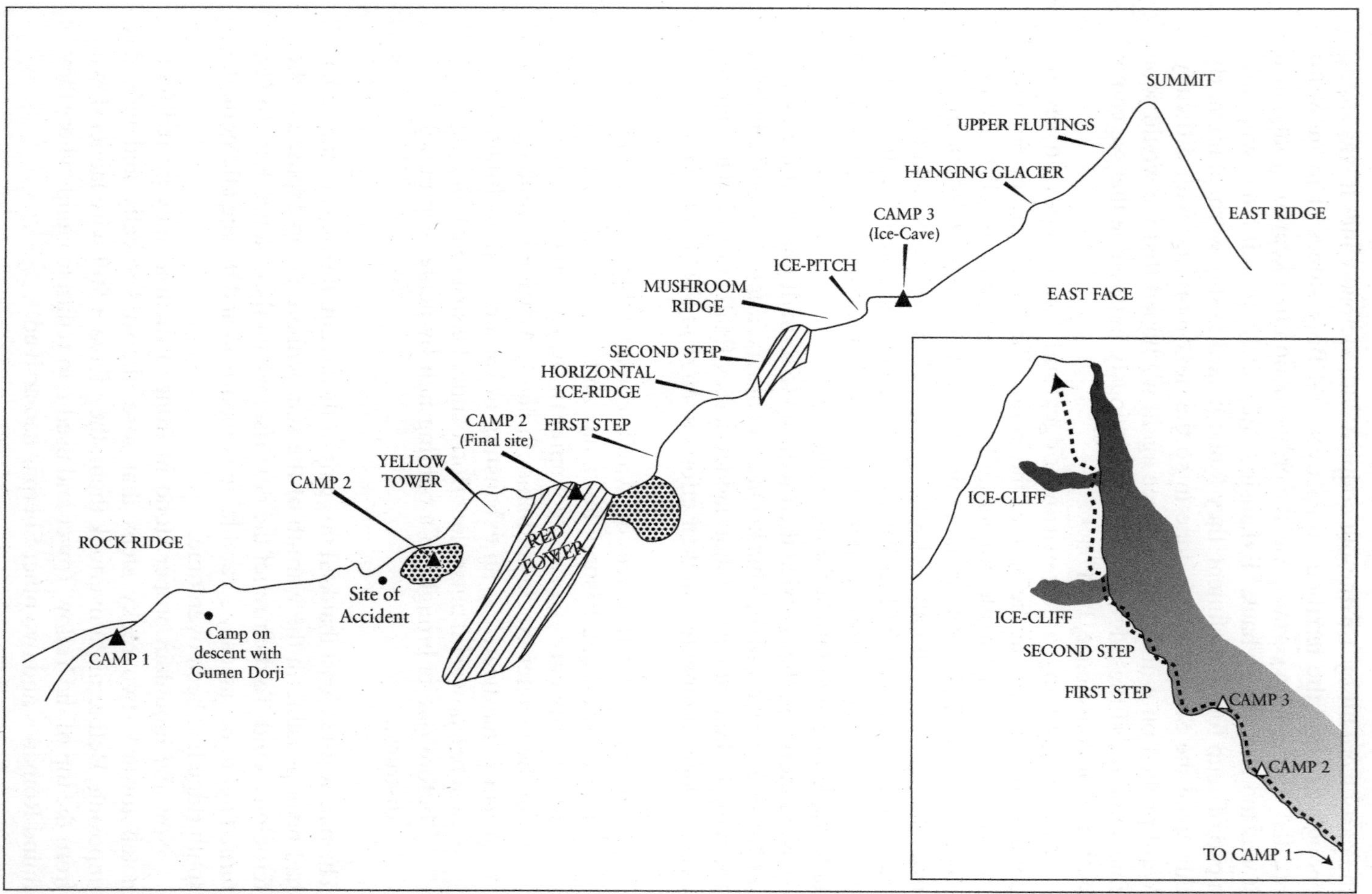


**Map 3. Ascent of Ama Dablam 1961** (based on map from Ward's article in *Alpine Journal* 1961)

The next day, the climbers took turns attacking the exposed 100ft face of the First Step in piercing wind. Although the trio eventually managed to overcome it, they ran out of daylight and could not make a start on the Second Step. Returning to camp, they found Mike Gill had joined them to make up their full complement of four climbers. The following day, the first of March, another wire ladder was fixed down from the First Step, which would save them over an hour each time climbing onto the Second Step. They also found a site higher up on an ice ledge where they set up Camp 2, some 1,500ft below the top.

That night however, during radio contact with Silver Hut, Pugh told Ward of a light aircraft which had crashed while landing in Mingbo at a recently laid out airstrip. Hillary had been responsible for its hurried construction, only the third of its kind in Nepal. To his credit, Ed had managed to build the short, sloping runway without access to machinery, using only manual labour provided by the villagers. (This was in response to an urgent request from the International Red Cross who needed to fly in much-needed aid suppliers for refugees crossing the border from Tibet into Sola Khumbu. Many were in a pitiful state, escaping the crackdown by Chinese troops begun two years earlier in their homeland.)

Frustrating though it was for Ward to leave the climb at this point, he went down to Mingbo the next morning to offer medical assistance. Bishop and Romanes also decided to go down the mountain for a rest and stay in the Green Hut, where room was available. Gill, who was still fresh, remained behind to stock Camp 2 with supplies and fix ropes to consolidate their route.

At the makeshift airstrip, Michael found neither the pilot nor his passenger was hurt, other than showing symptoms of acute mountain sickness. Coming into land, the plane had damaged its tail, but the pair managed to fix it with some wire and pieces of wood. The following day, after a nervous take-off they flew back to Kathmandu, allowing Ward to return to the mountain on 6 March, collecting Bishop and Romanes on the way up.

They found Gill had put in more fixed ropes and discovered a better site for Camp 2, which he had begun stocking. It sat on top of the Red Tower, some 400ft across a ridge and 150ft further up. This extra height would save them a second hour of climbing at the start of each day.

Waking up to heavy snowfall the following morning, the four spent a full eight hours with their two Sherpas moving the remaining stores to the higher site, where they built small rock platforms and pitched two tents. From here on, the route would be harder and as the Sherpas maintained it was now a 'Sahib path, not a Sherpa path', they were happy to leave the climbers to their mountain. After they left, Ward fixed more ropes with Bishop. However, he worried about having let the Sherpas return by themselves, given their lack of climbing experience, and was greatly relieved to hear by radio of their safe arrival.

Meanwhile, Gill and Romanes reconnoitred from the Second Step towards the glacier (the 'dablam'), only to return with gloomy news. They had encountered 'extraordinary mushroom towers of unstable ice' blocking the crest of the ridge and its sides. Beyond this there was a vertical wall of ice rising some 40ft, which would have to be scaled before they could get onto the glacier itself.

The next day, Ward and Bishop managed to get past the mushroom towers and climb the wall with the aid of pitons and an étrier. Eventually, they walked onto the acre-sized glacier shelf where they found the snow perfect for digging out an ice-cave. This meant they could leave the tents behind and lighten loads their considerably when they relocated to a higher camp.

That night, their last at Camp 2, they were in a position to discuss the possibility of a bid for the summit. They decided to remain together if it came to that, reasoning they stood a better chance of survival in case of an accident on the sharp end of the mountain. Moreover, the other scientists working at Silver Hut would probably not be able to mount a strong rescue operation.

Early the following morning they headed up with four days' provisions. They began work around four o'clock that afternoon on what was to be their final overnight site, Camp 3, sitting around 21,000ft. Six hours later, they had managed to dig out a small ice-cave, but it was backbreaking work. Following a sparse meal, they finally fell asleep at midnight, completely spent; Gill would later describe their efforts: 'It was a day I would forget if I could, a day of unremitting struggle against what Tilman calls "mountaineer's foot": the reluctance to put one foot in front of the other.'

The next morning, they were still too tired to contemplate a bid for the summit. Later that day, while their teammates worked on enlarging the cave, Ward and Romanes, being the fitter pair then, left to begin preparing the route up and explore what lay beyond the ice-cliffs. Running on their crampon points on concrete hard ice, they had to cross a dangerous-looking avalanche runnel, 20ft deep, formed by falling ice from the cliffs above. Once across, they worked their way onto the cliffs and horizontal ice-ridges where Michael recalls 'the exposure was monstrous'. Eventually, they reached the hanging glacier guarding the peak's upper flutings. It looked surmountable but they resisted any temptation to make a dash for the top, instead returning to their now bigger and more comfortable ice-cave.

The next day, 13 March, the climbers started out soon after dawn and retraced the route marked out the previous day by Ward and Romanes. Past the hanging glacier, they steadily ascended the steep flutings, cutting steps much of the way in near-perfect snow conditions. At half-past two that afternoon, four mountaineers stood on the top of Ama Dablam – the first to have ever done so.

How did Michael *feel* at that moment, after what was undoubtedly his finest mountaineering achievement? He makes no mention of it. Not in his expedition diary, nor *In This Short Span*, nor even in his unpublished manuscript; rather, letting the event simply speak for itself. In recognition of Ward's leadership, Gill would write: 'It really was Mike's climb. He saw the route, was the first to start climbing on it, and it was Mike who put the route up the first rock buttress which is the most technical part of the climb.'*

The summit turned out not to be the sharp point they had expected, but a snow cap some 30yds wide and 100yds long with a crevasse running along its length. Before heading back down, Ward went across to the north ridge which Mike Harris and George Fraser had climbed two years earlier, looking for any trace of them but found none. It seems unlikely they had managed to reach the top as their ridge abutted the mountain 100ft below it; as Gill described in *High in the Thin Cold Air*: 'We were appalled at the steepness of the final ice ridge and the ferocious severity of the knife-edge rock falling away below it. Why had they chosen this route, we wondered …'

As well as having ascended by way of a more favourable route, Ward's team had the advantage of being thoroughly acclimatised after their time at Silver Hut. In fact, the ascent of two peaks as difficult as Rakpa and Ama Dablam without supplementary oxygen demonstrated just how effective such acclimatisation could be. (Although a key finding from their research later would show that the hut sat too high for acclimatisation over the long term – as their next attempt on Makalu would prove.)

From the top of Ama Dablam, the climbers had fine views of the surrounding peaks including Everest and Makalu, and they were able to make out the Silver Hut as a dot far below. After less than an hour on top, as the clouds closed in, the four returned to their ice-cave. The next day as they started down, they began clearing the mountain of the pitons and over 1,500ft of fixed ropes they had used coming up. At Camp 2 they rejoined

---

* From a letter by Gill to George Rodway and Jeremy Windsor, as mentioned in their *Alpine Journal* (2010/11) article titled 'Ama Dablam – 50 Years On'.

their two Sherpas and continued their descent; but before they could get all the way down, disaster struck.

Pugh had been following their progress with a telescope from Silver Hut and on seeing them on the summit, had sent two more Sherpas up to assist. Above the Yellow Tower, Romanes cleverly installed an overhead rope pulley to hurtle their gear down to its base. Here, while the sahibs shouldered loads of 40lb, the Sherpas decided to carry almost double loads to save themselves another carry the next day. They set off first down the ridge, but the climbers soon caught up, only to find them gathered around Gumen Dorji lying prostrate in the snow. He had stepped on a loose rock which gave way under his heavy load and had fallen 10ft, snapping a leg at the shin. Cutting away his puttees, Michael diagnosed a compound fracture.

After administering Gumen a large dose of morphia, he straightened the protruding bone, put a field dressing over it, wrapped the leg using cardboard boxes, and finally used an ice-axe as a splint. The team then debated how to get the injured Sherpa safely down the steep slopes and remaining obstacles. Ward later recalled in *The Mountain World* (1962/63): 'The tension that always eases after climbing a difficult mountain now returned with relentless pressure.'

Since Gumen was the largest of the Sherpas, weighing around 120lb, none of the other three Sherpas could carry him. Romanes was also not physically big enough and Bishop was suffering from a bad abscess, which meant the task fell to Ward and Gill. Each of them struggled with Gumen on his back for ten minutes at a time, while the other protected his broken leg from knocking about. Romanes was tasked with belaying the carrier down while Bishop shouldered the climbers' personal gear, weighing some 90lb.

They arrived at the tower which had defeated Cunningham with darkness falling, but fortunately found a gully nearby to camp in. Ward remembers having to walk down its steep sides backwards carrying Gumen, while the others shouted instructions as to where he should place his feet. By this stage they had made radio contact with Pugh, who sent food and fuel up to Camp 1, together with a special wire splint for Gumen's fracture, which Romanes went down to collect.

That night, the climbers crowded into one of the two-man tents while the Sherpas slept in the other. It snowed constantly overnight, making the challenge of finding a way around Cunningham's Tower the next morning harder still. After discussing the problem interminably, they decided their only hope lay in executing a tricky pendulum traverse across the face of the tower with a heavily sedated Gumen strapped onto Gill's back, he being the younger and stronger one. Ward would swing beside them to steady the pair and keep them facing towards the cliff. Bishop would belay him from a rope fixed to the top of the tower, while Romanes did the same for Gill. Later, Michael described the operation as it played out:

> After a few hesitant movements Mike [Gill] made very rapid progress across the cliff, which was not quite vertical. By choosing a line that led across and downwards all his movements were made either across or in descent. It was an outstanding feat. Wally was masterly – and his judgement of the amount of tension needed to help Mike across awkward places remarkably exact, considering that he could not see him for long periods. There was no time to be frightened.

The manoeuvre, watched fearfully by Pugh and others at Silver Hut through their telescope, proved successful, aided by Gumen's complete inertness. As to the latter, Ward put it down to: 'Probably the combination of morphia, anoxia and the view, when he opened his eyes, petrified him.'

When they reached the end of the ridge below, they found help had arrived in the way of Milledge and other Sherpas. One of them, having a reputation of being among the strongest men in Khumbu, took over carrying Gumen seemingly without effort, although he still had to clamber barefoot over many boulders. Michael found out his name and immediately recruited Karma for the upcoming attempt on Makalu.

Although it began snowing heavily, the party arrived back safely, but Ward knew they had 'only just managed it'. A few days later, Gumen was flown out from Mingbo airstrip to Kathmandu for treatment, where he would go on to make a full recovery.

It was a month to the day since Michael and his team had first reconnoitred the mountain; a month of high drama which neither he nor the others would forget. Their achievement would make headlines in the mountaineering world, while one London newspaper article led with 'Killer Peak Conquered by British Surgeon'.

But an unexpected issue now arose as a result of their success, one that threatened to put the remainder of the expedition in jeopardy and caused Hillary a good deal of heartache. He had just returned from New Zealand with the spring party, which included two fresh climbers who were going to join the attempt on Makalu, thus marking the last phase of the Silver Hut Expedition. The Nepalese Government, however, in an uncompromising and sternly worded letter to Hillary, withdrew its permission for this final climb.

The authorities were incensed on learning of the ascent of Ama Dablam. They had only consented to expedition members climbing within the Mingbo Valley, on whose northern boundary Ama Dablam stands, but certainly not to bag its summit. The mountain represented a major prize (it features on Nepal's one-rupee banknote) and one which they could have charged another climbing party a substantial peak fee, but this opportunity had now been lost.

Before making the attempt, Ward had discussed it with Pugh; while Hillary noted in his account: '[I] had quite happily given them permission to reconnoitre the mountain – not believing for one moment that they would actually reach the summit during the winter months.'

On learning of the authority's displeasure, Hillary immediately flew to Kathmandu and spent the next nine days shuffling between government departments eating humble pie, while seeking assistance from the British and Indian ambassadors. Eventually, he managed to salvage the rest of their expedition after paying a fine and a royalty for ascending the peak totalling 4,000 rupees, equivalent to over US$500.

Despite the significant problems this affair caused Ed, including considerable loss of acclimatisation, Michael recalled: '[At] no time did he castigate me or anyone else. I think in fact that he was rather glad we had climbed Amadablam as it gave a cachet to the expedition which it badly needed.' It had come after Hillary's unsuccessful yeti hunt which, in the eyes of many, had cast their effort as something of a stunt. Not surprisingly, the scientists' slow and meticulous research work hadn't captured the public's imagination either. Whereas now, his expedition was receiving international mountaineering acclaim.

Years later, Jim Milledge would reflect: 'It was a climb of great technical difficulty and well ahead of its time. It was not repeated for [almost] 20 years …' Moreover, it marked the first ascent of one of the world's most iconic peaks, and one which would forever be linked to Michael Ward.

# 14

# At Death's Door

The ascent of Ama Dablam was followed by three hectic weeks at Silver Hut to complete the last of the scheduled research. It meant many twelve-hour days for Ward and the others before they packed up the laboratory equipment and vacated their high quarters.* This marked the completion of the expedition's second phase (its first being Hillary's yeti hunt). What remained was the third and final phase, an attempt on Makalu (27,825ft) without the use of supplementary oxygen – if successful, this would be the highest summit attained without its aid.

As mentioned earlier, the mountain would be tackled by some climbers from the winter party, all of whom were well acclimatised, plus Hillary and his fresh climbers. Both sets would be clinically observed to allow a comparison of their performance at altitude.

There were also some last elements of the scientific programme which had to be completed at an altitude higher than Silver Hut. This work would be undertaken on Makalu Col (24,500ft) and include measuring heartrate with a portable ECG machine and maximum work capacity using the ergometer. One can imagine the reaction of the Sherpas, faced with having to haul a one-wheeled bicycle up Makalu – as Gill later mused, 'truly the ways of the sahibs must have seemed strange' to them.

Rather than make a roundabout march to Makalu via the Barun Glacier, Hillary decided to take the shortest route, but this meant crossing three high passes around 20,000ft. As Pugh was having difficulty ascending and working at this height, he decided to remain at Silver Hut and asked Ward to take charge of the physiological team. After vacating the hut, Michael and two fellow climbers off Ama Dablam trekked some 10 miles east, crossing

---

* The hut was later dismantled and taken to the Himalayan Mountaineering Institute in Darjeeling where it was put to good use by its chief instructor, Tenzing Norgay.

the Hongu Glacier to meet up with Ed's team.* Hillary had already set up Base Camp (I) and was starting to prepare for the assault on Makalu.

Before joining them, Ward took a well-earned break with Gill for a week, descending to Shershen, a small village with a yak pasture nestled 14,000ft to the south. Although this time off gave them some opportunity to recuperate, he felt they still 'looked too fine-drawn' – an observation that would prove prescient.

When they returned to Base Camp together with Jim Milledge, they found the preliminary camps all the way up to Advanced Base Camp (III) had already been established. Camp IV (23,000ft) was now being set up, ready for the push onto Makalu Col. This col is a saddle which lies between the main mountain and a subsidiary peak Makalu II (25,192ft) about 2 miles away. Michael immediately noticed the change in scale here compared to Ama Dablam, as everything was further away and more exhausting to reach. He was slated to be on one of the assault teams, while Milledge took over as the medical officer.

Following two nights at Camp IV, Ward and Gill were tasked with fixing a route to the col. After losing a day inadvertently climbing a gully to a dead-end cliff, they managed to accomplish the task on 5 May. Hillary was delighted to hear this news as, other than the summit itself, he had expected the excessively steep route to the col would pose their biggest challenge.

By this stage, the altitude was beginning to wear Michael down, much more than his partner, and he 'felt ghastly', suffering from headaches and nightmares. Nevertheless, he was exhilarated by the surrounding view of the magnificent peaks from this desolate col. As they made their way back down, the pair fixed ropes to allow the next team with Sherpas to carry supplies and the bicycle ergometer up to establish Camp V.

Over the next two days, Ward descended first to Camp III then II at 19,000ft, and immediately began to feel better – but found Hillary taking a turn for the worse here. Initially Ed was suffering from a bad headache which Michael treated without difficulty, but a 'strangled shout' from his tent later that evening signalled something far more serious.

On examining him, Ward found he had suffered a stroke, with one side of his face paralysed and unable to speak properly. Milledge, who was in a nearby tent, confirmed his diagnosis. The two took turns sitting by Hillary's side that night administering oxygen by the light of a candle, which helped improve his condition to some extent. They decided he should retire to Shershen as soon as possible, and then be helicoptered out to Kathmandu,

---

* The fourth climber, Barry Bishop, did not go onto Makalu but stayed back to complete his glaciology study.

with both doctors offering to accompany him. As Ed mentioned later in their expedition book: 'Mike Ward spoke severely to me: I simply must go down below 15,000ft immediately and not come up for some months at least.' The next day Milledge and some Sherpas accompanied him down. As they left, the rest of the team were visibly shaken by their leader's sudden illness and departure.

Before leaving, Hillary appointed Ward, now the most experienced Himalayan climber and proven leader on Ama Dablam, to take charge of the assault on Makalu. Michael, however, had already agreed with Pugh to act as the scientific leader. With Milledge gone, he would also have to take over his share of the research work and act as medical officer. Already struggling from the effects of high altitude and long hours at Silver Hut, he acutely felt the weight of all this extra responsibility and workload.

Ward did receive one letter from Hillary, which arrived soon afterwards. It advised him that given his rapid improvement, rather than return to Kathmandu, Ed would stay in Sola Khumbu and build the schoolhouse promised to the Sherpas.* At least he undertook not go above 15,000ft, as Ward had sternly advised. The letter also contained Ed's proposed assault plan for Makalu, which was similar to one Michael had worked up.

Despite Milledge's departure, Ward felt the physiological work scheduled for Makalu Col should not be compromised, as it presented a rare opportunity which probably would not be repeated. (In fact, their measurements here, on the effect of high altitude on humans during exercise, established an altitude record that would not be surpassed for the next forty-six years). Ward decided his priority lay with assisting John West complete this work, rather than take part in the final assault. In making this call, he was putting research ahead of mountaineering and his own sporting ambition. He realised this decision could weaken their bid for the summit and leave him open to reproach from some quarters (he was indeed criticised by Hillary later). Nevertheless, Ward believed the rest of the team were experienced mountaineers and capable of succeeding without him.

The first assault was made by a team comprising Mike Gill, Wally Romanes, and one of the two fresh climbers, an American named Leigh Ortenburger. Ward's plan had the trio and most of the Sherpas carry loads nearing 26,000ft. They would establish Camp VI there before the majority of the Sherpas returned. The three climbers and remaining Sherpas would then take the loads across an intricate glacier running down from the summit

---

* This was the first of several schools and two hospitals Hillary would build in Sola Khumbu, endearing him to the Sherpa people.

and set up a final camp (VII) some 1,000ft higher. From this point, they and a second team would try for the top.

Unfortunately, the first team strayed off the path pioneered by the successful French expedition six years earlier. Worse still, because they were hit by bad weather and fierce winds, the climbers weren't able to establish the final camp. Instead, they could only dump loads 500ft above Camp VI (25,800ft), 700ft lower than planned, before stumbling back down, cold and exhausted.

Meanwhile Ward and West, assisted by an American Air Force physiologist and mountaineer Tom Nevison, assembled the ergometer in a tent on the col. Here, they replicated a set of experiments started even before the scientists had left for Nepal. This study would allow them to build a unique picture of man's adaptation to altitude, measured while working at increasing heights: sea level (London), 15,000ft (Mingbo), 19,000ft (Silver Hut), 21,000ft (Makalu Camp III), and 24,500ft (Makalu Col). Once these last tests had been performed, it marked the successful completion of the full programme, all done in the name of science. After the difficulties they would experience on the col, Ward could not help but remark: 'The few dots on a graph and the few figures added to a table, plus a few words in an article, seem ludicrously out of proportion to the effort involved.'[*]

By this stage, he had spent five days on the col and was feeling the effects of high altitude, compounded by the maximum work capacity tests he had subjected himself to. This meant any chance of joining a possible third team to the top was fast running out. Furthermore, as a doctor, Michael realised for the sake of his own health, he should be descending to a lower camp as soon as possible. However, when the first team returned beaten, he began revising the plan to include himself on a third assault party with the other fresh climber, New Zealander John Harrison, and another Sherpa.[†]

The second party had another New Zealander, Peter Mulgrew, who had earlier accompanied Hillary on the yeti hunt (and the Trans-Antarctic Expedition in 1955). He was accompanied by Tom Nevison, and a group of Sherpas. They started out from the col on 16 May and spent a difficult night at Camp VI. The next day they crossed the glacier with six Sherpas roped together in the lead. The Sherpas did all the trail breaking and load carrying between them, so as to conserve the strength of the two climbers. They had

---

[*] One finding would show the natural uptake of oxygen in the lungs extrapolated to the top of Everest to be around 1 litre per minute. This meant a fit climber, resting often, could theoretically summit without using supplementary oxygen.

[†] The accounts of Ward, Mulgrew and Gill differ here from Hillary's, who wrote that Ortenburger was to accompany Harrison, not Ward.

just located the stores dump left by the first team, when the last Sherpa on the rope slipped and pulled the other five down with him as none had taken the precaution of belaying themselves. Mulgrew and Nevison, following well behind, could only watch in horror as they slid over 300yds down the mountain with increasing speed. (With hindsight, Hillary maintained this fall was undoubtedly the turning point, not only for the summit bid but also the events that followed.)

The climbers believed all six Sherpas were done for, but to their immense relief the fall was arrested when the last two fell into a crevasse. After the Sherpas regained themselves, they found Ang Temba had hurt his ankle severely and probably broken it. As he was struggling to walk, he returned to camp with another Sherpa who had gashed his head. The rest of the party continued their climb, this time with Nevison leading and Mulgrew carrying an extra load – in the process both used up their reserve strength. They set up Camp VII at 27,000ft before the Sherpas headed back down, leaving the pair and their lead Sherpa, Annalu, to try for the top next day.

Following a cold and uncomfortable night in their tent, they managed to climb 400ft the next morning. But it took them over four hours to do so, and they were becoming increasingly tired and needed to rest for longer periods. Although Annalu had managed to keep up, his ribs were still painful from the previous day's fall (it was later learnt that at least one had been cracked). Yet with only 400ft left to gain the summit, the trio believed they could get there and return by darkness.

Suddenly, however, Mulgrew collapsed from a tremendous pain in his chest and remained immobile in the snow for half an hour. Although he urged the other two to go on, Annalu was in no shape to do so. Yet Nevison was, and this must have been a difficult moment for him. But he could see Mulgrew was ill and needed to return to camp. The three climbers, their summit bid now over, stumbled back down in gale force winds with Peter semi-conscious, often collapsing and coughing up blood, but worse was to come.

Mulgrew described his harrowing rescue a few years later in his book *No Place for Men.*[*] It began in earnest after he had spent four nights above 26,000ft, the last two without an air mattress which resulted in him being severely frostbitten. Ward wrote in the *Alpine Journal* (1963): 'That he had managed to live through the nightmare days of his descent was unbelievable. His will to live had triumphed where that of a lesser man would have failed.'

---

* Its Appendix describing the 'Medical Aspects' of what occurred is extracted from Ward's article 'The Descent from Makalu, 1961' in the *Alpine Journal* (1963). Mulgrew had suffered pulmonary thrombosis while, earlier, Hillary had a transient stroke.

For much of the time Mulgrew was carried down on the back of Sherpas, many of whom were otherwise employed as 'low-altitude' Sherpas. At the crucial stage of his rescue, Michael was unable to help because it coincided with his own rapid deterioration, and he later candidly admitted: 'My illness nearly killed Pete.'

Ward had gone up on 18 May from the col to Camp VI to examine Ang Temba's injured ankle and take charge of the earlier rescue effort after the Sherpas' fall. However, despite climbing with oxygen at the full 4 litres per minute, he could only just keep up with the Sherpa accompanying him who was not using oxygen, which again points to his rapidly deteriorating health. After assessing Ang Temba, he radioed the col for assistance to get him back down.

That night Michael suffered recurrent bouts of claustrophobia and by the next morning was hallucinating. He asked the two rescue climbers, Harrison and Ortenburger who arrived with other Sherpas to assist Ang Temba, why they had bothered coming up since 'Pete and Tom have reached the top', which he knew because 'A friend of Ed's told me'. In fact, around this time Peter had collapsed, and the situation high on the mountain for both him and Michael was desperate.

When the Sherpas left, carrying Ang Temba back to the col, Ward struggled down after them, but he wasn't using oxygen and soon fell far behind. Eventually, he collapsed face first into the snow and was only able to make camp after two Sherpas came back to assist him. Somehow, he managed to get into his sleeping bag fully clothed with boots still on but was soon shivering violently. He remembered nothing for the next forty-eight hours. During this time, the two rescue climbers for Mulgrew at Camp VI tried repeatedly to radio him for assistance and oxygen to be brought up, but Ward lay incapacitated.

When he came to, around eleven o'clock on the morning of 22 May, Michael was greeted by John West, who had come up to Camp V to assist. Although he was not a climber and had never been this high on a mountain, West would play a decisive role in the overall rescue operation. First, he and Tom Nevison extracted Ward from his sleeping bag. Then, after finally convincing him that he was not well enough to remain on the col, they began the tricky process of getting him down. Even using oxygen, and carrying only his diaries, it took Michael five hours to stumble down to Camp IV, arriving just before nightfall. The next day was worse, as he recalled:

> It is difficult to describe accurately the feeling of emptiness.
> Will-power had long since been expended … There is nothing
> that I have ever encountered that is anything like the fatigue

of high altitude … There were two of these little ascents – not more than 50 feet each. The second nearly finished me. The tetracycline tablets had given me diarrhoea and I was incontinent. I could not care less. I was switched off, an animal relying on reflexes.

He eventually made it down to Camp III and Mulgrew was carried in the day after, barely alive. A helicopter was arranged to land at Shershen and fly the two to Kathmandu, together with Ang Temba. Paradoxically, Ward was the most qualified doctor at the United Mission Hospital where they were taken. This was the same hospital he had helped out at on arriving in Nepal, but this time he was in no position to treat anyone. Although, from his specialist experience dealing with cases of frostbite, after examining Mulgrew's badly frostbitten legs, he did impress upon the medical staff not to amputate them until all other alternatives had been exhausted. Returning home to New Zealand, however, Peter would need to have both legs and several fingers amputated.[*]

Michael spent a week in hospital at Kathmandu recovering from his acute altitude sickness, as well as frostbite to his nose, fingers, and toes. He had lost much weight, and an X-ray taken there showed an enlarged heart which only returned to normal after three months. Still, he was lucky to be alive and arriving home he remembers: 'I was met by Jane and Mark, whom I had left as a baby, and who was now a strapping fourteen-month-old toddler. When I bent to lift him up to kiss him I found I had not the strength. I nearly wept.'

Ward had no doubt the injury toll from Makalu could have been far worse. As Gill noted in his book *Mountain Midsummer* about this disaster: 'We had come with the idea of finding out how easily a high mountain could be tackled without oxygen, and we had learned with a vengeance.' Ward and Pugh always advised mountaineers to take oxygen on high climbs as a precautionary measure. In the article mentioned earlier, Michael stressed: 'If medical oxygen had not been taken on Makalu in all probability there would have been three deaths.' He never relented about the importance of this basic precaution, as years later his grownup son Mark recalled:

> My father spent his whole career railing against those who
> resisted the so-called 'cheat' of having safety oxygen available

---

* With the use of prosthetic legs, Mulgrew would return to the Himalayas to help build schools and hospitals for the Sherpas. Tragically, in 1979 he was killed in a plane crash in Antarctica together with all 257 persons on board.

> at all high camps. Several superb mountaineers he had climbed
> with died needlessly on other people's expeditions, he felt,
> because they did not have back-up oxygen for emergencies …
> My dad felt events like these turned mountaineering into
> a blood sport, and his disdain for its practitioners knew no
> bounds.

The account of the Silver Hut Expedition was published soon afterwards, but unfortunately this did cause both Ward and Pugh some grief before its release. *High in the Thin Cold Air* was written jointly by Ed Hillary and another member, Desmond Doig, a journalist who had joined them from India where he worked for *The Statesman* newspaper. Part I of the book – more than half the text – discussed the failed yeti hunt; while Part II covered the rest of the expedition: the ground-breaking research undertaken at Silver Hut, the first ascent of Ama Dablam, and learnings from the Makalu disaster. This skew in emphasis would have been disappointing for Ward and Pugh, but there were other problems too. True to form, Michael makes no mention of the difficulties that arose during the book's publication in either his autobiography or his unpublished notes.

Harriet Tuckey, though, in the book about her father, devoted a chapter to 'The Battle of the Book'. Published fifty years after Hillary's account, she described what she believes to have transpired: During the writing process, Hillary had not sought input from either Pugh or Ward. Not even for the scientific aspects which Griff had led, nor the first ascent of Ama Dablam that Michael had. Neither Hillary nor Doig participated in the climb, and Ed inexplicably asked Mike Gill to write the piece about Ama Dablam. Yet despite Pugh and Ward's separate requests, Hillary would not share the draft manuscript with either of them.

After persevering, Michael managed to see the galley proofs shortly before the book was due for release in 1962 by two major publishers in Britain and America. He was taken aback by some sections relating to Griff and himself. It seems Ed had yet again failed to acknowledge Pugh as the expedition's scientific leader or give his scientists their due, while claiming credit for ideas that were not his. Ward was also unhappy about some remarks made about him after he took over from Hillary as climbing leader on Makalu. The aggrieved pair wrote to the publishers seeking changes to the text and threatening legal action, which 'had the desired effect' and without too much rewriting, as Tuckey pointed out:

> The amendments Pugh had asked for were very limited. They
> amounted to a paragraph in the preface introducing himself as

the leader of the scientific team and giving the names of the scientists which had been left out by Hillary. He also asked for minor alterations of emphasis to make the coverage fairer – he asked for Ward to be acknowledged as the leader of the successful ascent of Ama Dablam and judicially changed Hillary's use of the word 'I' to the word 'we' in many places.

Also telling is the comment by another member of the Silver Hut Expedition, Norman Hardie. Four months after reading a review of Tuckey's book by mountaineer Mark Horrell on his website, Hardie posted below it:

> I was consulted a few times by Harriet when writing this excellent book. I have read it with care and I found no inaccuracies and the review comments [by Horrell] about Hillary and the Silver Hut scientific results are absolutely true.

In the review that Hardie refers to, Horrell had written: 'Hillary … ignored much of Pugh's advice, misinterpreted many of his findings, and ultimately tried to claim credit for much of his research.'*

Putting aside this unpleasantness triggered by the expedition book, and of course the disaster on Makalu, for Ward, Silver Hut had otherwise been a rich and rewarding experience. And not only for him, as the youngest member of their party, Mike Gill, recalled: 'It was a special time remembered with great affection by those who lived through it.'

---

* Posted on 2 October 2013 on Horrell's website 'Footsteps on the Mountain' (https://www.markhorrell.com). The full text to do with Silver Hut reads: 'Hillary emerges from this episode as a *short-sighted and egotistical leader* who ignored much of Pugh's advice, misinterpreted many of his findings, and ultimately tried to claim credit for much of his research. He even stole the text of some of Pugh's dispatches and quoted them verbatim and uncredited in his book.'

Further note: In December 2022, I interviewed Pat Barcham, another mountaineer from New Zealand who went on the yeti hunt with Hillary during Silver Hut. When discussing Hardie's post, Barcham stated: 'Norman in my opinion was a very fair-minded man.'

# 15

# Exploring Bhutan

As much as Ward needed time to recuperate, he had to return to work following his long leave of absence. After a short break, he was back at the London Hospital as a senior registrar late in 1961.

His other imperative was to start documenting his own findings from Silver Hut. Rather than publish these in a series of articles as the other scientists were doing, he decided to combine all the various strands into an MD thesis, this being the prerequisite for gaining a higher Doctor of Medicine degree (Jim Milledge would do the same). This commitment, however, would mean going back to long hours of study and writing, which Michael undertook before and after his 'normal' workday at the hospital. He also made time to write detailed articles for various mountaineering journals describing the Silver Hut Expedition, his team's first ascent of Ama Dablam, and learnings from their disastrous experience on Makalu.[*]

Just as he was settling back down to a routine of work and study, an opportunity appeared out of the blue beckoning a return to the Himalayas. It involved the possibility of leading an expedition to the last remaining unclimbed peak over 8,000m, Gosainthan. Also known as Shishapangma, it stands at 26,335ft on the border between Nepal and Chinese-occupied Tibet. At the time, it was unclear whether the mountain straddled the two countries (it actually lies 3 miles wholly within Tibet), and a China-Nepal Boundary Commission was in the process of delineating the vague frontier of this area. Due to the uncertainty surrounding the peak's position, the Nepalese co-chair of the commission had suggested to Colonel Charles Wylie, who was still working in Kathmandu as military attaché, that his government might grant permission for a British party to climb Gosainthan from the Nepalese side.

Soon afterwards, Wylie was invalided back to London where he contacted Ward and the Alpine Club in July 1963 to discuss the matter. The club

---

* See the *Alpine Journal* (1961–63), *The Climbers' Club Journal* (1962), and *The Mountain World* (1962/63).

secretary then wrote to the Mount Everest Foundation (MEF), which had by this stage replaced the Himalayan Committee, outlining the opportunity. His letter also requested funding of £15,000 and nominated Ward as expedition leader. Encouraged by the enthusiastic response from the foundation, Michael quickly set about pulling together a small but experienced team. It included the likes of Chris Bonington and Ian Clough, both of whom had just ascended the North Face of the Eiger; Jim Milledge was pencilled in as their doctor; and John Hunt agreed to serve on the organising committee.

During this time, Ward was hunting down every relevant map and photograph he could unearth, trying to find a feasible route to the upper slopes of the mountain across its glaciers and snowfields. Just as his team was finalising plans, however, their hopes were dashed. A newspaper article in May 1964 reported a large Chinese party of almost 200 mountaineers had beaten them to it, placing ten climbers on the summit together with a bust of Chairman Mao. As Michael recalled: 'That was the end of British interest in Gosainthan, and all that remains of our aspirations are two large and bursting files.'

Disappointing though this abandoned venture was, another soon presented itself. One which would combine all of Ward's interests: mountaineering and medicine, together with the exploration and mapping of remote areas in high Asia, Pundit-style.

Ward was approached by a fellow doctor to accompany him to the Kingdom of Bhutan. Fred Jackson was a consultant cardiologist at the Newcastle General Hospital and also interested in mountain medicine. A few years earlier, he had carried out research on Ama Dablam using an ECG machine with himself as the test subject, in an effort to study how altitude affects the functions of the human heart. In early 1964, Jackson had visited the King of Bhutan, Jigme Dorji Wangchuck, to provide him specialist advice following a mild heart attack.

Jackson was due to make a follow-up visit shortly, and since the king lived permanently above 10,000ft, he approached Ward to accompany him, knowing his expertise in high altitude medicine. Of course, Michael needed little encouragement. He immediately began finding out all he could about this landlocked state nestled in the Eastern Himalayas between Tibet and India.

Bhutan is one of the world's tiniest independent kingdoms, and at the time it had a population of around 250,000 (today, approaching 800,000).

It is roughly the size of Switzerland and has the distinction of being the world's most mountainous country. Known to locals as Druk Yul, or the Land of the Thunder Dragon, its people are of Tibetan stock and the country predominantly Buddhist. Like Tibet, until recently it had a disproportionately high number of lamas and, as education was mainly confined to monasteries, the lamas exerted immense influence on lay people.

Until 1947, Bhutan's history had been heavily influenced by its southern neighbour British India, and thereafter by India. Its first two roads capable of carrying vehicles were built by 1965, and these further connected the two countries. Even today, Bhutan's people live mostly in its fertile southwestern valleys around the capital Thimphu. The south has also been settled by large Nepalese immigrant communities who make up over one-third of the country's population, which has often led to communal strife. In the north, following the failed uprising by Tibetans against Chinese rule in 1959, refugees had been crossing into the kingdom through a few high passes, but the frontier had been closed by Bhutan soon afterwards.

The whole northern region, which lies in the Great Himalayas, is sparsely settled and can well be described as 'unspoilt'. Other than being cut off from the rest of the country by high mountains, at the time, the little contact locals had with the wider world was by way of radio, but only if one was available. These areas were still unknown to most Bhutanese and simply marked 'Unsurveyed' on most maps. From all Ward could make out, no European had ever explored here.

Two English botanists, Frank Ludlow and George Sherriff, had undertaken six extensive trips through the valleys of central Bhutan from 1933 to 1949 and come to know the country better than any other foreigner. In his last year there, Ludlow had also travelled on his own through some parts of the northern region. On his return, his collection of birds, butterflies and plants was stored at the Natural History Museum in London. Before leaving, Michael managed to track him down at the museum, where he regularly worked on his specimens. During their meeting, Ward was able to obtain a sketch of Ludlow's journey north, although this was only a rough map since his focus was on Bhutan's flora and fauna rather than its actual topography.

Ward and Jackson departed from Calcutta (today, Kolkata) in the last week of July 1964 to the Indian border town of Hasimara. They flew out in a small Dakota but could only land after the pilot 'buzzed' a herd of elephants off the airstrip. Expecting to be helicoptered by the Indian Air Force from its base there onto the palace grounds in the Bhutanese capital, they soon learnt this would not be possible. The monsoon had already set in, reducing visibility and making any flight risky, so the pair had little option but to be driven there by Land Rover.

Although a little more than 100 miles away, the trip would take two days due to the steep road winding up into the mountains, made treacherous by heavy rain. Just before the halfway point, they encountered a massive landslide. It forced them to wade through knee-deep mud with their rucksacks, lugging their gear and medical supplies to another Land Rover which had been prearranged and waiting on the other side. From here, they continued their hair-raising trip with another seemingly crazy driver, zipping along a narrow road hewn into the walls of a ravine, even as boulders the size of cars hurtled down the roaring river below.

Eventually, they arrived at the confluence of western Bhutan's two main *chus* (rivers), the Thimphu Chu and Paro Chu. Since the king was due to visit the town of Paro in two days' time, rather than push on to the capital, they were driven to Paro instead (see Map 4). Here, they visited its imposing *dzong* built in 1646, resembling a diminutive Potala Palace.

In Bhutan, as in Tibet, a *dzong* comprises a military fort, an administration centre, and a monastery housing many monks – thus women are neither encouraged to enter nor permitted to remain after dark. They are usually large sprawling complexes made up of square, white-washed buildings with attractive red ochre stripes and golden roofs. Often sited on a hilltop with a central tower, their high, thick walls were built to repel invaders. Many were constructed centuries ago, having a timeless, mystical quality about them, and Michael explored those he could with avid interest.

He also observed the distinctive garments worn by the people. Many men and women, including those working out in the fields, wore loose, knee-length gowns similar to those worn by Tibetans. Made from the wool of sheep or yak, or sometimes from sheepskin, they looked warm and comfortable. These gowns are held together by a belt at the waist, which allows for all manner of articles to be stored in the front fold. Some people wore locally made boots, but many walked barefoot, even for long periods in the snow, reminding Michael of Man Bahadur.

The next day, he and Fred were driven to a nearby monastery where they met the king's personal physician Dr Tobgyel, who briefed them on his charge's health. The doctor was also the country's Director of Medical Services, and they found him to be an efficient professional and a thoroughly likable person. The king, whom they met soon afterwards, was also friendly and took them for a tour into the depths of the monastery. They wandered past prayer wheels rotated by hot air rising from ghee lamps, and monks reciting special prayers for their monarch over a number of days. The king explained they were doing so because, this being the Year of the Dragon, it was an inauspicious time for him so the monks' incantations would help ward off bad luck.

Later, the visitors had lunch with the queen before gathering around the boardgame Scrabble, which they had brought over as a present, and now played with some of her older children. They noticed how the servants held the royal couple in absolute reverence and bent low to the ground in their presence, regarding them as demi-gods.

The following day, the king arranged for the pair to be driven a few miles northwest of Paro to visit one of Bhutan's most iconic monasteries and sacred sites, Takhsang (or the Tiger's Lair). Built in the late seventeenth century around a tiger's cave, it clings spectacularly to a cliff face and is only accessible via a steep and narrow path. The Bhutanese believe the Indian mystic Padmasambhava (also known as Guru Rimpoche), who introduced Tantric Buddhism to this region during the eighth century, landed here on a flying tiger.

Eventually, after locating the caretaker lama, the doctors were able to explore the many rooms within the monastery, one of which was thought to have been used by Padmasambhava to meditate. Another purpose of this dark room was to house the ashes of other holy men. Fred persuaded the lama to let him take a photograph of a barely visible painting on one of its rock walls using a flashlight (today, no photography is permitted in the complex). When the shot was later developed, it showed a fierce looking god riding a tiger, recalling the legendary creature whose lair the monastery had been built around.

After Jackson and Ward had medically examined the king, they realised he would also need to be X-rayed. However, since no X-ray machine was available in Bhutan, one would have to be sent from India, together with technicians to operate it. They would have to be transported by road since the monsoon was still preventing all flights, and so take three weeks to arrive.

Despite the heavy rains, the doctors wanted to put this delay to good use by trekking north into Lunana, an unexplored region virtually unknown to the Western world. Even Bhutanese rarely visited there. The king had doubts about their ability to cross a high glacier pass to gain access to the area as one of his officers had recently failed in an attempt to do so. Yet they were heartened on receiving His Majesty's permission to go, and 'climb a mountain or two' while there. He would send his district governors a letter to ensure the visitors received whatever food and transport they required along the way. He also offered them camping equipment from his army, promised to provide maps, and made his personal bodyguard available to accompany them. Jigme, or 'Jimmy', came from Lunana but hadn't been home in almost ten years, so was keen to join the doctors.

Unfortunately, when Ward received the quarter-inch scale map from the king, it proved practically useless for their purposes, and Jimmy's recollection of the tracks and villages in this remote area also turned out to be scant. However, after a long discussion with him, Michael was able to draw a rough sketch of their proposed route north, but it was literally done on the back of an old envelope. He intended putting this right by making a 'route map' of their trek, by estimating the distances he marched and using a prismatic compass to take bearings.[*] In doing so, Ward would apply techniques perfected by the Pundits, which he had first used during the 1951 Reconnaissance. Fortunately, on this occasion he would have more time and be under less pressure to complete his task.

In anticipation of making such a map, before leaving for Bhutan, Ward had practised in London's Richmond Park, learning to take compass bearings and estimate distances by counting his steps as he walked at a consistent pace. No doubt, this generated amused looks from other park users and was a source of bewilderment for his toddler son. Michael would then compare his results with the actual lie of the land as shown on a local map, and in this way improve his technique. Of course, the terrain in Bhutan would be more challenging, and he would have to contend with monsoonal rains and extreme heights while route surveying.

Following their meeting with the king in Paro, Ward and Jackson travelled to the capital and began preparations for their departure. Here, they had the opportunity to discuss the few routes available to them with some army officers.[†] They advised the doctors to take the longer track to Lunana up the banks of the Mo Chu, as the gorges along its twin river, the Pho Chu, were currently impassable. This would mean heading directly north first, via the Gasa Dzong to the region of Laya and its border post, then travelling east along the frontier to enter Lunana.

While in Thimphu they also visited the main hospital and met the doctor in-charge, who explained the difficulties faced in treating patients in Bhutan. Western medicine was typically distrusted by locals, who invariably sought traditional cures first and often only came to hospital when it was too late. Making a round of his wards, they were able offer him advice on treating some of the seriously ill patients. Michael even offered to perform an amputation on a patient whose leg had become badly infected

---

[*] A route map is not a complete map in itself but helps fill in the details of an area being surveyed. Being rudimentary, it contains inherent errors, even under the most favourable conditions.

[†] In his diary, Ward noted Bhutan's army comprised 6,000 men and 90 officers.

after sustaining a compound fracture, but the man could not be convinced of the dire need for such drastic surgery.

On 5 August, the two doctors began their trek from the capital, accompanied by Jimmy and another of the king's bodyguards, an officer named Yeshey Dorji who would also act as interpreter. They took a cook along and some muleteers leading seven animals loaded with their gear. The mules would be later exchanged for yaks, essential in the high mountains but which struggle to survive below 10,000ft.

The pair carried large umbrellas to shelter from the continuous rain that would barely let up for the three weeks they were away. The first bloodsucking leeches appeared once they passed 7,500ft, some even finding a way to steal into their sleeping bags. Often, they walked through deep mud and up steep slopes. The inevitable occurred when Fred skidded and wrenched his knee, which was soon swollen and gave him trouble for days.

Their march on the first day was particularly long and arduous, especially for the muleteers who followed well behind. At one point, these men had to unload their animals and carry 120lb loads while negotiating a narrow, steep path in the dark. It was ten o'clock that night when they walked into camp, complaining loudly. Due to the slowness of their baggage train, Fred and Michael would often charge ahead, but nothing ever went missing from their luggage.

The party camped in settlements along the way, and both doctors took time out to examine any villagers in need as best they could. In addition to dispensing medicines, the treatment they administered included extracting teeth and attending to eye infections. Lack of facilities was a constant problem, however, as in the case of a woman needing a heart operation (she later died from cardiac failure). Nevertheless, Michael took medical notes of the diseases prevalent here, which would form the basis of his study on health conditions in the high Himalayas.

Two days out from Thimphu, after crossing a precarious cantilever bridge, they arrived at the Mo Chu and the entrance to its spectacular gorge. Ward described the hair-raising track confronting them:

> The river here was confined between cliffs seldom more than a few yards apart, and through these it projected itself as from a hose. The path which we now followed lay entirely on the western bank and sometimes dropped to the river bed, but was more often thousands of feet above it. This gorge was of true Himalayan proportions; the steep cliffs adjacent to the river were 2,000 or 3,000 feet high, with the country above slanting back for another few thousand feet, the overall drop being two or more vertical miles.

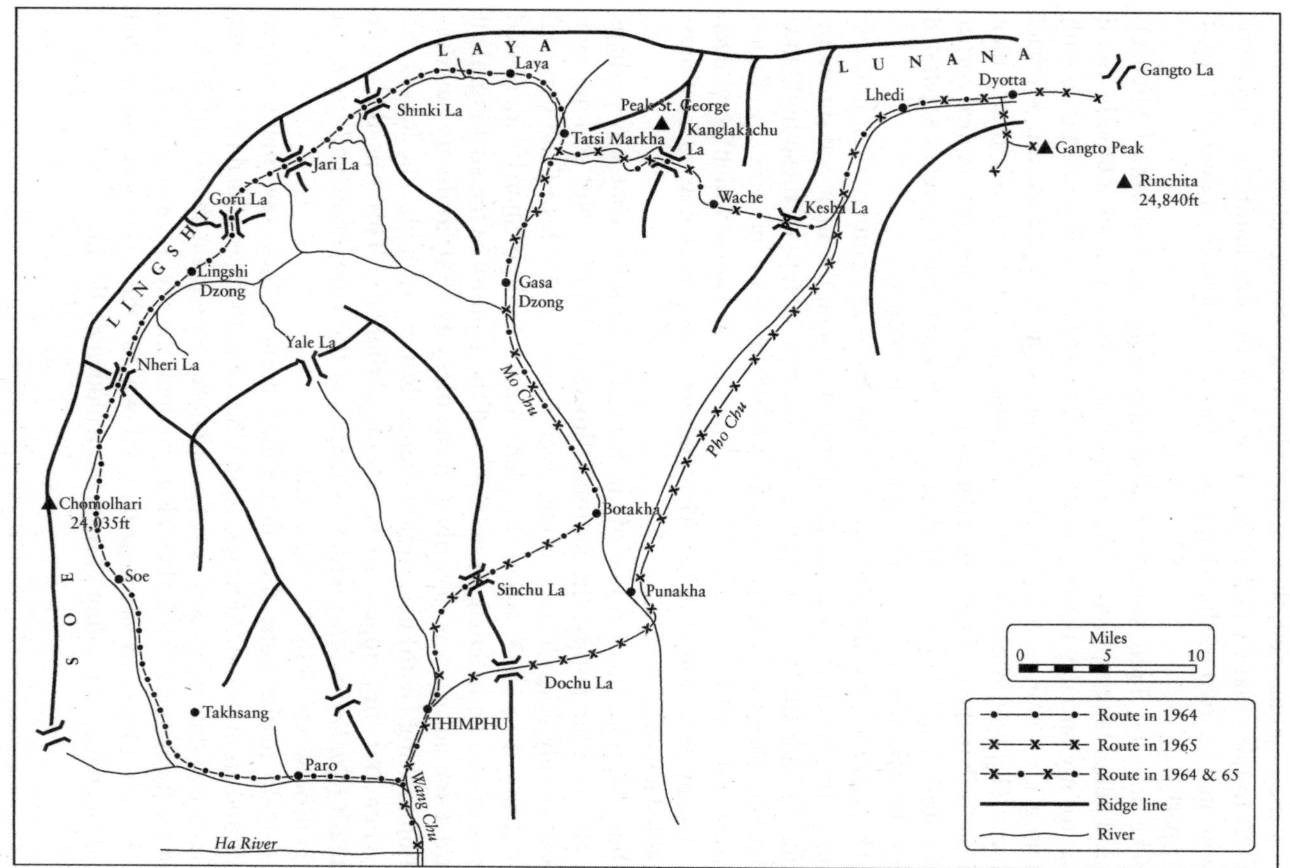


**Map 4. Exploration of Bhutan 1964 and '65** (based on maps from Ward's articles in *Alpine Journal* 1965 and '66)

Continuing their march north, the party reached Gasa Dzong, the main administrative centre of the northwest, sitting 9,300ft above sea level. Here, they exchanged their mules for yaks before climbing another 3,000ft to the village of Chamsa. As well as the yak handlers, they were now joined by two of the king's own hunters whom he'd sent to bolster their party.

The next day Fred turned 50, which prompted him to ask of Michael: 'You'd better take a photo of me. I have never been in such a bloody awful place for my birthday before.' In describing Fred, as he appeared then with thinning grey hair, spectacles and a preoccupied, academic air, Michael wrote: '[He] would be more at home pottering about in a laboratory than setting forth in the middle of the monsoon to some remote, unmapped corner of Central Asia.' Throughout their trip, although eleven years separated them, the two men seem to have got along fabulously.

This day also saw them arrive at the northernmost point of their journey, close to the Tibetan border in the district of Laya, the main yak-breeding region of Bhutan. Ward was struck by the raw beauty of these highlands and the 'tremendous smell of juniper'. To this memory, he adds a profusion of colourful wildflowers, including carpets of edelweiss which grew even larger than those found in the Alps and were so common as to be almost regarded a weed.

Interestingly, he also records in his diary spotting what was perhaps the elusive blue poppy, the national flower of Bhutan. Not so long ago, it was simply considered a myth, even linked with tales of the yeti. All that changed in 1933, when the plant hunter George Sherriff identified specimens in an isolated, eastern part of the country.[*] One striking plant Ward came across was described in his diary as 'Extraordinary science-fiction looking [with] pale yellow-beige flowers 3ft high. The leaves can be eaten and they appear to be a sort of rhubarb.' This was the noble rhubarb (*Rheum nobile*) which is native to the Himalayas and grows at heights between 13,000 and 16,000ft.

Adding to the butterflies that flitted around, they saw many native birds and animals too. At times, Ram Chukor partridges glided through the valleys, and they came across herds of *bharal* (mountain sheep) which they shot for fresh meat. Once, they chanced upon the small but rare Himalayan musk deer (*Moschus leucogaster*), known for the expensive musk that males secrete, but hunting these was forbidden by the king.

---

[*] Another variety, *Meconopsis baileyi* was first found and named in 1912 by Lt. Col. F.M. Bailey.

Looking out from the mountains, the yak pastures stretched out before them, dotted with black tents put up by the herders. These tents were surprisingly waterproof even though the yak-hair cloth used was woven with a relatively wide mesh. The herders similarly plaited their version of snow goggles from the tail of yaks, to protect their eyes from glare reflecting off the snow.

The doctors were able to hire fresh animals from the herders; but were always watchful of the vicious mastiffs these men bred and kept half-starved, to guard their tents and herds. The yaks represented their wealth. Each could be sold for 500 rupees, but were also capable of earning around 800 rupees annually through hire charges amounting to five rupees per load per day. These beasts were crucial for transport in the highlands, and adept at forcing a trail through snowbound tracks and passes. There were no roads or vehicles here, as Michael noted: 'The only wheel that is used in the Himalaya until recently has been the prayer wheel. No transport in high valleys uses this crucial item of technology.'

As they continued on, Ward kept up his route survey. He estimated distances marched, noted the names of villages and geographical landmarks such as adjoining streams, and measured the height of passes they crossed using his pocket altimeter. Whenever visibility allowed, he took compass bearings of distant peaks, but cloud cover often hampered his survey. The rain was incessant throughout most of the trek, as Michael regularly noted in his diary; one typical entry being: 'At the moment I am sitting in the rain – pouring down.'

Eventually, the party arrived at the high glacier pass the king had warned them about, the Kanglakachu La, which marks the gateway into Lunana. This pass sits at almost 17,000ft, but for the two mountaineers its crossing did not prove overly difficult; although everyone was showing signs of cyanosis – a blue tinge to skin, lips or nails due to oxygen lack. The other side of the pass, however, was so steep they needed their ice axes to descend as the path zigzagged down to the upper reaches of the Pho Chu.

At the river's head lay four lakes among the glacial moraine. Jimmy told them how one of the larger lakes had burst its moraine dam some years earlier and he had nearly drowned in its aftermath. The resulting tidal wave had wreaked havoc and death downstream in central Bhutan, especially in the town of Punakha. This was once the country's winter capital and lies at the confluence of the Pho Chu and Mo Chu (meaning 'male' and 'female' rivers respectively). Further down the valley, they saw for themselves the incredible force unleashed by this dam break as large, uprooted trees, their roots black with decay, still hung upside down from the branches of other living trees.

Two days later, after negotiating a few more passes, the party finally arrived in Lhedi. Although this was one of the bigger villages of the district, it numbered less than fifty persons, and the total population of the eleven settlements making up Lunana at the time was only 520. Ward learnt people here only travelled beyond their district to trade produce down in Punakha, and to buy rice which doesn't grow well above 7,000ft. One other reason was to undertake compulsory work in central Bhutan as an alternative to paying tax. This duty lasted up to a month, and usually involved working on the roads, where every rock used was broken by hand.

Otherwise, people seldom left their valleys, and for many months of the year were cut off from the rest of the world by heavy snowfall and the encircling mountains. Yet the doctors saw little evidence of genetic disorders caused by inbreeding or congenital abnormalities, and were told close relatives did not marry.

In Lunana, they based themselves in Lhedi, making use of a newly built schoolhouse which as yet had no teacher. Here, they held 'sick parades', attending to the various ailments presented by villagers, many of whom had never been examined by a doctor. In all, they would manage to see about 250 patients in Bhutan.

The next day, while Fred rested his knee, Michael went further up the valley with Yeshey, all the way towards the Tibetan border; probably being the first Westerner to have explored this far. As well as surveying the area, he was trying to identify two peaks named Kangri and Kula Kangri. The pair were shown on a Survey of India map and other charts as lying within the 'Unsurveyed' border region, and had also been identified by one of the Pundits during a secret mission.

While hunting in the basement of the Royal Geographical Society in London, Ward had come across photographs of both peaks, but these had been taken many years earlier and from somewhere in southern Tibet. Although they were marked as the two highest mountains in Bhutan on some maps, their location was uncertain. Locals were also vague about where they might lie, which was not surprising as Kangri simply means 'mountain' in Tibetan. As he visited the remaining villages in Lunana, Michael was able to include new placenames on his route survey. He felt frustrated, though, at not being able to see beyond the valley due to impenetrable clouds, and could not spot either of the two Kangris.

After returning to Lhedi that night, he joined Fred and many of the villagers in a big party which continued until dawn, with singing and dancing around lamplight. Michael learnt each dance had its own meaning, depicting everyday tasks such as planting and harvesting. He saw them performed by either men or women, usually dancing in small groups.

The next day, the two doctors began their trek back to Paro, from where they would be transported to Thimphu. Earlier, a telegram had arrived from Dr Tobgyel advising them the king was in good health and the X-ray machine had arrived.

Once again they had little difficulty crossing the Kanglakachu La. But this time, they couldn't match Jimmy and the hunters' pace as they charged madly up to the top of the pass in pursuit of a herd of wild goats. Here, visibility was again hampered by intermittent cloud, so the pair decided to climb higher to get better views. Sending the others ahead with the yaks to the village of Rodofu in Laya, they scaled a small outcrop and were immediately rewarded, as Ward recalls:

> I could hardly believe my eyes at the vista from the top of this. For some reason we had not thought that we would get a view towards the west, but we had a glorious and unforgettable sight of Kangchenjunga, yellowed by distance, with, a great deal nearer, Chomolhari, a pure snow cone.[*]

This view spurred them towards some rock needles nearby, which Ward promptly named Aiguilles de Rodofu. They roped up and climbed the closest spire, measuring 17,825ft, which he called Peak St George.[†] From its top, around two o'clock that afternoon, they were finally able to get a panoramic view, looking west from Nepal all the way round into southern Tibet. Spending an hour on the summit, Michael took bearings of visible peaks and a series of panoramic photographs by rotating his camera – information that would be used later to prepare a map of this area.

Some 30 miles to the east, he could see two high mountains which looked to be the two Kangris. What he saw were probably Gangkhar Puensum (24,840ft) and Kula Kangri (24,698ft). The latter lies in a disputed border region with Tibet, while the former is Bhutan's highest peak, also known to Lunana's inhabitants as Rinchita. (It is thought to be the world's highest unclimbed mountain because from 1994 the kingdom prohibited the climbing of any of its peaks above 20,000ft for religious reasons, before banning mountaineering altogether in 2003.)

---

[*] Straddling Tibet and western Bhutan, Chomolhari (24,035ft) is the country's second highest mountain.

[†] Named after Edward St George, a lifelong friend of Bhutan's king. He had been instrumental in arranging their trip to the kingdom; and later, Ward asked the king's permission to include both names in his map.

As Ward pointed out in his article for the *Alpine Journal* (1965) titled 'Bhutan Himal', the mountains he saw were separate from those lying in Assam. Thus, he determined these constituted a separate range which he now designated as Bhutan Himal – one which geographers had previously believed (incorrectly) to be a part of the Assam Himalaya. Ward went further and subdivided the Bhutan Himal into six sets of mountains, including the Chomolhari, Rodofu and Lunana groups. These ranges bounded Bhutan's northern frontier along the main Himalayan watershed. With binoculars, he and Fred could see across to many other unnamed mountains, leading Michael to comment: 'It was amazing that in 1964 we were probably the first Europeans to see many of these peaks.'

Finding their way back down to Rodofu took them longer than anticipated, and the pair only arrived late that night after stumbling along the river valley. Fred's knee was troubling him again, so Michael wore his white hat to give him something to follow in the darkness. Leading the way, at one point he crashed into a sleeping yak which was just as surprised as he was, but there was one bit of relief Michael recalled: 'With great forethought Fred had realised that the tubes in which jelly is kept for use with E.C.G. machines were watertight, and he had filled one of these with whiskey.'

The pair eventually found their campsite, after hearing shouts from an anxious search party. Yeshey was especially relieved to see them, as the king had made him personally responsible for their safety. To pacify Yeshey and explain their need to summit such mountains, they used a touch of subtlety: 'We described our ascent of this peak as a form of pilgrimage which the Bhutanese, being Bhutanese, well understood.'

From the border post in Laya, the doctors were able to send telegrams via Calcutta to their wives back home advising they were safe and well, and another to the king in Thimphu. Taking stock of their itinerary, the pair realised time was running out as they were scheduled to leave for England by 1 September. This was only ten days away, and they needed to attend to the king's X-rays before then. It meant having to cut their return trip from ten days down to six.

However, rather than return the same way, following the Mo Chu south, they wanted to explore a new route which the king had suggested. This ran along Bhutan's western border and passed beneath Chomolhari. They decided to take this route without compromising their shortened itinerary by making a rapid march to Paro with Yeshey. The rest of the party would follow a couple of days behind with the yak caravan and most of their baggage, swapping to mules when they left the highlands.

Now, the trio had to push hard across several passes, but at nights the doctors continued to make time to see sick villagers and dispense medicine – Michael was even asked if he could treat a yak with a broken hind leg. At one point, from a distance they saw what appeared to be a herd of strange-looking yaks. Later, they learnt they had sighted the takin (*Budorcas taxicolor whitei*), Bhutan's national animal, which is protected from all hunting.

After Laya, the next district was Lingshi with its grand old *dzong* sitting on a hilltop. It had withstood many Tibetan sieges in the past, and there was treasure reportedly stored in its underground rooms. Ward's diary also records another area off limits: 'There was a particularly holy part of the temple where we were not allowed to go because if we did, and were not holy enough, we would die.'

The forward party soon arrived below the southern face of Chomolhari but, to their disappointment, saw little of the peak as it was covered in cloud. From this point, the doctors resolved to get to Paro the next day, even though they were told by locals it would take another four days. Starting out at five o'clock the next morning, they pushed on as fast as possible in relentless rain, despite Fred's knee flaring up again. Luckily, they managed to cross a rickety bridge over a swollen stream just before it was washed away.

Michael was ahead of the others as darkness fell and hadn't realised the significance of a man carrying a basket who he passed coming the other way. Eventually, to his surprise, he stumbled onto a Land Rover belonging to Dr Tobgyel, who had sent his driver out to meet the returning party, as was customary. He had been waiting at a *dzong* some miles before Paro and, incredibly, had brought out a bottle of champagne sent by the king. It was in the basket Michael had seen yet rushed past, but the man entrusted with it arrived a little later with Fred and Yeshey. At this point in his unpublished autobiography, Ward finishes recounting his first visit to Bhutan with two short sentences: 'We finished the bottle. It was a fitting end to an unbelievable journey.'

On their return, Michael and Fred described their experience and medical findings in an article titled 'Medicine in Bhutan' published in *The Lancet* (1965). In addition to this, Ward's 'Bhutan Himal' article detailed the geographical aspects of the expedition, including a sketch map of their travels and photographs of many unrecorded peaks. It had been an eye-opening visit, but the kingdom had more to offer Michael yet.

**16**

# Return to Bhutan

W ard had often thought of putting his excursions into the Himalayas to greater use by combining them with his passion for mountain medicine and exploration. A way to achieve this was by studying the medical condition of its inhabitants in remote regions. This led him to a meeting with the convenor of the British effort within the International Biological Programme (IBP) begun in 1964. He explained the work of this organisation to Michael and its goal of exploring 'the biological basis of productivity and human welfare'. The programme would eventually run for a decade, investigating how humans adapted to different environments around the world – insights that would help improve their health and wellbeing.

The Human Adaptability section of the IBP was particularly interested in examining isolated communities, such as those existing at extreme altitudes in the Himalayas. Not only were they often unaffected by the modern world, but also largely unprotected from natural environmental hazards. These communities were thought to closely represent conditions under which mankind has lived for a large part of its existence. With the modern world rapidly encroaching, the study of their habitats and lifestyles was clearly a matter of urgency. Furthermore, a study of people from the high Himalayas would allow medical comparisons with members of their ethnic group living at lower levels in Asia, which itself should prove valuable.

After becoming aware of the IBP, Ward discussed the possibility of researching the people of Sola Khumbu and began collecting information about them. He soon realised, however, that the Sherpas were not isolated enough, as many of them moved about and some lived in Darjeeling for part of the year. Whereas, he had seen firsthand the seclusion of the northern Bhutanese, which made them an ideal group. In fact, at the time, they were probably the most isolated high-altitude community in the world.

Before leaving Bhutan at the end of August 1964, he and Jackson had talked to the king and Dr Tobgyel about the possibility of returning the following year to examine the inhabitants of Lunana as part of the IBP's

Human Adaptability studies. Theirs would be more of a preliminary study, to ascertain whether further comprehensive work should be carried out at a later date. Ward followed up their request with a formal letter to the king, and after receiving an enthusiastic response, began organising a small scientific expedition soon after returning home. The pair were able to secure grants to fund this work from various institutions, including the Royal Society (not to be confused with the RGS) and the Medical Research Council.

They decided to take a third doctor along to assist with the medical fieldwork, and also the onerous report writing to be completed on returning home. Initially they approached Griff Pugh, but he was recovering from an accident and unavailable. Fred then suggested a friend of his named 'Dick' Turner, a doctor and Reader in Medicine at the University of Edinburgh, who was keen to join them. Initially, Michael had concerns about Dick's lack of high-altitude experience and age, being six years older than Fred but, as events would prove, he need not have worried.

The timing of their departure and the imperative, this time, to arrive before the monsoon set in was hampered by two events. The first involved a political struggle which had broken out in Bhutan soon after Ward and Jackson returned home, when the prime minister there made a grab for power while the king was away overseas. Eventually the situation was resolved, but only after the prime minister was exiled and replaced by the king's half-brother.

The second complication arose with the outbreak of the Indo-Pakistan war at the start of August 1965. It prompted fears China would enter the fray and help East Pakistan (today, Bangladesh) isolate India's northeast frontier provinces from the rest of the country, which would effectively cut off Bhutan too. Fortunately, the warring parties agreed to a ceasefire within seven weeks of hostilities.

The resolution of both events opened the way for the three doctors to fly into Calcutta on 3 October, soon after the end of the rainy period. This was still cutting it fine though, as they would have to cross the Kanglakachu La, complete their work, then leave Lunana before snow blocked their exit and stranded them there for the duration of winter.

Well before leaving home, they had shipped over all necessary medical equipment and supplies. Among their gear was an ECG machine for cardio-vascular testing, a spirometer to measure lung-function, a hand centrifuge to remove serum from blood, plus all manner of medicines and test supplies. They also shipped out a small refrigerator, to be used for storing fresh blood samples, which they were planning to obtain in Thimphu just prior to their return.

Clearing all these items through customs in Calcutta proved to be a frustrating exercise. This burden fell to Michael while his two colleagues went ahead to Thimphu to begin organising their trip north. Bhutan, with no customs facilities of its own at the time, relied on India for this function and to collect tariffs on its behalf. Being a medical visit, no duty was payable, but Ward required a telegram from Delhi confirming this before their goods would be released.

Some of this holdup was due to confusion in the aftermath of the Indo-Pakistan war, but Michael also detected an anti-British feeling (India had wrested its independence in 1947 but was partitioned in the process). He used the delay in Calcutta to catch up with a few doctors and surgeons he knew, visiting their hospitals and offering advice where he could. At the end of it all, though, he recalled: 'Rarely have I spent a more taxing ten days'.

This frustration is reflected in his diary which, unusually, has no entries after 9 October and restarts with the exclamation: '18 Oct.! Left for Hasimara at 2.30am.' From this airfield on the Indian border, Ward caught a flight to the Bhutanese capital to be reunited with the others. But when their baggage was unpacked, they discovered the ECG machine was missing, together with a chest of medicine and some personal items. Thankfully, Dr Tobgyel was able to loan them an ECG unit, as it was critical for completing their medical programme.

With the cold weather closing in, the doctors wasted no time organising themselves and two days later were marching north with their muleteers. They were accompanied again by Yeshey and Jimmy. This time, they also had Jimmy's younger brother Nado with them, as well as a second interpreter named Kinley, and a cook. Once they had climbed high enough, their mules were exchanged for yaks, which lumbered along at an unwavering pace. They found some of the makeshift bridges being replaced now that the waterways had subsided, after the monsoon floods had done their usual damage. At times, the yaks had to swim across when these bridges were unsteady. Although sure-footed on rocky terrain, in one instance a yak did tumble over 150ft into a river. To everyone's surprise, it got up unharmed, even as some of its load was smashed.

Their yak caravan followed the same route out taken the previous year. This repetition, together with better weather, gave Ward an ideal opportunity to improve on his old route survey. His diary is filled with entries of bearings taken of mountains now visible, and diagrams of the overall topography together with the distances marched between various stages.

At nights, the doctors continued their 'sick parade', examining villagers and dispensing medicines. Sometimes they had to deal with more serious cases, such as treating a boy with a lacerated face and shoulder which had become infected. They learnt he had been attacked by a bear, which his father had fought off by ramming a knife down its throat. There were a lot of bears in this area and, together with snow leopards, posed a real threat to the locals and their livestock.

On the last day of October, ten days after leaving the capital, they arrived once more at the high point of their route into the northern region, the Kanglakachu La. This time they encountered more snow and wind, forcing them to double march over the pass and into the Pho Chu valley. The yak handlers used their animals to break a trail through the snow, up to 3ft deep in places. These hardy men walked barefoot without suffering frostbite or any apparent discomfit, only protecting their eyes with their yak-hair goggles.

The party soon found themselves strung out, with each man looking to his own strength to keep pushing on in the cold and wind. At one point Kinley collapsed, vomiting blood, and had to be carried by Jimmy for a while. Michael, too, found the going rough compared to Fred and Dick. This was probably due to being less acclimatised after his enforced stay in Calcutta at sea level, and he described the effect on him later in his scribblings:

> Felt very lonely and bereft and hoped that someone would wait. Feeling very weak and wobbly, muscles and bones, jelly, no substance … Tottered feebly up the pass – the scrabbling on snow covered rocks was horrible … Masses of snow on far side – weather much worse – black clouds boiling – wind increasing – snowing … I took one Purple Heart [Drinamyl tablet]. Only time I have ever taken a stimulant mountaineering as feeling so other worldly that I could not control my limbs …

The fierce struggle continued not only up the pass but down the other side. Their descent was made more treacherous by having to walk over rhododendron leaves which had frozen onto the rocks and then polished to a fine degree of slipperiness by the yaks in front.

Three days after entering Lunana, the party arrived at the village of Lhedi. The doctors would again base themselves at the school, which they found still in want of a teacher. They were welcomed by the villagers and their *Gup* (headman), who worked hard to make their stay comfortable and kept up a free supply of firewood. Although the schoolhouse was constructed with baked mud bricks, its one wooden wall let in piercing draughts through cracks between the planks, which they managed to cover up with cellophane bags. A stove in the middle of the room generated some warmth, but it caused a pall of smoke to collect in a thick layer below the ceiling. After enduring this for a few days, a brazier was fashioned from of an old paraffin tin which warmed the space sufficiently and allowed them to work from this room during the day. Ward's diary also mentions: 'A fine loo has been made overlooking the river, covered all around but with an open view outward.'

There was plenty of good, local food to eat, including vegetables and cheese, supplemented by yak meat and wild goats they managed to hunt. After the latter were shot and skinned, Michael would examine their hearts for any signs of enlargement caused by their high habitat.

One day, Kinley went out to hunt a snow leopard that had been killing yaks. He was unsuccessful, but the next day the villagers set a trap using two bows with arrows dipped in poison made from wild herbs. This time the creature was hit, as evidenced by the blood stains left behind, and was expected to die within half-an-hour. Although the locals didn't possess firearms, archery is Bhutan's national sport and Michael saw young boys practising with 5ft bows made from bamboo. They fired off 3ft long arrows and were able to regularly hit a small wooden target placed 100yds away.

The day after arriving in Lunana, the doctors started gathering medical data in earnest for the IBP study. They used non-invasive techniques which had been standardised, thus allowing their results to be incorporated with similar studies from other parts of the world. Working from dawn until well after dark, they began examining as many of the 500 or so villagers residing in Lunana.

To begin the process, with help from an interpreter, a medical history was obtained from each person. From the women, this included obtaining an account of pregnancies, miscarriages, and stillbirths, as well as infant and childhood mortality. Everyone was photographed, and a Polaroid print given to them to keep. These were probably the first and only pictures of themselves many would hold or own; and as Dick commented: 'It was entertaining to watch their expressions as they recognised each other's faces.'

Detailed physical examinations followed, including height, weight, blood pressure and anthropometry (body) measurements. Throat and nasal swabs were taken, together with a urine specimen for later analysis. Michael worried about ensuring all these samples were labelled well, noting 'Dick is so disorganised and may well forget something or lose it'.

In recording demographic data, because the Bhutanese used a different method for determining their age, these could only be estimated with the *Gup*'s help. He also proved invaluable in organising the people to be tested. This made a welcome change from their interpreter Kinley, who was often surly and uncooperative, despite the mountain of work needing to be completed.

Fortunately, the villagers weren't at all hesitant in having their blood sampled, although in this case children were not asked to participate. When they did collect blood, the doctors had to improvise after discovering their hypodermic syringes and needles were among the items lost in Calcutta. Luckily, the Vacutainer blood collection tubes with needles had arrived safely. They found these worked just as well, and thus were highly recommended in their report to the IBP for future field work. Using vacuum flasks, the samples were kept between 0–5°C, but one of the main difficulties faced during this process was separating blood from serum. This problem was exacerbated when the handle of their centrifuge broke, but Fred managed to fix it by making another handle from wood.

He and Dick were expert at using the ECG machine and were able to evaluate the incidence of cardiovascular disease among the population soon after testing them. They found no evidence of coronary heart problems, and surprisingly little incidence of disease in general for that matter.

However, goitre (a swelling in the neck due to an enlarged thyroid gland) was so commonplace in Bhutan that people simply accepted it as a part of life even though it is unsightly. Mostly caused by iodine deficiency, in Lunana the doctors noted over half the population was afflicted to some degree and many terrible cases of goitre were evident. They took soil samples back home to test for iodine content. (Very low levels would be confirmed; but after the sale of non-iodised salt was banned in Bhutan in the late 1960s, the incidence of goitre largely disappeared by the year 2000.)

An important test carried out with assistance from almost seventy villagers was to look at their ventilatory capacity. This was done by measuring the volume of air they could force out from their lungs using the spirometer. Their results would be compared later with Indians and Europeans residing at lower altitudes. One of the doctors' most interesting findings in this regard was that, despite living at high altitude, the villagers did not suffer from chronic mountain sickness caused by continual oxygen lack.

Another interesting set of data was obtained by taking fingerprints from about one-third of the adult population, after thoroughly scrubbing the engrained dirt from their hands. This information was being collected because little information on dermatoglyphics (the study of ridge patterns of the skin) was available for Himalayan peoples.

For the first three weeks, the doctors based themselves in Lhedi, 12,000ft above sea level. They relied on the *Gup* to ensure everyone present was seen, not just a select sample which would otherwise skew the data collected. He sent runners to the various settlements asking the villagers to come. To reach more of the population, the doctors spent a final week in the village of

Dyotta, 10 miles further up the valley and sitting 1,500ft higher. Eventually, they were able to examine over 80 per cent of Lunana's residents (around eighty-five were away, many labouring in lieu of paying tax).

During their stay in Lunana, Ward also made daily climatic recordings, including temperature, wind direction, and level of snowfall. He was lucky to witness a near-complete eclipse of the sun on 23 November that lasted for over two hours, which he described as having 'an eerie feeling' about it. The locals regarded this obscuring to be a bad omen for the king and his high officials, so they promptly lit fires, beat drums, and prayed until the sun returned.

When he had a moment, Ward questioned the *Gup* about yetis and whether any were seen in this area. According to the headman, these creatures stayed high on the mountains and weren't a danger to locals. Ward's diary shows the *Gup* referring to them as *lagi michum*, meaning 'children of the mountain'. He described them as small in stature, having a monkey-like face, covered in long hair, and with feet pointing the wrong way around.* On occasion, the *Gup* had come across footprints and even seen a creature some years ago, but this was from about 150yds away. (In 2003, Bhutan setup a national park, the Sakteng Wildlife Sanctuary, to protect its yeti – or *migoi*, as it is known to locals – whose existence they believe in fervently.)

Whenever he was out trekking or climbing, Michael continued to gather data for his route survey, and sometimes Fred helped by measuring distances and taking bearings. He also filled his diary with details describing the customs of the Bhutanese, including their traditional dress, diet and religious practices. In terms of the latter, to his surprise he saw plenty of evidence of the old Bon (Tibetan) religion, which pre-dates Buddhism, still being practised. Sometimes the things he heard could be confronting, such as when he asked how they dealt with their deceased. Although adults were mostly cremated, bodies of young children were cast into the river or left out for vultures, a form of sky burial.

Ward learnt that over three-quarters of the families owned their homes and a little land. He was interested in the way their houses were constructed and observed 'every house we went into was remarkably clean and tidy'. Out in the fields, he noted their farming methods and saw firsthand the many challenges villagers faced before the introduction of modern aids. All these details amounted to a 'human survey', and one that would represent

---

* Interestingly, the earliest accounts of yetis given by porters on the 1921 Mount Everest Expedition also described their feet as turned backward, to enable them to climb steep slopes easily.

an invaluable historical record of the Bhutanese and their Tibetan-based culture, as Eric Shipton had noted:

> For, whatever its imperfections in terms of modern democracy and in spite of its material poverty, the Tibetan theocratic system seems to have produced a people as content, as tolerant, as courageously independent and as free from cramping taboos as can be found anywhere. Today Bhutan is almost the only place where this remarkable culture still thrives on its native soil.*

Ward would also have the unique opportunity of comparing northern Bhutanese with the Sherpas of Nepal, being the first explorer to travel extensively through both these isolated communities. He also met with Tibetan refugees who had fled to Bhutan over the years. Although some managed to establish themselves and had fared well, he witnessed the plight of others not so fortunate, many of whom were relegated to the worst jobs by locals in exchange for appalling living conditions.

By the last week of November, all medical work for the IBP study had been completed. Michael and Fred were now free to explore further afield and climb some of the lower peaks in the area. From the tops of these, Ward took bearings and panoramic photographs to confirm the topography of the surrounding mountains. While Dick, Jimmy and the others left with a large party of villagers going to trade in Punakha, he and Fred organised a side excursion. They wanted to spend a few days trekking further along the valley hoping to find a route into the district of Bumtang located in central Bhutan.

Following their month of intense work and constant stream of people waiting to be examined, Michael recalls 'how peaceful it was … the change to solitude was reviving'. After hiring a porter, the pair headed south. But in no time, they encountered powder snow up to 5ft deep lying under a thin crust, which they virtually had to swim through to continue on. Not having snowshoes, Michael's toes were starting to get frostbitten, so they were forced to admit defeat.

Instead, they clambered up an 18,000ft peak towering above the surrounding yak pastures, which they named Yak Peak. Two days later, they climbed another mountain of similar height from which they could see over the Gangto La, the now-closed border crossing into Tibet, and named it Gangto Peak. These were both first ascents, and from their tops Michael searched with binoculars

---

* From Shipton's foreword to Dr Peter Steele's book *Two and Two Halves to Bhutan*. Steele visited there in 1967 to conduct medical research for the IBP and climb mountains – similar to what Ward had done before him.

for another route into Bumtang but could find none. Nevertheless, by taking bearings of other mountains observed the previous year from these two peaks, Ward was able to link his surveys from both years. This would be an important aid for any cartographer drawing a map from his data.

The pair did consider trying to break fresh trail down the main southbound valley, but as Michael recalled: 'However, it was winter and the snow was atrocious. In addition, we felt in honour bound to return by the more conventional route.' They knew the gorge going up the Pho Chu towards the Kanglakachu La was already closed by snow, so they followed the river downstream to Punakha instead. It too had a difficult pass, the Gongu La, sitting at 16,850ft. This was the route Dick and the traders had taken, using yaks to force a way through the snow.

On the way to catching up with them, the two doctors stopped at villages for food and *chang*, sometimes accepting too much of the latter. Once they treated a man badly mauled by a mastiff, who then fed them in gratitude. A little earlier, their porter's wife had joined them, carrying the same load as him and proving more than capable, not least because she drank less *chang* than the three men. As they marched, Fred collected rhododendron seeds, while Michael continued his route survey over this new ground.

On 10 December, four days after turning south for the Gongu La, they finally caught up with Dick and the yak caravan, joining them on their march to Punakha. When they arrived there, the doctors visited its monastery, which is Bhutan's most revered and stands prominently at the confluence of the Pho Chu and Mo Chu. The next day they were back in the capital, Thimphu.

Their first task here was to check the many test specimens collected in Lunana had survived – and were greatly relieved to find them all intact. However, they knew that due to the long trip, the blood samples would be in poor condition by the time they reached home. So, they took another set of samples from twenty nurses at the hospital, which they stored in the refrigerator brought from London for this purpose.

One of their last duties was to debrief the king and Dr Tobgyel about the expedition before leaving. (Sadly, the king died a few years later at the age of 44, from long-term heart problems.) The trio returned to London on 17 December, where Michael was met at the airport by Jane; but where he learnt to his dismay that none of his letters and telegrams from Bhutan or India had reached her.

Ward's two visits to northern Bhutan collectively represent ground-breaking work on a number of accounts: its contribution to medical science and the IBP study; its human survey of an isolated, high-altitude community; the exploration and mapping of a remote section of the Himalayas; and the first ascent of a number of unknown peaks. Yet he ends this account of Bhutan in his typical understated way: 'Next day I went back to full-time clinical work, as did Dick and Fred. In the year to come we managed to collate and analyse our results and, with the help of many others, present these in the form of a report.'

As well as their extensive 'Report of I.B.P. Expedition to Bhutan', which was republished by the Royal Society, within two years the doctors jointly reported on their other medical results. On analysing the data gathered in Lunana with the help of colleagues, the remainder of their findings would be published in various medical journals detailing their blood and serum work, ventilatory capacity measurements, and an analysis of the fingerprints taken. In an article for the *Alpine Journal* (1966), Ward summed up the value of this work: 'It is particularly satisfying that our research programme revealed a number of ways in which the health of the population could be protected and improved.'

The doctors also gave numerous lectures and published some work separately. Ward's most important personal contribution appeared in *The Geographical Journal** (1966) in an article titled 'Some Geographical and Medical Observations in North Bhutan'.† It included a large foldout map of northwestern Bhutan drawn by the chief draughtsman at the Royal Geographical Society using Ward's survey data from both journeys. Thus, a reliable route map of this little-known region was finally available to geographers, mountaineers and, more importantly, the people of Bhutan. It also represents probably the last exploration map ever published which relied on Pundit-style techniques.

Michael later followed up his geographical work with an article titled 'Exploration of the Bhutan Himalaya' for the *Alpine Journal* (1997). In it, he added a history of this portion of the Great Himalayas and the expeditions undertaken there by earlier explorers, including the Pundits he had emulated. In a rare show of emotion, he ended his article with what this all meant to him:

> It is given to few mountaineers to see for the first time a hundred-mile stretch of an unknown and unexplored part of the world's greatest mountain range, to climb four of its peaks, to map it and to re-name it.

Ward's experiences in northern Bhutan would spur him on to making further contributions to the twin pillars of research and exploration. Although he would not return to the Land of the Thunder Dragon, his legacy here remains significant.

---

* The official journal of the Royal Geographical Society.

† This article was based on two lectures he gave to the RGS, one of which was the Dickson Asia Lecture for 1966.

# 17

# Writer and Scholar

Ward's return from Bhutan marked a significant shift in his involvement with the mountains he loved, away from high altitude climbing and towards mountain literature, medicine and leadership. Over the years, he had been building an impressive library – the motto below the striking shield of his *Ex Libris* bookplate reads *Transcendere per scientiam* (Transcend through science).

Michael had a keen interest in mountain literature and poetry, as have many other mountaineers (and mystics) from the inception of this 'sport'. Through the written word, they have sought to define the essence of mountains and what it means to them, although not always successfully due to its elusive nature. In an article for the *Alpine Journal* (1976) titled 'Mountain Literature – then and now' Ward laid out his thoughts:

> The purpose of mountaineering literature is threefold: first it is simply to report and record; secondly it seeks to describe the motives and emotions of the climber; and lastly to distil that element of beauty which we find peculiar to mountain country and which may profoundly affect us.

Ernst Haas, in the opening lines of his *Himalayan Pilgrimage* wrote: '[Of] a fact that had long intrigued me: that the highest mountains in the world seemed to have inspired the highest levels of the human spirit'. Michael had experienced the highest of mountains, and hoped to capture this spirit in his first book *The Mountaineer's Companion*, an anthology he edited. It was published in 1966 when he was 41 – a relatively young age for a literary undertaking such as this.

Originally, the book had been commissioned by Maurice Temple Smith, an old acquaintance from his days at Cambridge who had since become a publisher under his own name, although the book was eventually released by Eyre & Spottiswoode. Ward had begun working on it a few years before his travels in Bhutan. In its introduction, he explained how he viewed this 'pastime' and his approach to its compilation:

> Mountaineering is classified as a sport, but this always seems to me to be an inadequate description; for some it's a way of life … It has even been claimed by mentors as a very desirable alternative to military experience, offering as it does 'the glory of conquest without the humiliation of the conquered' … All of the material included in this collection has been chosen because I found it interesting or enjoyable or both. To attempt any other method of selection would have turned a pleasing occupation into a dreary task.

Divided into nine parts, this 600-page anthology spans a wide range of mountain literature and poetry. Beginning with 'The Nature and Fascination of Climbing', it then quotes pieces from climbing in the Alps and Britain. This is followed by expeditions to the Himalayas, especially Mount Everest but including lesser-known peaks, and then to 'Other Ranges'. The anthology ends with 'The Secret Mountains', an eclectic mix of mountaineering incidents and anecdotes.

In this final section was an item which Ward probably could not resist. It was Bill Tilman's 1938 summary of all the available evidence concerning a creature which dogged Michael for much of his life, the yeti. On this topic too, his son Mark has related an interesting story:

> I recall, aged around 9 or 10, venturing with him into the Harrods bookstore and discovering for the first time the Tintin series of original graphic novels. I scanned the brightly illustrated covers which promised exciting adventures underseas, in the jungle, on a crashed asteroid, and even in space. Where to begin?
>
> My father spoke: "Well, you're going to have to pick one of them."
>
> Then my eye fell upon the only possible choice: [*Tintin in Tibet*]*

---

* The cover shows Tintin's party encountering a line of yeti footprints in the snow. Mark thought the similar photo of his father from 1951 might have influenced Hergé to write this story (now translated into over thirty languages).

The cover scene was eerily similar to the one my father had lived through in real life.

I beamed as I handed the book to the cashier.

"My dad met a yeti once," I proudly announced as she rang me up.

The cashier smiled indulgently at me and then my dad: "Oh really, how interesting."

My father, with the smallest hint of a grin, handed over his money and said not a word.


Soon after *The Mountaineer's Companion* was released, in a long and often critical review in the *Alpine Journal* (1967), Bill Murray had this to say:

[This] anthology is the most radical yet to come on the market, and this on three counts. Firstly, to make room for new writers, many once-revered heads have rolled from his chopping-block … Secondly, the editor has cut free from that long-lasting defensive attitude, which manifested itself as (an only apparent) literary snobbery … Thirdly, the editor departs from precedent in more often using long passages to give a complete incident. All this adds up to a more satisfying book, strongly built to a clean design … Michael Ward compiled this book in the hope that his pleasure in mountaineering and its literature could be shared. His hope is fulfilled.

Ward had discovered from his earliest venture into the Himalayas that, although he loved the mountains, climbing on its own was insufficient to hold his full attention; that 'something was missing'. By combining this love with writing and his interest in mountain medicine, he found his true calling.

The years following Bhutan were spent furthering his knowledge of high altitude physiology. Finally, in 1968, seven years after his return from Silver Hut and working beyond his 'day job' as a consultant surgeon, he completed his 25,000-word doctoral dissertation, noting: 'Writing the thesis turned out to be a dour and exacting voyage of discovery through [many] libraries'. Titled *Diseases Occurring at Altitudes Exceeding 17,500 ft*, it had taken longer to complete than he had hoped, but so had his recuperation after

Makalu. Nevertheless, it would have been a proud moment when the thesis was accepted by his old university, Cambridge, and the degree of Doctor of Medicine conferred. Although Michael says little about this milestone, it demonstrated his scientific ability through original research – as opposed to his clinical ability as a surgeon.

During these years of professional development, Ward was climbing whenever he could, returning to his old haunts in Britain and the Alps. He also began taking up a leadership position within the mountaineering fraternity. In 1967, the Alpine Climbing Group which he had helped found fifteen years earlier merged with the Alpine Club. It only came about, however, after a long and vociferous debate among the latter's members, some of whom were less than impressed by these 'young Turks'.

The following year and the next, Ward was elected Vice President of the Alpine Club, the world's oldest mountaineering club founded in 1857. In spite of this honour, there is some suggestion he may have felt let down by never being elected its President, despite being eminently qualified (Michael, of course, maintained his silence). If so, this was perhaps due to lingering tension with some of the old Everest guard, stemming from his disagreement with John Hunt.

Ward kept extensive diaries of his climbing through the years. Unfortunately, other than his key expeditions, most have been misplaced or lost. Even those still extant are often difficult to decipher due to his doctors' scrawl, exacerbated by the often challenging conditions under which many entries were scribbled down. The other issue was, as his old friend Jim Milledge observed: 'He not only eschewed the computer, he hadn't even got into the typewriter age!'

Michael's diaries, covering the first half of his life until 1965, provided the source material for his autobiography *In This Short Span*. At its core were his five expeditions to the Himalayas involving Mount Everest, the Silver Hut, and Bhutan. When it was published by Victor Gollancz in 1972, the book was well received by readers. Mountaineer and author Raymond Greene (brother of novelist Graham Greene), who was also the doctor on Everest in 1933, began his review by noting in his opening paragraph:

> Michael Ward is well on the way to becoming a Very Eminent Surgeon. After reading this book one wonders whether perhaps this is rather a pity. There are a lot of Very Eminent Surgeons but not many writers of adventure stories like this, and presumably this, his first, will also be his last. The world will force him into beating his ice axe into a scalpel.

Whether he was right about Ward's talent as a writer is up to readers to decide, but he has been proved wrong about this being Michael's last contribution to mountain literature, as we shall see.

In a longer review of 'The Books of the Year' in the *Alpine Journal* (1973), then President of the Alpine Club, David Cox, in his opening paragraph, quickly made the link between Ward's first two books:

> A few years ago Michael Ward gave us his anthology, *The Mountaineer's Companion*, a book which revealed something of his appreciation and wide knowledge of mountain literature. In its introduction he rejected as inadequate the classification of mountaineering as a sport ... he argued that different people, or even the same person, might climb for very different reasons. His new book, *In This Short Span* ... illustrates remarkably this point ... In visiting the Himalaya, Ward has been equally fascinated by climbs of the highest technical difficulty ... by journeys of exploration in country where 7000-m peaks are known to exist but have never been firmly placed on the map, by medical work among primitive hill people and by the physiological problems for Europeans of high-altitude mountaineering.

Cox also commented on his understated style: 'Michael Ward writes with great restraint and with a factual directness which often conveys more than would the same story told in a more dramatic way.'

Even as he was writing about mountains and the struggles to climb them, Ward continued publishing medical articles on high altitude physiology through various journals. In 1975, he co-instigated a symposium for mountaineers, expedition doctors and physiologists, where he presented two papers of his own, 'Everest Without Oxygen?' and 'Frostbite'.

That same year he published *Mountain Medicine*, the first textbook to appear in this growing field of study. It was welcomed by medical practitioners, researchers, and students alike, and of *direct* benefit to people living and working at higher altitudes, as well as climbers. Moreover, as he pointed out: 'The mountaineer at altitude acts as a model for those at sea-level with oxygen lack due to chronic heart and lung disease.'* Thus,

---

* See his article 'Mountain Medicine and Physiology: A Short History' in the *Alpine Journal* (1990).

his text would also be of *indirect* benefit to people struggling with such medical conditions right across the world.

In his unpublished autobiographical notes, Ward candidly noted Pugh was better qualified to write this book, but he could not be convinced to do so, not even as co-author. It remains a standard and definitive text on this subject – a sixth edition was released in 2021.

In the years after transitioning from doctor to consultant surgeon, Michael worked at various hospitals in the capital, often taking on a teaching role. From 1975 onwards he went further, to become Lecturer in Clinical Surgery at the London Hospital Medical College, an internationally renowned teaching hospital.

In the second half of the 1970s, Ward partnered up with Professor Edward Williams. They began studying the effect of strenuous exercise, such as climbing, on a medical condition which leads to the swelling of body tissue known as 'oedema'.* Although mountain sickness is caused by oxygen lack, it can manifest as oedema of the lungs (pulmonary) or brain (cerebral). The pair were joined by a small group of British medical researchers, including Jim Milledge, and they light-heartedly called themselves 'The Worshipful Company of Gentleman Physiologists'. Over several years, the group conducted a number of field trips in North Wales, the Lake District, and Switzerland, particularly to study the onset of pulmonary oedema, which is thought to account for most deaths from high altitude illness.

However, as Michael had experienced firsthand on Makalu, both forms of oedema can be life threatening at altitude. This is especially so for cerebral oedema, as the increased pressure on the brain due to the rigidity of the skull can lead to death rapidly. The researchers already knew oedema could be caused by oxygen lack, but were now discovering that severe exercise could also trigger this condition. Mountaineers were therefore doubly susceptible, hence the special interest in its research by the mountaineering fraternity. Ward understood well what was at stake here, as he noted in the *Alpine Journal* (1993): 'At sea-level if an athlete fails to produce an Olympic-class performance he may lose a race or a title; near the summit of Everest he may lose a limb or his life.'

During a 25th anniversary reunion of the first ascent of Everest celebrated by some of the team in Nepal, Michael was even making clinical observations as their group trekked from Darjeeling to Sola Khumbu over

---

* Oedema occurs largely as water (which makes up 65 per cent of body weight) moves from the inside to the outside of cells within the body.

a number of weeks. The other four members probably wondered (good-naturedly?) whether they'd ever get away from his infernal tests.

That same year, Ward became Chairman of the Mount Everest Foundation for a period of three years. It was during this time he began organising his next major expedition. He was returning to the high peaks of Asia, but this time to one located far west of the Himalayas, and his primary role would shift from one of climbing to leadership.

# 18

# China Opens its Doors

In his writings, Ward often expressed fascination with Central Asia and its history, beginning with the ancient Silk Road and its network of overland routes, as caravans plied their trade between distant empires. This rich history, including the extraordinary travels of Marco Polo, continued through the centuries as kingdoms rose and fell, and borders were reshaped often through violent conflict. Eventually it evolved into the Great Game between the Russian and British empires, and it was during this time the Pundits were dispatched by the Survey of India to secretly map unknown parts of Central Asia.

Michael longed to explore here in their footsteps, across a land once known as Turkestan. In the 1800s, it had been split up into a western half controlled by Czarist Russia, and an eastern half which China repossessed. The two sides were divided by a formidable natural barrier, the Pamir Mountains, known locally as Bam-i-dunya, or Roof of the World. His interest in the eastern half, which the Chinese had renamed Xinjiang (meaning New Frontier), was further piqued by Eric Shipton during their long talks while on the reconnaissance of Everest.

Prior to this, Shipton had been based in the secluded city of Kashgar, which lay on the province's far west at the entrance to the Pamirs. He explored the area extensively and in 1951 published a book *Mountains of Tartary*. This is a sparsely populated and arid region with its necklace of oasis settlements encircling the deadly Taklamakan – one translation of this desert's name suggests 'None who enter, return'. Ward was also determined to visit here, as he recalled in his introduction to Chris Bonington's expedition book *Kongur: China's Elusive Summit*[*]:

> [Shipton] often talked of his years as Consul General in Kashgar. Every journey that he made on horseback outside

---

[*] All quotes involving Mount Kongur, unless otherwise stated, are from Bonington's book. As well as its introduction, Ward wrote the chapter on the scientific work undertaken and contributed to two of the appendices.

this oasis town could bring him within minutes to the borders of the known world. This laid a train of hope that smouldered for thirty years. Expeditions are created by individuals and our venture in Southern Xinjiang bore the imprint of my desires, wishes and interests.

To this end, years before leading a party there, Michael began lobbying authorities in Peking (today, Beijing). Starting in 1972, with the help of British diplomats, including a former prime minister who led a mission to the Chinese capital, Ward sought permission to enter and climb in the province, but his many letters and requests were repeatedly knocked back.

Five years later, he became acting Chairman of the Mount Everest Foundation, then continued as head of the organisation for a three-year stint. The MEF's stated objectives are: '[To] encourage and support expeditions for exploration and research in the mountain areas of the world ... by making grants to appropriate expeditions.' Ward wanted to mark his chairmanship by taking the first British party into Communist China and attempt one of its major peaks. Like the reconnaissance of 1951, here was another example of him wanting to seize the initiative and tackle something new and different. He specifically disregarded returning to Everest, explaining: 'Central Asia is so vast that to return again and again to well-known areas would show a lack of imagination and enterprise.'

Ward had been reading about China's scientific work on the Central Asian plateau through various journals such as its *Scientia Sinica* and noted how the Chinese sometimes combined research with climbing. In 1975, for example, they installed a survey tripod on the summit of Everest and remeasured its height after nine climbers made it to the top. Michael felt this might be a way to approach them, hoping they would be more inclined to permit a dual-purpose scientific and mountaineering expedition, as long as it stayed clear of politically sensitive border areas.

By this stage, many of the world's premier peaks had already been climbed, some multiple times. The highest mountains of China, however, had largely remained untouched, often due to internal political turmoil and the country's isolationist policies. A European party hadn't visited the Pamirs in Xinjiang province in over fifty years. By the end of 1976, China's decade-long Cultural Revolution was over, and the country was beginning to open up again. Three years later, Ward learnt it was about to allow foreign climbers access to its mountains. Now, he redoubled his efforts to secure permission, even seeking help from senior diplomats in both capitals. In acknowledging Michael's early initiative and unique skills, Bonington would write:

> For it was he who had not just dreamt of going climbing in China, as many of us mountaineers had done over the years, he had actually worked at it … Only a medical scientist with an extensive knowledge of both field research and mountaineering could plan and co-ordinate this type of party.

The late Prince Philip, too, in writing the foreword to *Kongur* singled out Ward's early 'vision and determination'.

China had initially listed eight mountains it was opening up to foreign parties. Since only one of these had yet to be climbed, Ward's focus, with the MEF's unanimous backing, was firmly on Kongur. The mountain stands at a height of 25,326ft, some 120 miles south of Kashgar and 20 miles off the Karakoram Highway, the high road connecting Xinjiang with northern Pakistan. Also known as Kongur Tagh, it is highest of the three main peaks in the area – the other two being its close neighbour Kongur Tiube (24,541ft) and, lying roughly 25 miles to the south, Mustagh Ata (24,757ft). This group of peaks is usually regarded as part of the Pamirs, but can also be thought of as a northward extension of both the Karakoram range and Kunlun Shan.[*]

Mountaineering had formally become a sport in China only in 1956, yet its climbers had notched up some early successes, most notably an extraordinary ascent of Everest four years later.[†] However, the Chinese had yet to attempt Kongur, and when asked about this Michael learnt: '[They] admitted that it had posed unusual problems. They described it as enigmatic, and weather conditions were notoriously fickle.' They had not properly photographed the mountain or able to provide anything more than a sketch map of the area. There hadn't been any recent survey showing the approaches to Kongur either, or even around the region containing the three peaks. Neither did Shipton's book reveal much helpful information.

The best information Michael found about the peak had been published over fifty years earlier in *The Geographical Journal* (1925) by the British Consul-General at the time, Clarmont Skrine. Like Shipton, he had been based in Kashgar and was the first Westerner to visit large parts of this

---

[*] Kongur Tagh means Brown Mountain, Karakoram means Black Mountain, and Mustagh Ata means Ice Mountain Father; while Shan refers to a mountain range.

[†] This ascent in 1960 was initially disputed by Western climbers but is generally accepted today.

area. Skrine was able to photograph Kongur, but only from 40 miles away. And although he undertook a survey around the mountain, his training in the use of a plane-table and other survey equipment consisted of a crash course completed in two days. His subsequent article 'The Alps of Qungur' included a map compiled by the Survey of India's drawing office from his topographical data. Skrine's information was a good starting point, but not much more. Frustratingly, it seemed as if Kongur was an unknown name in an unknown place.

By this stage, Ward had enlisted 46-year-old Bonington, a member of the MEF Management Committee, and earmarked him as the expedition's climbing leader based on his already formidable list of ascents in the Himalayas. For his part, Michael would lead a small team of medical scientists and was expected to be named overall leader. He first met Chris in 1963 after inviting him to join the expedition to Gosainthan, which had fizzled out when a Chinese team beat the British to it, as mentioned earlier.

A few years later, after Bonington's successful 'Eiger Direct' climb via its North Face, Ward had treated him in a London hospital for frostbite, having become a specialist in treating cold injuries and preventing amputations. But even on this occasion, he didn't get to know him well. Michael was older now and, as the pair connected properly for the first time, Chris's impression of him in this latter stage of his life is interesting:

> Although there was only a difference of nine years in our ages, I somehow felt that he was of a different generation. How much of this was the shock of white hair and the half-frame granny glasses he used for paper work, and how far his manner, I am not at all sure. Michael has an analytical and enquiring mind. He is impatient and does not suffer the slow or lazy gladly. He has an instinctive sympathy for academic training.

Together, they flew out to Peking in February 1980 to hold talks with the Chinese Mountaineering Association (CMA) and its vice chairman Shi Zhanchun, who had led China's successful Everest team two decades earlier. They were fascinated to be in the heart of Communist China for the first time. Upon landing, the pair were driven past a never-ending stream of cyclists enroute to the massive Tiananmen Square, and saw the ancient Forbidden City with its huge portrait of Chairman Mao set over the gate. Sometime later, Ward would have the opportunity to meet the country's then-paramount leader, the reformist Deng Xiaoping.

During this trip, he and Bonington were well looked after by their hosts, who included sightseeing tours in between their long meetings which were much appreciated. In return, Michael delivered a lecture at the Institute of Research in Sports Medicine on 'Exercise Oedema and Mountain Sickness'. Following his talk, Ward was pleasantly surprised to learn his textbook *Mountain Medicine* had been translated by the Chinese and read with interest by their high-altitude researchers and mountaineers.

On the second day of negotiations with the CMA, matters quickly came to a head as Bonington recalled:

> After the usual courtesies, Mr. Shi came to the point. First …
> we could have Kongur. 'When do you want to climb it?' he
> asked. This was almost too fast for us. We had been planning
> on an expedition for 1981 and said so. Mr. Shi smiled and
> said, 'Well in that case someone else might climb it this year.
> Surely though, you will need to make a reconnaissance?' This
> is something we hadn't even thought of.

After a hurried conversation with Chris, Michael took Shi's hint to make their presence felt on the mountain as soon as possible, thereby staking their claim and shutting out foreign parties. At this point, they were also advised that although the CMA was prepared to assist them, it had decided not to join the venture.

The next few days were filled with interminable negotiations, thrashing out details to do with planning, logistics, costs, and a multitude of other issues, often working into the early hours of the morning. Finally, on 26 February Ward signed a protocol with the CMA for a British reconnaissance of Mount Kongur that year, followed by a summit attempt the next, during which time medical research could also be undertaken. Watching on as the documents were exchanged, Chris wrote: 'There is no doubt that Michael's age and presence, as well as his status as a surgeon and scientist, impressed the Chinese.'

Although Ward was thrilled with their rapid progress, signing the protocol had meant committing considerable MEF funds even before sponsorship had been found. He and Chris estimated the reconnaissance, followed by the main effort, would cost around £180,000 – a figure which represented almost the entire capital of the foundation.

Michael was greatly relieved, therefore, when Jardine, Matheson & Co. agreed to underwrite the entire project, as a way of commemorating its 150th anniversary since the company's founding in the Far East. Based in Hong Kong, this large and wealthy trading enterprise had also opened an office in Peking recently, from where it was able to provide them invaluable assistance with organisation and logistics within China. Moreover, its office in London became their administrative home base, leading Michael to gratefully acknowledge: 'There are not many expeditions that have had this advantage.'

The money side of things was further assured when the Medical Research Council and St Bartholomew's Hospital made substantial grants towards the scientific programme and agreed to provide sophisticated medical equipment for use in the field.

Returning home, Ward began working furiously with Bonington to put the reconnaissance together, scheduled to get underway in three months. For this first phase, they decided to take one other member with them, choosing another Englishman named Alan Rouse whom Chris knew well. 'Al' was an outstanding rock climber, who had also made notable climbs in the Himalayas. He was almost 30 years old, and Chris described him as having 'an essentially buoyant nature with a bubbling enthusiasm and self-confidence'. Despite the difference in their ages, the three worked well together, not only in organising the equipment and supplies needed for a two-month recce, but throughout their time in China as well.

In the last week of May, Michael flew out to Peking before the others to take part in a meeting organised by Academia Sinica, China's equivalent of the Royal Society. He had been extended an invitation after his well-received lecture during his initial visit. This first-ever multidisciplinary symposium focused on the Tibetan Plateau* and was attended by over 300 scientists, many from outside China. Ward chaired various meetings, and this time spoke on 'Exercise Oedema and Altitude'.

Chris and Al arrived a week later, prompting a quick trip to the Great Wall, on which the pair demonstrated the art of rock climbing to CMA members new to the sport. Soon afterwards, they flew deep into Central Asia, first stop Urumqi, capital of Xinjiang province. Ward used the three-day break here to visit its hospital and give a lecture at the Xinjiang Medical College.

Their party included a liaison officer named Liu Dayi, an accomplished mountaineer who had participated in the 1960 Chinese expedition to Everest, although he did not summit. Jardine's manager in Peking, David Mathew, had decided to come along too, but only as far as the mountain to help the visitors get started. In Urumqi, they picked up their interpreter

---

* Also known as the Qinghai-Xizang Plateau.

Peter Chen, a graduate from Peking University who had been forced to spend many years working here as a labourer. He had been exiled to this far-off place years earlier by the communists, suspicious of his bourgeois background and the fact he was half-Burmese.

On 7 June, all six flew to Kashgar, where the three climbers were among the first Westerners allowed in since the proclamation of the People's Republic. Here they encountered a different China, far less developed but also less constrained: donkey carts shared the road with modern vehicles; market stalls with all manner of goods proliferated the city; and more people wore their traditional dress rather than the drab communist garments.

The local people of Xinjiang are predominantly Uyghur and followers of Islam, with physical features and headwear displaying their Turkic ethnicity. Not so long ago, they were nomadic pastoralists. Today, they remain altogether different from the Han Chinese, who have been migrating here in increasing numbers since China regained the province in 1877. When the expedition arrived in Kashgar, there was little hint as to where the emerging ethnic strife between the two peoples could lead.*

As no restrictions had been placed on their movements, Michael and the others eagerly wandered through the old quarter of the city and its iconic Grand Bazaar, considered the best in Central Asia.† Talking with locals through their interpreter, the visitors were impressed by the general well-being of the people, as well as the education and health services provided by the provincial government. They toured the now rundown British consulate where both Shipton and Skrine had once worked, gathering intelligence for their empire from this remote listening post wedged between the Russians and Chinese.

After three days in Kashgar, the party headed out before dawn for Mount Kongur, in a bus loaded with all their gear, food, and a local cook. The road they took was once part of the southern arm of China's old Silk Road, encircling the Taklamakan Desert. It soon deteriorated into a dusty track, signalling the approaching mountains. The massif itself lay some miles directly south of the Karakoram Highway, but they continued counter-clockwise around its outer slopes onto the Pamir Plateau, finally stopping at the twin Karakol Lakes. At a height of almost 12,000ft, on its idyllic shores, they set up five tents and a cooking shelter.

---

* From around 2017, the Chinese government began detaining hundreds of thousands of Uyghurs in internment camps.

† Unfortunately, Chinese authorities tore down much of the bazaar in 2022 to make way for new construction.

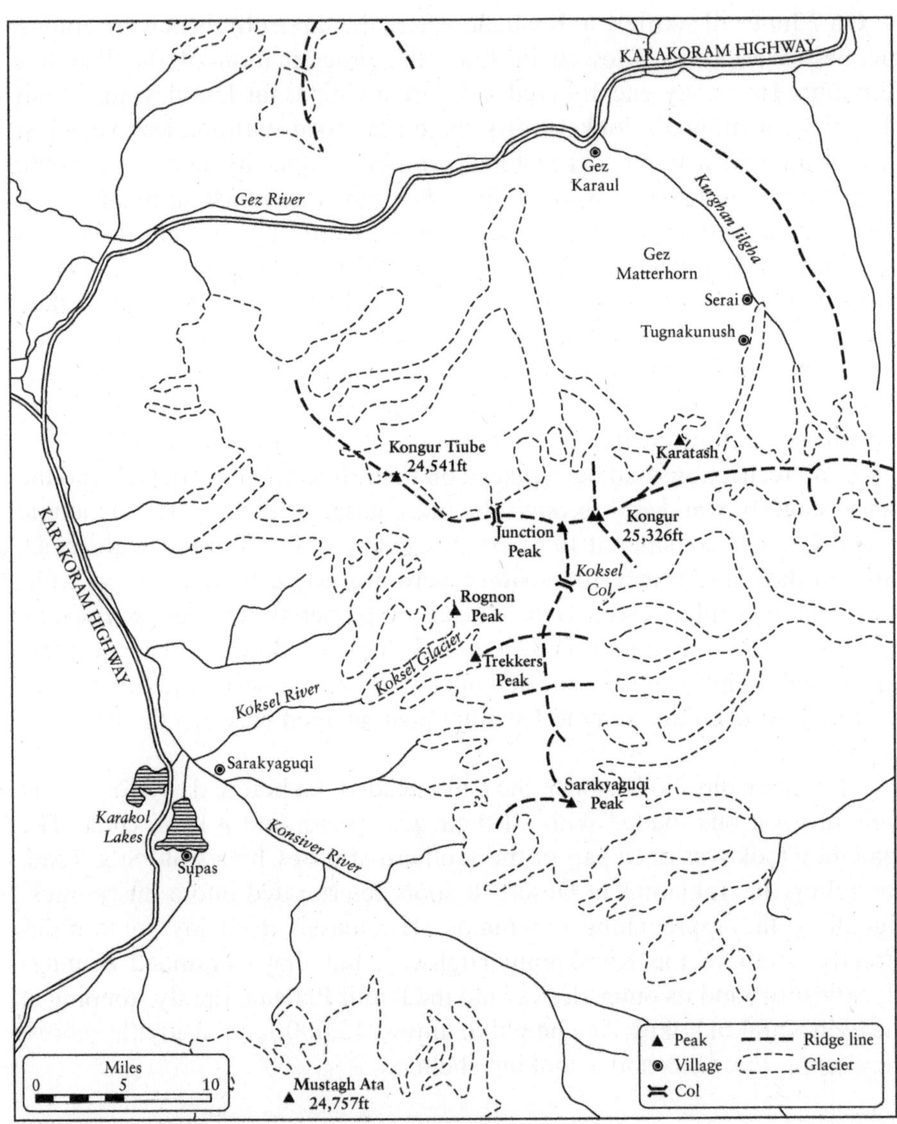


**Map 5. Mount Kongur Expedition 1980 and '81**
(based on map from *Kongur: China's Elusive Summit*)

The views of the surrounding mountains, lakes and endless pastures were nothing short of magnificent. To the south, even closer than Kongur lay the imposing cone of Mustagh Ata, whose summit Shipton and Tilman had fallen short of attaining by some 200ft in 1947, beaten back by bad weather.

During their three-day lay over here, Michael used the time to visit a nearby Kirghiz village. Its people were semi-nomadic, and many still lived in their traditional yurts made from heavy woollen felt draped over a circular latticework of wood. As part of this excursion, Ward was looking for the incidence of goitre among the locals, just as he had done in Bhutan. He was surprised to find little evidence of it, even though 200 miles south, on the other side of the Karakorams, over 70 per cent of inhabitants were afflicted to some degree. Even more puzzling was to learn from village elders that goitre had never been present here, despite it being recorded in other parts of Xinjiang (Chinese authorities only began iodising salt in this province from 1949). Ward made a mental note to investigate this further when the opportunity arose.

On 12 June the party broke camp early in the morning, crossing the main Konsiver River before its waters began to rise dangerously, fed by glacial meltwater as the day warmed. They began moving northeast towards Kongur, accompanied by a dozen yaks and their owners, which the Kirghiz rode and used to haul the expedition's gear. The herders were amazed to see the climbers choosing to *walk* the hills all day long with their rucksacks. To their way of life, it was demeaning for a man to walk any distance or carry a load, and which bordered on madness if there was a suitable animal available, even though the climbers soon outpaced the yaks. They marched up the slopes along a tributary of the Konsiver, the Koksel River, and then alongside the large glacier that feeds it. Eventually, they found an ideal spot by a trickling stream where Base Camp was set up around 15,000ft.

Two days later, Al, Chris and Michael set out expectantly with some gear, including a three-man tent made from the recently invented Gore-tex material. They carried sufficient provisions for a week-long outing; as Chris recalled: 'It was deeply satisfying to be on our own, just the three of us, on the brink of a journey of discovery, knowing that very soon we would stand where no one had been before.' (Skrine had simply marked the area south of Kongur as 'Unexplored' on his map.) Such thoughts often bring out the natural competitiveness in climbers, with some setting a blistering pace, wanting to be the first to see over a mountain pass or even what lay around the corner – this group was no different.

By this stage, Michael's lack of acclimatisation and his age were beginning to tell as the tempo picked up on the higher slopes. The other two generously lightened his pack at their own expense but this incident rekindled a nagging doubt in Chris's mind as the climbing leader: How would the scientists cope when they all attempted the ascent next year? To his relief, Michael soon confirmed his team would concentrate on medical research, leaving any summit bid to the others. His thinking was influenced by his experience on Makalu: 'Having both a scientific and mountaineering aim could pose very great problems, as I knew from previous Himalayan expeditions. Both were demanding and jealous masters.'

Michael was still not feeling well when they made camp on the col, so he stayed back for a couple of days while the other two explored further, all the time scanning Kongur's upper slopes for a viable route to its summit. In the process, they made a first ascent of a lower peak, naming it Sarakyaguqi after the nearby village. From its top (20,342ft) the pair could see across to ranges in Afghanistan, Pakistan, and the Soviet Union; as Chris wrote: 'We were in a veritable Aladdin's cave of unclimbed summits.'

After their return to the col, the next day the trio set off back towards Base Camp, but on the way down disaster struck. His youth getting the better of him, Al had broken into a carefree run down a slope when he fell heavily, wrenching his ankle and was in considerable pain. A quick examination by Michael, even as the ankle began ballooning, showed his ligaments were torn but luckily no fracture was evident. There was no way Al could continue walking down the mountain, which meant arranging for some form of evacuation. Michael stayed with him in their tent while Chris hurried down to Base Camp, before taking Liu Dayi with him to the nearby Kirghiz encampment to seek help.

Although they eventually managed to get Al back to camp, first by yak and then donkey, it turned out to be a long and tortuous process. From the outset, they were frustrated by Chris and Liu not being able to speak each other's language. Their miscommunication played out dangerously when the pair had to make multiple attempts crossing the Konsiver and were swept a long way downstream, nearly drowning in the process. When they finally reached the Kirghiz, since Liu could not speak their language either, he could not explain their predicament to the herders. Thankfully, despite their three-way language difficulties and some false starts, all ended well. Under Michael's watchful eye, Al recovered sufficiently at Base Camp not to require an immediate return to Kashgar for X-ray. Any further climbing, however, was out of the question for him, which left Chris and Michael to complete the reconnaissance.

Much time had already been lost. The yaks were due in a week to cart their gear back to Karakol Lakes, so the pair needed to work quickly and complete their investigation of Kongur's southern slopes. Fortunately,

Michael was back to full strength now and able to carry loads equal to Chris.

Over the next six days they trekked into the Koksel Glacier, dodging flurries of falling stones on the way up, before entering the expansive basin sitting above it. Using crampons, they climbed Koksel Col (19,000ft) and finally onto a subsidiary summit lying on the South Ridge, which they dubbed the Pimple. From here, a knife-edged rocky ridge extended towards Kongur, but it was unclear whether the top could be reached from this direction. The almost constant cloud-cap and complicated ridges frustrated their efforts to get a decent look upwards.

Before they could explore further, bad weather had them snow-bound in their tent for a day, which they spent reading a two-volume biography of the Duke of Wellington – Michael settling for volume two (he was also a fan of spy novelist John le Carré). With time running out, the pair decided to return to Base Camp but immediately ran into a total whiteout, which called for expert orienteering skills as Chris explained:

> Fortunately Michael had brought his compass, and just before the whole Koksel Glacier filled with cloud, he took a vital bearing … There were no features, no wind, no sound. Michael started off in front, and I followed keeping the rope between us taut … Our progress was desperately slow, and, with nothing to measure it against, we did not seem to be moving at all. Our fear of hidden crevasses was heightened by this sense of uncertainty.

When Chris took a spell upfront, he soon realised just how harrowing it was leading into a void with crevasses lurking all around. It wasn't until late afternoon they were finally out of trouble, with Chris recalling: 'The shared danger and effort, increased both our respect for each other and confidence in each other's performance.' There was also a funny side to their ordeal: Looking back up the slopes soon afterwards, they watched as the cloud cover simply rolled away – had they waited a few hours, they could have come down in perfect visibility.

The next morning, they broke camp and while the yaks lumbered along with the others, the climbers and Liu, all lightly dressed, forged ahead again. Around midday, on reaching the Koksel River at their intended crossing point, they waited hours for the others only to realise they must have forded earlier on, further upstream. By now it was too late to cross the river as it had swollen dangerously, so they were forced to spend the night where they were.

All their gear was with the yaks and the temperature soon plummeted to around freezing point; as Chris described: 'We had no food and no shelter. Michael, the veteran mountaineer, was the only one of us to observe the adage never to be parted from your sleeping bag.' Yet seeing Al cold and still struggling with injury, he handed it over to him. What probably impressed Michael's companions even more, was the half-bottle of whiskey he produced from his pack as they huddled around a small fire, faced with an uncomfortable night.

The next day, they were back at Karakol Lakes to meet up with the bus and retrace their earlier trip. Travelling along the Karakoram Highway, clockwise this time, they disembarked at Gez Karaul which lies north of the Kongur massif. Here, the whole village turned out to greet them, and they were treated to a sumptuous Kirghiz feast washed down with many bowls of *kumis* (fermented mare's milk).

With Al still out of action, Michael and Chris spent two days on an initial recce of Kongur to get a better look at its northern slopes. Following their return, on 7 July the whole party was transported up the banks of the Kurghan Jilgha on the backs of Bactrian camels. These long-legged animals proved their worth when fording streams and rivers, and by carrying twice the load of a yak. Since neither Skrine nor Shipton had travelled along the Kurghan Jilgha, the climbers were probably the first Europeans to explore up this river.

Their destination was a small village named Tugnakunusk, made up of a cluster of yurts. Its six families each posed in their finery for photographs, taken by Chris with his instant camera. The visitors would spend a week here, getting a rare insight into the everyday life and customs of a Kirghiz commune; and at nights they heard folk songs accompanied by traditional stringed instruments and a mouth harp.

Tugnakunusk lay by a glacier within a dramatic cul-de-sac valley, in the shadows of the Kongur massif. For a full week Chris and Michael probed the area, searching for a route up. At one point, while descending over steep rocks, Michael had a minor fall which resulted in the little finger of his right hand becoming dislocated and the bone puncturing his skin. Luckily, it wasn't serious and after bandaging the wound, the pair continued on. In the process they ascended another nearby peak, almost 18,000ft high which they named Karatash. From its top, they confirmed that although Kongur could be climbed from the north, 'it was not a route for the first ascent of a mountain'. In an article written for the *Alpine Journal* (1981) Ward noted:

> [Kongur is] a very complex mountain with four definite and
> differing aspects … it was to take us 40 days in the field to get

some idea of the mountain's shape, size and character. In many respects the best views that we got were those from a distance of 15–25km.

Back with Al, the trio decided the expedition next year should proceed from the south, by way of the Koksel River and up its glacier. The only matter left to complete was their formal report to the MEF, a chore Chris recalled well:

> In this respect Michael provided the discipline of the scientist. I suspect that Al and I would quite happily have basked in the sun, gossiping and reading, and putting off the inevitable paper work until we got back to civilization. In the event, writing up our findings while they were still fresh in our minds, and before the diversions we would face on our way back, was invaluable.

The reconnaissance party returned to Kashgar before the three climbers flew home on the first day of August. In less than a year's time all three would be returning as part of The British Mount Kongur Expedition.

# 19

# First up Kongur

T he combined team for Kongur, with Ward as overall expedition leader, flew out to Peking on 13 May 1981. His scientific team included three other experts in various fields of high altitude physiology, all of whom were competent mountaineers as well. There was Jim Milledge, his old colleague from Silver Hut; Edward Williams, with whom he had been researching the effect of exercise on oedema; and finally Charles Clarke, a neurologist in his thirties.

Bonington's climbing team also comprised four members, who were among the cream of British mountaineering at the time. Al Rouse had returned, his ankle now fully recovered; and the other two, Peter Boardman and Joe Tasker, came as a formidable pair with recent ascents in the Himalayas. In fact, Michael had pretty much chosen this eight-man team with Chris's input even before the previous year's reconnaissance mission.

Two more members, again both British, were added later. The first was cameraman Jim Curran, an accomplished climber in his own right, who would film the expedition. The other was David Wilson, a diplomat based in Hong Kong who could speak Mandarin and Cantonese and would act as a second interpreter.* In China, the team was joined by five local personnel comprising a local interpreter, two high-altitude assistants, a cook, and once again their trusty liaison officer Liu Dayi.

Before all this eventuated, back in London, there had been many more hands to help with organisation this time around, including the offices of Jardine Matheson in both countries. This proved to be a big weight off Michael's back since he was still encumbered with significant work commitments. On top of which, he had been assisting his team with the experiments they would conduct at altitude, some of which were complex

---

* David went on to be the penultimate Governor of Hong Kong and later, Lord Wilson of Tillyorn (who wrote the foreword to Sale's book subtitled *Michael Ward and the Pundit Legacy*).

and time consuming. They trialled these tests thoroughly on each other first, knowing how much could go wrong on the mountain itself.

In fact, the all-important exercise test was started nine months prior to the expedition leaving London. It established each of the eight individual's baseline performance at sea level, including their lung capacity, heart rate and general physical condition. This evaluation could take up to two-and-a-half hours of continuous monitoring to complete, and involved two observers for every subject. Moreover, it had to be redone if the slightest mistake was made. Milledge had put everyone through their paces in his laboratory, wired up on a treadmill with a heavy pack on their backs. These tests were similar to the unpopular ones performed using the bicycle ergometer two decades earlier at Silver Hut. Once again, despite being told the test wasn't a competition, the climbers in particular could not help comparing results and mocking each other's fitness levels.

Three months before the expedition had flown out, all the climbing gear, scientific equipment, and food was airfreighted to Peking and then sent on to Xinjiang by train. When the team arrived in China, Ward and Milledge made a side trip to Shanghai to deliver a lecture at the Institute of Physiology, prior to joining the others at their camp by Karakol Lakes. Here, they met up with a small trekking party that would accompany them as far as Base Camp. It included Jardine Matheson's chairman and four senior executives, all of whom had assisted in getting the expedition off the ground. Of course, Ward lost no time roping them in as participants in some of the tests as well.

While the rest of the team headed up towards Base Camp, which was to be established close to the old one, Michael stayed behind with David Wilson to supervise the loading of the yaks and camels. The scientists had brought two of every piece of critical equipment with them and never let the same animal carry both items. Once loading was completed, the pair crossed the Koksel River with the baggage train. They were accompanied by a small flock of sheep to provide the expedition with meat, but these animals would not be coaxed into the water. So, with some difficulty, Michael ferried them across one at a time in a little rubber dinghy. This comical episode was caught on film by Jim Curran, noting the operation was 'surely a first for a London surgeon'. Ward's profession had obviously made him apprehensive, as after their first meeting Curran recalled in his autobiography *Suspended Sentences*:

> I found Michael almost a caricature of the successful London surgeon, formal, dry and precise. I wondered how we could possibly get on together on a long expedition. In the event, I

couldn't have been more misled: once we left civilisation, he underwent an almost miraculous transformation.

This year with a bigger party, Base Camp was better equipped and luxurious by comparison. Other than individual tents, the members had a large communal tent with folding tables and chairs, a boxful of books, and a cassette player blasting out music. There was even an old-fashioned wooden thunderbox which, according to Chris 'was certainly the loo with the best view in the whole of Central Asia'.

After visiting some unspoilt areas and bagging a nearby unclimbed peak, the trekkers returned to Hong Kong, leaving the others to begin the serious task of tackling a high mountain and a demanding scientific programme. Ward's team wasted no time setting up their field laboratory tent with its small power generator, and began work focusing on three particular areas.

First was the effect of altitude on two hormone systems which could lead to acute mountain sickness. Edward Williams would study this by analysing blood samples taken from both teams. The potential problem he faced was that the results from these tests would not be known until six months later. Thus, any errors he made now could not be corrected, requiring him to be extraordinarily meticulous. Interestingly, Michael observed that although Jim their cameraman worked in a different field altogether, he faced similar stressful challenges with little margin for error and no 'comebacks'.

The second area questioned whether the physiology of the climbers, by being repeatedly exposed to extreme altitudes, was becoming closer to that of Sherpas. This would be examined during exercise by measuring oxygen consumption using a Douglas bag, and heart rate by ECG.* Since a treadmill wasn't available for use here, the subject was made to step up and down a 1ft high block at an increasing pace, before maximum work rate was simulated by loading him with a rucksack full of rocks. As this exercise was carried out in open air, it sometimes meant having to work in a snowstorm but this didn't faze Ward, who noted: 'Luckily snow did not affect any of the apparatus and melted on the subject's body.' However, since low outside temperatures did prevent some instruments from functioning, it tested his patience as work could not get underway until the day warmed up, usually around eleven in the morning.

The final area of medical interest was the effect on a person's brain from ascending too quickly to high altitude, which can result in cerebral oedema.

---

* However heavy their workload, the climbers' heart rate was found to stay below 150 beats per minute – whereas Sherpa rates can reach 200, confirming their bodies have increased efficiency in transporting oxygen at altitude.

It would be investigated by observing and photographing the blood vessels and optic nerve located at the back of the eye.* This was Charlie Clarke's area of expertise and he, too, had begun his work months earlier by first testing expedition members at sea level at St Bartholomew's Hospital. At Base Camp, sited around 15,000ft, he made good use of the specialist equipment brought over, including an ophthalmoscope and a retinal camera. In his diary, Pete Boardman described undergoing this particular test:

> Move into a darkened tent. Generator whirring, twenty minutes after anaesthetic and dilator put in my eyes. A new guillotine-type machine held in front of my eye. It's very dim and my forehead is propped so I can't move. Blinding flash photographs, yellow and blue … Then he pumped some yellow green glowing dye into my blood, and a few seconds later it reaches my eyes through the blood vessels. He takes more photos.

The other effort Charlie led was fulfilling a promise Michael had made to staff at the Royal Botanic Gardens, Kew, which owned no specimens from this part of Central Asia. Eventually, the team managed to collect over 150 plants for its herbarium, including many alpine and desert flowers, grasses, lichen, and moss.

Most days, the scientists were kept busy with their testing programme, which they performed on each other as well. Afterwards, they would compare results with the climbers, but this needed them to submit to the tests also. Although they did oblige, and readily so, understandably they were more interested in acclimatising as quickly as possible, their thoughts firmly fixed on the big climb to come.

Bonington, who was sixteen years older than the oldest in his team, was careful to conserve his strength. He picked up flu which had infected others in the camp but, in his case, it turned into a serious case of pneumonia. This laid him up for a few days and there were fears he might be forced out of any summit attempt. To his relief, Michael eventually declared his chest was clear of infection. Chris discussed the pros and cons of the various routes and climbing strategies with his team, and would afterwards explain his plan to Michael, which worked well for both leaders.

---

* This is the only place in the body where they can be observed without surgical procedure. The optic nerve is an extension of the brain thus, like blood vessels, it also swells during cerebral oedema.

One bone of contention among the climbers was the prickly question of what constituted an alpine-style climb, since this was the method they had all agreed to use on Kongur. Al was a purist in this regard, against the use of any form of siege tactics. For him, this meant seeking no assistance from the scientists to establish an intermediary camp or even employing a small number of fixed ropes. He and Chris had had heated discussions about this issue during their reconnaissance the previous year, but Michael had chosen not to get involved then, or now. Although he was the overall leader, and as much as he wanted to see the climbing team achieve its goal, he believed this issue was for the four climbers to resolve. In the end, they settled for at least understanding how each felt about the subject – the other three taking a more practical approach rather than splitting hairs, as they felt Al was apt to.

The climbers established Advanced Base Camp in the Koksel Basin on 5 June and then began their acclimatisation programme over the next few weeks. They ascended the col and various peaks and ridges as they worked their way towards Kongur, retreating when the weather turned against them. Once, after a difficult session battling the massif, on returning to camp Chris found two letters in one of the tents. They were from Michael, who had walked up from Base Camp the previous day, left them messages, then returned.

The first letter congratulated the team on their efforts thus far. The second revealed something about how Ward as a doctor could be misunderstood by his patient – perhaps just as Hunt had on Everest, and Hillary on Makalu. It was addressed to Chris, worrying about his fitness following his bout of pneumonia, and asking him to think carefully before joining the others on any summit bid. Chris recalls having mixed feelings on reading it:

> It was probably a subject more easily covered in writing than in conversation and I could appreciate and understand his concern both as a doctor and leader of the expedition. At the same time though, it was like a douche of very cold water at a moment of elation at the end of our first foray on the mountain ... I showed [the others] the letter, which probably was not very fair of me, for they had little choice but to reassure me, but I think that their reassurance was genuine. They cheerfully declared me officially well and said I could start demonstrating it by breaking trail on the way back.

On 23 June, after almost a month in the mountains and a short rest period at Base Camp – where they were subjected to more testing – the climbing team moved back to Advanced Base Camp. Now they were ready to start the assault proper, with Curran there to film them. Ward came up for a few days with Milledge to assist where they could.

As the four climbers moved high up the mountain the wind became vicious. At one point, they slept fully clothed at night, expecting their tent to be ripped apart or blown away at any moment. Eventually, they got high enough to get a good look at the top, as Chris wrote:

> Suddenly, it looked very remote, very big and very hard … Even the view we had had from the South Ridge two days earlier had not alarmed us, since our concentration was entirely absorbed by the slope immediately in front of us. We had somehow brain-washed ourselves into thinking that the South Ridge was the challenge and once this had been solved, we had almost climbed the mountain.

They dug a snow cave at around 23,500ft and spent the night there out of the wind, deciding to make a dash for the summit the next day, leaving their rucksacks behind. All that day, however, they were unable to find a way to the top over the sharp snow ridges and rocky pinnacles. With time running out, they returned to the sanctuary of their cave. The next morning, after an acrimonious discussion about whether to make another attempt, with food and fuel running low the majority voted to go back down. As they neared Advanced Base Camp, they saw a figure coming to greet them:

> [It] was Michael Ward. We all felt guilty, dreaded having to break the news to him. 'Go on Chris, you're climbing leader. You'd better justify your title. You tell him,' someone said. And I did. Neither Michael's face nor voice registered any disappointment and he immediately asked for all details.

At Base Camp, the climbers took a well-earned rest and helped themselves to plenty of food. There was no shortage of the latter, but the scientists were keen to continue their testing regime and record how the higher altitude and strenuous exercise had affected each of them. Although they did submit to the tests, Chris and Al weren't well enough to subject themselves to maximum work capacity tests, knowing they would be returning for another tilt at Kongur in a few days' time.

Time, however, was against the team. In terms of the climbing season, the best weather conditions would soon be gone. Just as worrying was the presence of a Japanese expedition in the area, which had permission to climb Kongur from the north starting mid-July. At Base Camp, Chris learnt the Japanese team had already climbed Mustagh Ata and were now heading their way.

Determined not to be usurped, the climbers started back up the mountain on 4 July, taking with them ten days' supply of food and fuel in case they had to wait out bad weather. They would supplement these supplies with a cache they had left behind in the snow cave before their retreat.

Despite Al's purist concerns, the scientists did help them get started, with Milledge and Wilson carrying loads further up the Koksel Basin. Ward and Williams had gone out a day earlier to retrieve some gear the climbers had left behind on Koksel Col since this time they planned to use a different route up the mountain, via its Southwest Rib rather than the South Ridge.

The story of how all four climbers made the first ascent of Mount Kongur on 12 July 1981 has been amply described by Bonington in the expedition's book, and need not be repeated here except in brief:

Over the next few days they negotiated the sharp ridges, which they found even more dangerous this time around as they were covered in thick snow, and the climbers were weighed down by the extra provisions. When the weather turned foul, they found a gully and managed to hollow out shallow 'coffins' as the snow was not deep enough to dig a proper cave. Here, with a storm raging outside, they were forced to hunker down over four nights and three days. Often, the coffins had to be rebuilt after they collapsed; and inside, there was so little fresh air left at times their portable stoves would barely light.

On the fourth day they emerged, weakened by days of inactivity and having survived on half-rations, but fortunately to a fine morning with clear skies. Wasting no time they made for the top, but the going was hard as Chris described: 'This was real climbing, steeper than the North Face of the Matterhorn, more like the North Wall of the Eiger in winter.' Shortly after eight o'clock that evening, in a fierce wind and bitterly cold, all four climbers stood on the summit. Before leaving, Chris buried a card in the snow from Michael which had been given to him bearing a message of peace, recalling it was 'the only token of our presence that we left behind'.

In the meantime, Ward had come up to Advanced Base Camp to await the climbers, accompanied by Curran who would capture their return on film (he had also given Tasker a camera to use when nearing the top). During the eight days the pair waited, Jim came to see two very different sides to Michael, as he described in his autobiography:

> He had a strong interest in the arts and an extremely inquisitive
> mind, full of probing and intelligent questions ... Michael had

rarely been on an expedition without the presence of Sherpas to look after the sahibs. Consequently he had the greatest trouble with even the simplest domestic chores. Despite his manual dexterity as a surgeon, he never managed to master the art of striking a match, let alone producing a meal. I willingly took over all the cooking in exchange for washing up and digging snow for brews.

Michael agreed with this assessment of his abilities, noting in his unpublished notes: 'I am not allowed to carve at home being considered not domesticated – a view I share. I can however boil water and pour wine.'

As the days wore on, Ward became increasingly anxious for the safety of the climbers. Since they carried no radio, he was unaware they had taken shelter in snow coffins. Meanwhile, after their successful ascent the team spent the night in another snow cave which they dug close to the top. The next morning, however, they looked across to Kongur's second summit and began to wonder whether that one might be the taller of the two. As Pete said to the other three: 'We'll kick ourselves for the rest of our lives if we don't make sure we've been to the top, and the only way to know is to go there.'

This took the best part of another day, only to confirm that the second summit was lower than the first by about 100ft. Not long afterwards, during their descent, Pete was momentarily knocked unconscious by a football-sized rock which his rope dislodged while abseiling. But for his glove getting caught in the karabiner, he would have probably slid off the untied rope-end and fallen thousands of feet to his death.

By this stage, Michael and Jim were desperately concerned for the climbers' wellbeing and ascended partway up the Southwest Rib to look for them. They were about to return disappointed late that afternoon when, as Jim described:

> Michael stopped for one last look through the binoculars. 'I can see them,' he announced quietly but with intense emotion. I realised how worried he must have been and for a moment both of us were very near to tears of relief … I filmed the four as they approached and passed me, striding through knee-deep snow but looking all in. 'We've done it,' croaked Chris.

Bonington later admitted: 'Despite our thorough reconnaissance, we seriously underestimated the complexity of the climb.' While Ward, in his article for *The Geographical Journal* (1983) describing the climbing team's historic ascent, ended with the simple statement: 'It was a close-run thing.'

The six returned to Base Camp for a final feast with the others. Here, many toasts were drunk from a case of champagne sent out by Jardines, which happened to arrive on the big day and with only one bottle broken. Soon enough, though, they would have cause to reflect on the fine margins between success and failure. This was cruelly highlighted upon learning all three members from the Japanese team, who had set out for the top after them, were never seen again. (The following year, Pete Boardman and Joe Tasker were also killed on Everest; and Al Rouse, although he became the first British climber to summit K2 in 1986, died during the descent.)

Unlike the climbers, whose expedition was now over, the scientists' work was, in many ways, just beginning. The data gathered from their physiological tests would have to be analysed back home before the results could be published over the coming months and years in various specialist medical journals, often collaborating with other scientists. Ward would also publish a general article in the *Alpine Journal* (1982) describing his team's efforts, titled 'Science on Mount Kongur'. In concluding their expedition book, discussing the disparate teams involved, Bonington noted:

> The aims of these groups could so easily have begun to conflict.
> That they didn't was partially due to the personalities involved
> and partially to the way that Michael Ward had interwoven the
> research and climbing programme … It was certainly one of
> the happiest expeditions that I have been on.

The party returned safely to Peking on 22 July. For Michael, it had been a coming together of his passion for medical science and mountaineering, made possible by his ability in organising expeditions to high Asia. He had also been the driving force behind the reconnaissance effort which had resulted in the first ascent of Kongur, just as he had done thirty years earlier with Everest.

This time, in recognition of his efforts, he was awarded the Founder's Medal of the Royal Geographical Society for 1982. First begun in 1832, this is one of two gold medals the society awards annually, which over the years has represented the premier recognition for geographical science and discovery in the world. Ward's citation read: 'For high-altitude medical research and leadership of the British Mount Kongur Expedition.'

# 20

# Across Tibet

**W**ard's last adventure in high Asia would involve traversing Tibet with a group of international geologists. But before this, there were a couple of notable events: Two years earlier in 1983, he was made a Commander of the British Empire (CBE) for his services to mountaineering and medical research. The following year, Michael participated in a study conducted at the United States Army's high altitude research facility in Colorado together with seven other medical scientists-cum-mountaineers.

His visit to America were with two old associates, Jim Milledge and Edward Williams, who had organised the expedition as a follow up to their work on Kongur. Back then, they had noticed by chance that some members had abnormally high blood pressure on the mountain compared to what they recorded at sea level. To investigate this anomaly further, the scientists secured use of the army's laboratory set up at 14,000ft on the summit of Pikes Peak in the Rocky Mountains. Here, they observed the effect of exercise and sudden exposure to altitude on blood pressure. They also investigated the biochemical mechanisms associated with these changes during acute (1–5 days) and chronic (5–20 days) exposure. These were the same mechanisms involved in mountain sickness and oedema of the lungs and brain, which they had been studying for years.

Following his return from Colorado, events began to move rapidly. Out of the blue in May 1985, Ward received a call from the secretary of the Royal Society sounding him out about joining a geological expedition to the Tibetan Plateau. Although surprised at being considered, since Michael knew next to nothing about geology, he was immediately interested, for three quite different reasons:*

Not only did the prospect of travelling through this inaccessible country sound fascinating, but it would also allow him to visit key sites where

---

* Much of the material for this chapter is taken from Ward's unpublished autobiographical notes completed in 2005.

the Chinese were conducting high altitude medical research and see their progress firsthand. Finally, by traversing the plateau as the expedition intended doing, he would have an opportunity to follow in the footsteps of one of his lifetime heroes, Kishen Singh.* In an article for the *Alpine Journal* (1988), Ward described this Pundit's four-year mission begun in 1878 as 'the most substantial and important journey in the history of Central Asian exploration'.

The day after the phone call, Michael attended a meeting at the Royal Society's headquarters in London where the project was discussed in more detail, including the makeup of the British team. He was to be its medical officer, and made his first contribution that same day when the question of setting an age limit for possible members came up. A few were over 70, prompting concerns about how they might fare on the plateau after prolonged exposure to abnormal altitude and cold. Ward was able to reassure the others this should not be a problem, drawing on his experience in the highlands of Bhutan where some inhabitants lived beyond the age of 80, often in rudimentary conditions.

Michael learnt this was to be a joint effort by the Royal Society and Academia Sinica, representing the first large-scale cooperative effort by scientists ever conducted in the central and northern parts of the plateau. The team from the Royal Society would be led by Professor Robert Shackleton, and eventually numbered ten scientists including two Americans and a Swiss. Many of them were leading specialists in geology and palaeontology.

Similarly, some of the best Chinese academics would participate, fifteen in all, led by Professor Chang Chengfa. He had been instrumental in the project's conception and would be in charge overall. His government would issue entry permits into Tibet and be responsible for logistics and supplies within China. An old hand, Chang had already spent around twenty years studying the plateau's geology. One of his team would also act as interpreter, while Michael's role would be to ensure everyone maintained good health during the two months spent in the field.

The aim of the expedition, soon referred to as 'the Geotraverse of Tibet', was to better understand the geological events occurring on the plateau. Together with the Himalayas and other mountains of Central Asia, it had begun forming around fifty million years earlier after a collision between the Indian and Eurasian tectonic plates, as the earth's crust crumpled and thickened some 50 miles. This process continues today, lifting the region – and with it, Mount Everest – by approximately half an inch annually.

---

* Ward's notes contain many pages describing Kishen Singh's achievements, which he was also intending to use in his book about the Pundits.

When the plates first collided and the ground subsequently rose, the prehistoric Tethys Ocean above the seabed drained away leaving behind some of the deepest gorges on Earth, known locally as the Sword Slashes of Buddha.

By carefully examining the plateau, the geologists hoped to gain a better understanding of the colossal forces involved in its formation, particularly as this is the only point on the planet where convergence is still occurring between continental masses. Although this tectonic plate collision and its sometimes dramatic consequences, such as large earthquakes, were already well documented, the basic geology of the region was not. This lack of knowledge was due in part to Tibet's physical and political remoteness. Previous fieldwork carried out here had mostly been of a reconnaissance nature, in contrast to the detailed research already completed across other mountain ranges in the world, such as the Alps in Europe.

In preparation for the geotraverse, Chinese organisers arranged for the large trucks and four-wheel drive jeeps that would be used by the expedition to be driven 3,000 miles from Peking to Lhasa, in readiness for the team's arrival there. Members flew into the Tibetan capital at the start of June 1985, immediately becoming aware of its 12,000ft elevation as they struggled for breath and suffered headaches. Michael felt the effects of this altitude too, initially experiencing partial blindness in one eye due to a swollen eyelid – a condition he had previously encountered on Everest after gaining altitude too quickly.

During the team's short stay here, he explored the capital and its surrounds, all the while recalling the first visit to this once-forbidden city by a Pundit over 100 years earlier. It had resulted in Nain Singh (older first cousin of Kishen Singh) being presented with the Patron's Medal of the RGS – the twin award to Ward's recently bestowed Founder's Medal. When Nain Singh had arrived here in 1866, the city had around 15,000 inhabitants and was dominated by monks, whereas now Ward saw many Han Chinese who had migrated into Lhasa, swelling its population to over 100,000 (today, around 900,000).

Like every other visitor, Michael was immediately struck by the splendour of the Potala Palace, once home of the exiled Dalai Lama, which dominates the city from a hilltop on its outskirts. For a long while he stood alone watching crowds of pilgrims as they slowly circumambulated the palace, intoning their sacred Buddhist mantra *Om mani padme hum* (Praise to the jewel in the lotus). Among them were the exceptionally devoted who chose to prostrate fully and touch their foreheads to the ground after every three paces. Ever the medical scientist, Ward made a mental note of the relative absence of goitre among these pilgrims, and later learnt from a local physician this affliction was more prevalent among country folk.

The city is built on the banks of the Kyi Chu (meaning River of Happiness), a tributary of Tibet's primary river, the Tsangpo. Although he saw children happily splashing about here, he also witnessed the corpse of a man float by – a traditional method used to dispose of their dead (another being to dismember the body and feed it to vultures).

In the heart of Lhasa, Michael walked to the holiest shrine in Tibet, the Jokhang. Entering its dark halls lit by flickering butter lamps, he made his way to the giant statue of Buddha, in front of which pilgrims prostrated. The smell of their unwashed bodies, mixed with ghee, incense, and smoke from yak dung fires prickled his nose, but he found it less unpleasant than the odours often encountered in the modern hospitals he worked at. At the time of his visit, a large square was being constructed in front of the Jokhang which, he observed, required the clearing of many houses belonging to locals by the Chinese authorities.

Nearby, Ward visited the Mendzekhang, or House of Medicine and Astronomy, and was shown around by the director of the college. First built in 1916, it remains the main hospital for teaching traditional medicine in Tibet today, and is also responsible for preparing the country's annual astrological calendar. Michael learnt there were around 1,000 practising doctors in Tibet at the time, a third of whom were women. They attained qualification after completing a four-year training programme, during which over one-third of their time was spent studying Western medicine. Most Tibetans, however, preferred traditional medicine, as did about half the Chinese immigrants.

Michael was told they believed the basis of good health depended upon the maintenance of harmony between the body's three vital functions or 'humours', these being wind, bile, and phlegm. Illness was diagnosed through a careful study of the pulse, which indicated the nature of any imbalance present; while the traditional medication prescribed by doctors came from herbs gathered and prepared by college staff.

In the capital, Ward visited the home of Dr Sun, Director of the Tibet Institute of Medical Science. He was a leader in high altitude studies among Chinese scientists, having published numerous papers in Western journals, and Michael was flattered to hear he had read his textbook. They discussed research at the Institute of Physiology in Shanghai, which was often conducted to coincide with Chinese expeditions to peaks such as Mount Everest. Dr Sun took him on a tour of the local hospital, a massive structure built to withstand Lhasa's ferocious climate, leading Ward to observe:

I could not help comparing this with the latest 'modular' hospital building in which I was working [in London] that had just been constructed. In this, the room in which the surgeons changed before operating had a leaking roof that remained unfixed for more than a month, and the floors and walls were already showing signs of wear and tear after only a few months.

Dr Sun also took Michael to the local markets, where he noticed traders from all over Asia, prompting the realisation that Lhasa had only ever been a closed city to Europeans, not others. Among a myriad of exotic goods being sold, he saw the skin of the endangered snow leopard on offer. Another surprise was coming across a fine mosque, which unlike in Xinjiang, seemed out of place in this overwhelmingly Buddhist country. Later, he met the deputy mayor at a dinner party who turned out to be a Muslim. From him, Michael learnt there were up to 3,000 of his brethren living in the city, which was home to other mosques as well.

A few miles outside the city limits, Ward visited the Drepung Monastery, established in 1416. It is the largest in Tibet and houses thousands of monks, many of whom had suffered persecution during the Cultural Revolution. In more recent times, their activities have been curtailed and kept under surveillance by the Chinese authorities. During the visit, in the courtyard below, he witnessed a novice being rigorously subjected to an oral examination by other monks. It reminded Michael of his own final assessment in clinical surgery many years ago, when questions were similarly fired at him by a panel of examiners.

The full expedition party left Lhasa on 8 June in trucks and jeeps, ascending the Tibetan Plateau which, like the Pamirs, is often referred to as the Roof of the World. Covering an area of almost a million square miles, ten times the size of the United Kingdom, it is the world's largest and highest plateau with an average elevation of around 15,000ft. Because it sits in the lee of the Himalayas and receives less than twelve inches of annual precipitation (mainly as hail), it is an arid, treeless steppe. Being far removed from the moderating effects of any ocean, the whole country experiences extreme shifts in temperature. As Ward and the others soon discovered, a clear sky can cloud over within minutes and give rise to hailstorms; but although it freezes most days of the year, the ground remains essentially free of snow.

Their convoy intended travelling across Tibet by closely following the new road linking Lhasa with Golmud, the second-largest city in the neighbouring province of Qinghai. It lay over 700 miles to the north, and this trip would reveal a geologic cross-section through the predominant northwest–southeast grain of the plateau.

A few hours out from Lhasa, Michael saw workmen laying pipes to harness a series of thermal springs which run across southern Tibet. This

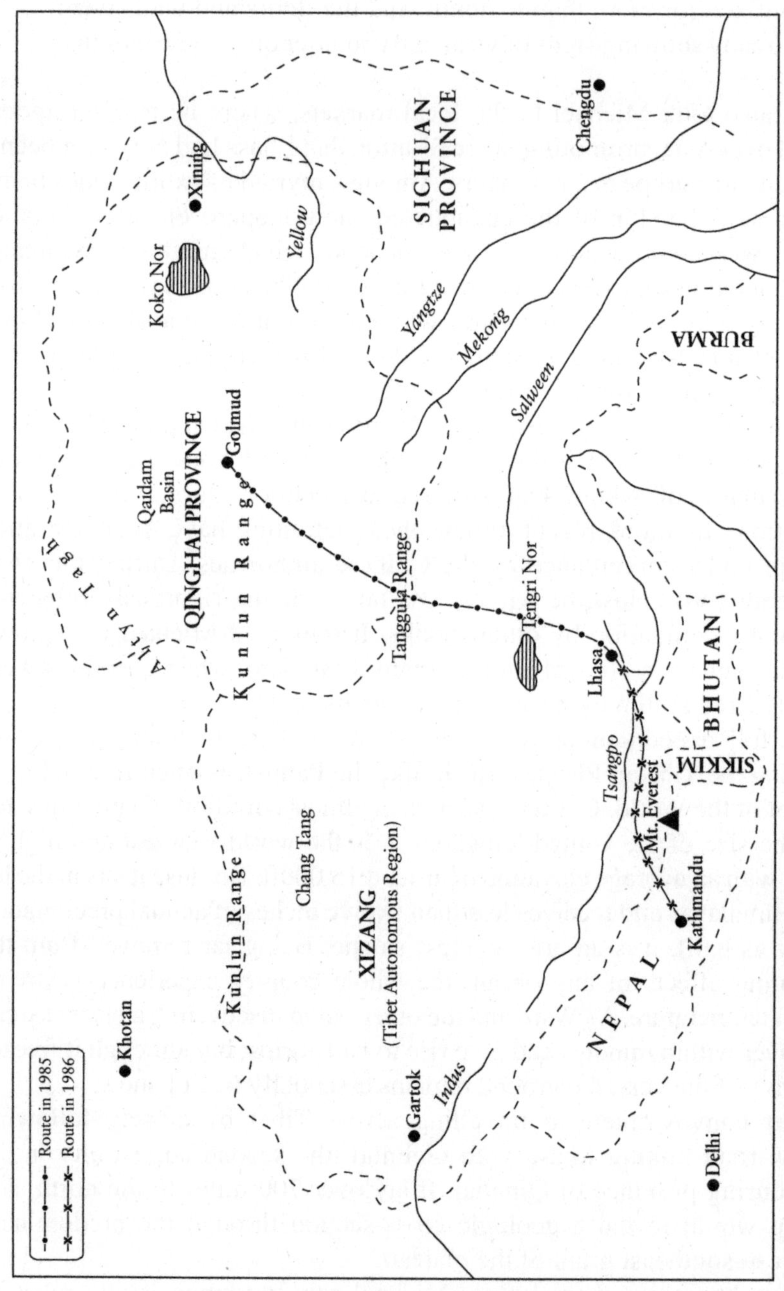


Map 6. Geotraverse of Tibet 1985 and '86 (based on map from Ward's article in *Alpine Journal* 1986)

reminded him of Kishen Singh's account of one of his journeys when he had witnessed an unusual geyser close by, on the banks of a tributary to the Tsangpo. The jet of water, which was close to boiling, shot 60ft into the air before turning into a freezing pillar of ice some 30ft in circumference. The Pundit had noted how the river was so hot here it remained unfrozen 3 miles downstream.

A hundred miles north from the capital, the party veered off the main road in their jeeps to visit the serene Tengri Nor (or Namtso), a large salt lake renowned for its beauty, as Ward described:

> I saw an immense eagle perched on a rock – perfectly capable I would have thought of carrying off a newborn lamb. They were also clusters of yellow poppies. In the sun, it was quite warm. The waves of the Tengri Nor glistened silver and the sky was huge and bright blue with white cumulus clouds hurrying across it. Then the sun was hidden, and the temperature fell rapidly, and sleet started to fall on us.

Beyond the lake, the expedition moved onto the Chang Tang (or Northern Plain), the highest and most isolated part of the Tibetan Plateau. The severe climate here has reduced it to being sparsely populated, mainly by nomadic herders known as the Changpa (people of Chang), who are among the highest-living inhabitants on the planet.

Within a decade, much of this plain would be set aside as one of the world's largest nature reserves, and home to some of the last remaining herds of wild animals such as the yak, kiang, mountain sheep, gazelle and antelope. As well as observing various flocks from a distance, the expedition encountered Bactrian camels and domesticated yaks. The latter are vital to the Changpa's survival and especially treasured for their milk and wool. They are also used as a means of transportation and the production of heat from dung fires.

Driving across the Chang Tang, the convoy crossed the Tanggula Pass at 17,000ft where a *chorten* (Buddhist shrine) and brightly coloured prayer flags marked the border with Qinghai. Ward was interested to learn of some Tibetans who, until recently, mined high grade quartz crystals in the Tanggula Shan at altitudes approaching 20,000ft. They had worked in this range continuously for up to four months during summer over a period of three to five years, living in tents and without suffering mountain sickness. This made them the highest altitude workers in the world, surpassing miners in the Andes who lived around 17,500ft, which until then was believed to be the upper limit for permanent human habitation.

As the convoy drove across the plateau, it gathered data for making a route map, just as Kishen Singh had done a century earlier, except the Pundit had *walked* the whole way and counted every pace he took. In a vehicle with an odometer, measuring distance becomes infinitely simpler of course, and the main road to Golmud over the plain runs dead straight for many miles at a time. As they worked, the members also gathered information for making geological maps of the region, which they would prepare upon returning home. When completed, these detailed multi-coloured maps would represent a key element of the expedition's output.

After entering Qinghai, the tarmac road deteriorated into a dirt track, muddy in the sun and frozen in the shade. To their relief, a little further on the expedition chanced upon a hot spring which provided its members with their first bath since leaving Lhasa.

This part of the plateau, as explained to Ward, was a virtual 'geological terra incognita' and the team was kept busy. One thing they were careful not to do was commit the cardinal sin of 'jeep geology' – observing rock formations from afar using powerful binoculars rather than actually driving out there. No matter how distant, the geologists would repeatedly walk over rough terrain to knock off samples with their hammers, all of which Ward observed 'could be very bruising and tiring over an eight-hour day'. Despite this, there were no serious injuries or illnesses for him to treat, other than monitoring everyone for the effects of altitude and fatigue.

During the day, Michael usually had some free time while the geologists went about their work, but in the afternoons the altitude didn't stop the Brits playing cricket, using a geological hammer as a bat. The bemused Chinese preferred to stick to their board game of Mah Jong.

Ward had a lot in common with one of the expedition members, the Swiss professor Augusto Gansser who had explored northern Bhutan, and the two shared many stories. Gansser had also made an unauthorised foray into southern Tibet disguised as a pilgrim, where he found seafloor rocks on the plateau which confirmed this area once lay on the bottom of the Tethys Ocean.*

Eventually the convoy approached the Kunlun Shan, a range which stretches some 1,250 miles in an east–west direction and separates the Tibetan Plateau from the Tarim Basin and its dreaded Taklamakan Desert. Ward had already explored the western extremity of this range during

---

* The RGS awarded Gansser its Patron's Medal in 1968 'for geological exploration and mapping in the Himalaya'.

his trip to Mount Kongur and now saw its eastern end in Qinghai. The expedition would spend about three weeks here, thoroughly studying the geology of the area.

Their first base was a lorry depot at Budongquan, just below the climb to a pass through the mountains. Michael described it as a 'miserable spot with no heating of any sort' and their rooms were damp and freezing despite it being the middle of summer. At times, the weather was so foul they were confined to barracks. One afternoon, he went out for a walk on his own and ran into a blizzard, experiencing dangerous whiteout conditions. It was only his trusty compass and orienteering skills that eventually got him safely back to the depot.

Still, Michael knew his cold room was better than being stuck in a small tent on a mountainside, as he had often experienced. This wasn't so for the geologists who, for once, were silent as the cold subdued their normally good-natured debates at night. Ward found them to be 'a very lively lot, but intellectually seldom strayed from geology' (the language barrier meant he was talking here about members from the Royal Society). During their fieldwork, when he assisted as best he could, Michael relates an interesting incident:

> I once picked up what to me was an obvious piece of coal and thinking this unusual showed it to them. None were prepared to say it was a piece of coal, even after close inspection. 'Carboniferous' was the best diagnosis I could get according to one professor on the party. 'Truth' in geology seemed to be the majority opinion of whatever group of geologists happened to be discussing at that time.

Observing the geologists at work, Ward learnt a lot about their science and methods. They were particularly interested in understanding the origins of a gap in the Kunlun Shan, several miles wide through which the main road passes. Along the floor of the surrounding Xidatan Valley runs a fault line, he was told, similar to the infamous San Andreas Fault in California. It indicates that the eastern portion of the Kunlun Shan is still moving away, albeit ever so slowly, triggering major earthquakes during the process and a reshaping of the landscape.

Over the course of a few days, Michael helped the team search in the Xidatan for rocks of identical composition lying on both sides of this divide. By finding such samples, the geologists would be able to prove the two sections of the Kunlun were in fact part of the same range. Then, by measuring the distance between the rocks, they could estimate to within a few million years, how long ago this split had occurred, and the forces involved in separating the range apart.

During their search, Ward and others were thrilled to discover a drovers' route, unmarked on their map, lying a few miles further down the valley. It was well-watered and provided an alternate path across the mountains. Along the way, they met Tibetans on horses herding yaks, camels and other livestock. Their caravan included many sheep carrying saddlebags filled with produce; again, reminding Michael of the Pundits who had used sheep to good effect: as baggage animals, for food when required, and to complete their disguise as traders.

Back on the main road, the vehicle convoy continued to follow the ancient trade route into Central Asia first mapped by Kishen Singh. After crossing the Kunlun, the party established its second base on the other side of the range at another truck depot, Nachitai, which sat some 5,000ft lower. Ahead lay the Qaidam Basin, a closed depression almost one-half the size of the United Kingdom. It contains many saline lakes and wetlands (Qaidam means 'salt marsh'), although around one-third of the basin is also desert. The expedition halted here for ten days to finish the last of its geological work. Then, after driving 60 miles to Golmud, the geotraverse was concluded and the geologists returned to Peking before dispersing home.

Ward decided to stay back in Golmud and tour the local hospital. The doctors here, starved of contact with the non-Chinese medical world, were keen to hear from him. Despite contracting laryngitis, he croaked his way through a few lectures with the help of an interpreter, remarking: 'My hosts could not have been kinder, but I was a rare animal to them.'

Afterwards, Michael travelled by train 400 miles due east to Qinghai's capital, Xining, the largest city on the Tibetan Plateau. Here, he visited the High Altitude Medical Research Institute which had been opened the previous year. By now, he was running a high temperature and sweating profusely, but he managed to deliver all his scheduled lectures and 'field questions which came thick and fast'.

On 4 August, some miles outside of Xining, Ward visited Kumbum, the second-most revered monastery in the country and an important centre for traditional Tibetan medicine. Unlike the leading Drepung Monastery, it had largely escaped destruction during the Cultural Revolution. He toured its 'immaculately clean and well kept' hospital which smelt of herbs, before sharing a traditional meal with the director, finished off with the usual yoghurt made from yak milk.

The next day Michael visited China's largest lake, the Koko Nor (or Qinghai Lake) and its tranquil surrounds. It was the final excursion of his initial travels across Tibet, and he captured the change in scenery here, so different from the bleak plateau:

> Descending to the shores of the lake we went through many miles of grassland where herds of yak, sheep and horses grazed. It was a sunny day, the wind was warm, and the air felt thick in pleasant contrast to the crisp, thin air of the plateau, and it smelled salty.

After the outcomes of the 1985 geotraverse were discussed at a conference in Beijing, another was quickly organised to extend its scope from Lhasa all the way south to Kathmandu, to begin in September 1986. Ward was again invited to join members from the Royal Society and Academia Sinica as the expedition's medical officer.

Unlike the previous year, this time he was called upon to attend to a serious health issue, which occurred even before the combined team left Lhasa. One of the British geologists, Nigel Harris, had crackling noises in his lungs yet wasn't running a high temperature, which suggested the onset of high altitude pulmonary oedema. Although Harris was reluctant to leave, Ward had no option but to order him down to lower altitude immediately, putting him on the next flight out of Lhasa. As soon as he was on the plane, which was pressurised to the equivalent of 8,000ft, Harris began to recover quickly and was able to rejoin the team in Nepal and continue his work normally.

For Michael, one of the highlights on this second leg of the geotraverse was to finally see the grand waterway of Tibet, the Tsangpo. He had keenly read about the various Pundits who had surveyed it downstream from Lhasa, attempting to solve 'the riddle of the Tsangpo'. Back then, this question had confounded explorers and geographers alike, and was one of the great mysteries of the time: did the Tsangpo flow into the Brahmaputra as it debouched onto the plains of India? Or did it perhaps join up with one of the other five major rivers of China and Southeast Asia, which also have their headwaters originating from these highlands?

In 1913, the British officer and one-time master spy in Central Asia, Lt. Col. F.M. Bailey finally provided irrefutable evidence that the Tsangpo and Brahmaputra were in fact the one and same river.* Years before Ward, he had

---

* For his efforts, the RGS awarded Bailey its Patron's Medal in 1916.

explored Bhutan, and his wife and mother were the first European women to have entered the country. Ward visited Bailey's widow in Norfolk prior to joining the geotraverse and listened avidly as she related her husband's many adventures.

This time, much of the journey across southern Tibet followed the trail taken by prewar expeditions to Everest, allowing Ward to view approaches to the mountain from the north. Their first major halt was Shigatse, Tibet's second-largest city. Here, he visited the Tashilhunpo Monastery founded in 1447, which is the traditional seat of the Panchen Lama.* Michael again witnessed a never-ending line of pilgrims circumambulating the monastery's revered walls. This part of Tibet had also been visited by the Pundits, and he was able to compare their descriptions of its holiest shrines with what he witnessed now, after the destruction perpetrated by Mao's Red Guards.

While the geologists worked along the banks of the Tsangpo, he visited Shigatse's hospital. It had 270 beds and was staffed by Chinese doctors caring for Tibetan patients, many of whom were suffering from upper respiratory infections. After the tour, Michael noted: 'By European standards it was pretty dismal, but I am sure it was better medically than it has been prior to 1949–50 when there was little modern medical treatment and only the fit and lucky survived.'

On the last day of September, the convoy travelled further south to Shekar Dzong, which many of the prewar Everest parties had also visited. Unfortunately, Michael found its original monastery had not withstood the ravages of the Cultural Revolution. One morning before dawn, he led a small group up an immense rock pinnacle nearby, hoping to get views of the Himalayas and its highest peak, but they were thwarted by low cloud.

The expedition now skirted west of Everest through a spectacular defile; along a road he considered to be 'a marvel of engineering' but susceptible to terrible landslides. Finally, the party entered Nepal across the Friendship Bridge at the border town of Kodari. With the capital only a day away, the full geotraverse, Golmud–Lhasa–Kathmandu, was finally over.†

On the last day, Michael recalls their drive meandering along 'one of the most beautiful gorges I have ever been through' – another Sword Slash of Buddha, and a fitting end to his last adventure in high Asia.

---

* Although second in spiritual authority only to the Dalai Lama, the appointment of the current Panchen Lama in 1995 by the Chinese authorities – in defiance of the Dalai Lama – has been controversial.

† The expedition's 400-page report *The Geological Evolution of Tibet* was published by the Royal Society in 1988.

# 21

# The Final Quarter

◇◇◇◇◇◇◇◇◇◇◇◇◇◇◇◇◇◇◇◇◇◇◇◇◇◇◇◇◇◇◇◇◇◇◇◇◇◇◇◇◇◇◇◇◇◇◇◇

After his time on the Tibetan Plateau, there would be no more major climbs or expeditions for Ward in the last quarter of his life. Although now a year past his 60th birthday, this did not stop him being thoroughly active, not where his two passions – mountaineering and medicine – were concerned.

On his return, he wrote 'Across Tibet' for the *Alpine Journal* (1986) followed by almost forty articles for various publications, as well as contributing to several others.* These included pieces on Everest and the Himalayas, Central Asia and Tibet, exploration in high Asia and, of course, his beloved Pundits. In 1989, his seminal textbook *Mountain Medicine* was expanded to report on information now available from Russia and China. This time it was co-authored with his two old friends from Silver Hut, Jim Milledge and John West, and reissued as *High Altitude Medicine and Physiology*.

While still fit and climbing, Ward became President of the Cambridge Alpine Club and served for over a decade (1986–95). Meanwhile, after a lifetime with the National Health Service, and being asked to stay on three more years beyond the statutory retirement age, he eventually put away his scalpel in 1993. Of his medical abilities, Milledge would say: 'He was highly regarded as a teacher and an all-round surgeon'; and of his nature, Westmacott added: 'He was in fact a caring man, to the benefit of his patients and his friends, but might have been embarrassed to admit it.'

That same year, after many years of involvement, Ward became Master of The Worshipful Society of Apothecaries. Established in 1617 by royal charter from King James I, this society has, among its other activities, licensed doctors to practise medicine since 1815. He served as its head for two years and helped develop courses for medical practitioners in the management of disasters, particularly for Third World countries.

---

* See Bibliography for a full listing of Ward's books and articles.

Although Ward had a congenital kidney abnormality which required an operation in his later years, he largely enjoyed good health. Even in his seventies, for example, while attending a conference in Peru he walked the Inca Trail to Machu Picchu, backpacking his own gear uphill all the way.

But in September 2002 he suffered a cruel blow: While out driving on an almost clear road, his car was struck by another after its driver lost control around a bend, killing the two occupants of the oncoming car. Michael, although blameless, was lucky to have survived. His injuries included a fractured skull, spinal damage, cracked ribs and a collapsed lung. After being cut out from the wreckage, he had to undergo many hours of surgery. During his long period of recovery, Ward continued writing as best he could. The following March, he underwent open heart surgery, but various complications arose during his recovery period.

Despite these difficulties, the next year Michael marked the 50th anniversary of the first ascent of the world's highest peak with the publication of his book *Everest: A Thousand Years of Exploration*. It represented the culmination of a wide-ranging study over many decades, of a mountain that had loomed so large in his life. In its preface, he noted: 'I have written this monograph on the mountaineering, mapping and medical aspects of the exploration and ascent of Everest because no contemporary publication gives a comprehensive account of these three interwoven strands.'

During its research, Ward had benefited from access to rarely available information from the archives of the RGS due to his being a recipient of its Founder's Medal. Afterwards, mountaineer, writer and physiologist George Rodway would reflect:

> This, his last book, stands as testimony to one man's exceptional, multifaceted talents. This unique work brings together the historical chronicle of Mt. Everest's mountaineering, geographical and medical aspects into a definitive, coherent story.

Another climber and author Doug Scott reminded readers: 'No one was better placed to write this book since Michael Ward did so much to pioneer the way to the summit.' And travel writer Jan Morris added: 'I am more convinced than ever that this book is the *most* interesting ever written about Everest.'

Unfortunately, Michael struggled to recover from his car accident despite Jane's constant care at their home in West Sussex. Together, they had designed and built a beautiful house and gardens in the picturesque village of Lurgashall. Just when it seemed he might pull through, on

7 October 2005 Ward died suddenly at home from a ruptured heart (aortic aneurysm).

His son Mark, on his website, recalled: 'Jim [Milledge] gave a most moving, and entertaining, address at my father's funeral ... it was remarkable for its celebratory nature.' In reading the tributes to him, Mark wrote: 'I was stunned to see *The New York Times* give him equal space with the legendary civil rights activist Rosa Parks.' He then went on to sum up 'dad':

> He was a daunting figure in his accomplishments and no-nonsense disposition. His competitive streak, combined with a disregard for the niceties, could make him seem brusque, somewhat remote. But, in truth, he was a man of deep feeling: a remarkable man from a remarkable generation of men who ... were always looking to the far horizon, then tried to figure out the most interesting way of getting there.

Among the many obituaries published in journals and newspapers, one in *The Guardian* ended by pointing out: 'He was by choice something of an outsider to a mountaineering establishment in this country which remains substantially in his debt.' Ward's own words – the final lines from *In This Short Span* – suggest a fitting epitaph:

> The summit attained is a simple physical achievement but the mind and spirit reap their own harvest, formless and immeasurable. This is what we carry over into our everyday lives.

# Appendix

## CLINICAL NOTES FOR HILLARY AND TENZING

<u>HILLARY AND TENZING</u> (Open Circuit Oxygen)

Camp 4 to South Col to Camp 4.

21/5   <u>CAMP 4 (21,200 ft) → CAMP 7 (24,000 ft)</u> Using Open Circuit Oxygen
Took 4¼ hours (¾ hr rest at Camp 5, 22,000 ft) using 4 litres/minute.
From Camp 5 to Camp 7, Hillary carrying 48 lbs including oxygen set and personal gear. Tenzing was carrying slightly less.
Hillary felt that he had a heavy load but his legs kept going and he was not panting.
Arrived at Camp 7 with no unusual fatigue.
Camp 5 → 6  1 hr, 25 mins.
Camp 6 → 7  1 hr.

<u>Night</u> at Camp 7. No sleeping oxygen. No sleep for either Tenzing or Hillary. Breathless on lying down in tent, which lasted 20 minutes. Before taking set off, stood around for a minute or so. No sense of change.

22/5   <u>CAMP 7 (24,000 ft) → SOUTH COL (26,000 ft) → CAMP 4 (21,000 ft)</u>
Left at 8.30a.m. and in 6 hrs to South Col. Arrived 14.30 hrs.
Tenzing using 4 litres/minute all day. Carrying 2 bottles of oxygen = 32 lbs weight altogether.

Hillary:  1 hr at 4 litres/minute
          4 hrs at 3 litres/minute
          1 hr at 4 litres/minute

For the last two hours both Hillary and Tenzing carried an extra 11 lbs. Noted little difference in going, just slower. Not more breathlessness, with extra weight. They chucked away a used cylinder.
Both Hillary and Tenzing were making the route [for Sherpas carrying loads to the South Col]. They found this fatiguing.
They left some oxygen sets on the South Col and descended without oxygen. The first 1,000 ft on return were fatiguing but then improved and continued down to Camp 7 and Camp 4 the same day.
At Camp 4 Hillary was very tired, but capable of normal speech and thinking.

<u>Fluid and Food</u>
Hillary:      ½ cup of tea plus a few grapenuts for breakfast
            Camp 7  ½ cup of fluid
            Camp 5  1 cup
            Camp 4  3½ cups
            Almost 6 cups x 300 mls = ?1800 mls/day

Hillary:    Mask not used from South Col down. Husky voice at camp.
Tenzing:  Mask used from South Col to Camp. Voice not husky.

__HILLARY__ (Open Circuit Oxygen)

25 /5   __CAMP 4 → CAMP 7__
in 3¼ hours using **Open Circuit Oxygen** weighing 17 lbs.  Feeling very fresh at 4 litres/minute.
Slept on oxygen at 1 litre/minute for 8/9 hours.
Slept well but woke when oxygen stopped.

26 /5   __CAMP 7 → SOUTH COL__
in 2¾ hours on 4 litres/minute carrying 38 lbs altogether.  On South Col removed oxygen set and walked 200 ft up hill without fatigue.
Slept on oxygen 1 litre/minute.  Bloody night as it was very windy.  Most uncomfortable night that he had spent at altitude.  Very cold.
Wearing:  String vest
      wool vest
      2 Shetland pullovers
      windproof jacket
      wool gloves
      down jacket
      short cotton underpants
      long wool underpants
      down trousers
      socks
      H.A. boots.
      Ear muffs
      New Zealand outer sleeping bag.

27 /5   __ON SOUTH COL__
Off day.  Wind very bad.
Felt OK.  Eating ++.  Drinking +.
No oxygen used.  Got oxygen bottle ready for next day.  Felt OK at the end of the day.
Slept on oxygen 1 litre/minute.
Much warmer and more comfortable night.  Still slightly cold –29°C.

28 /5   __TO CAMP 9 (27,800 ft)__
Left with Tenzing at 10.00a.m. 4 litres/minute.  Hillary load 49 lbs.  Tenzing load 44 lbs.
At 27,300 ft (Hunt dump) took extra load and carried 63 lbs from 27,300 ft → 27,800 ft.
Increased oxygen uptake to 5 litres/minute for 30 minutes.  Appreciable difference - feel more energetic, everything goes more easily.  Like changing gear.
At 2.30p.m. reached campsite at 27,800 ft.  Hillary and Tenzing took off oxygen from 2.30p.m.- 5.00p.m.  Worked on campsite.  Hard work clearing tent site.  Snow and ice.  Had to cut rocks from ice.
Had to sit every now and again to rest.  Pitched tent.  Brewed up.  Soup, sugar.  Tin of apricots, jam, biscuits, sardines.
Hillary sat up all night.
Used sleeping oxygen for 4 hours.  1 hour here and there.  On oxygen they did doze.
–27°C at 3.00a.m.

---

204

29 /5   <u>CAMP 9 → SUMMIT → SOUTH COL</u>
Left at 6.30a.m.
Load 30 lbs. 3 litres/minute +. South Peak 9.00a.m. Very hard work getting to South Peak. Dumped one bottle of oxygen so carrying 20 lbs from South Peak to Summit. From South Peak to Summit Hillary led all the way. Took 2½ hours. Step cutting not hard work.
Did back and knee between rock step and ice (Hillary Step). Most energetic thing that they did. Tenzing rather tired. Hillary going well. More step cutting to the Summit. On Summit at 11.30a.m. for 15 minutes. Hillary removed oxygen for 10 minutes and took photographs. Felt slight weakness but nothing more. Could move around slowly and carefully. Mentally no confusion. Passed urine on Summit and ate Kendal Mint Cake. Tenzing removed oxygen for about 5 minutes on the Summit. Left Summit at 11.45a.m. Went back to South Peak in 1 hour from Summit. Down steep bit of ridge, snow in dangerous condition. No falling off. A bit tired but making good time.
At 27,800 ft Camp made quick brew of lemon juice. Arrived Camp at 2.00p.m. Left at 3.00p.m. Dumped empty oxygen bottle and took bottle with 1000 lb pressure. On 2 litres/minute carrying about 20 lbs weight, down to ridge to Couloir. Felt tired but took it slowly.
At Couloir had to cut steps down it. By Hillary. Tenzing kicked steps.
Oxygen working until he met Lowe on the South Col. Then it stopped. Little difference noted but going uphill noted a marked weakness. This gradually wore off.
Both Hillary and Tenzing were very tired but arrived much fresher than other parties going above South Col.
Sleeping oxygen. 1 litre/minute for 8 hours. A bad night.

30 /5   <u>SOUTH COL → CAMP 4</u>
Legs very tired. Used 4/litres minute down to Camp 5. From Camp 5 - Camp 4 without supplementary oxygen. Not clinically dehydrated. *ON EXAMINATION*

<u>Fluids:</u>
27/5   7-9 mugs in 24 hours
28/5   2 mugs + ½ pint
        1 cup soup, 1 cup coffee, 2 mugs lemon, 1 mug at 1.00p.m.
        1 mug at midnight.
29/5   1 mug, 1 mug soup, 3-4 oz sugar
        Pint/mug of lemonade
        ½ pint. 1 mug + sugar
        1 mug soup. 3-4 mugs
        Biscuits, sardines.

# Acknowledgements

Foremost among those I sincerely thank is Stuart Leggatt of Meridian Rare Books in London. Upon learning I was writing this biography, he told me no mountaineer was more deserving and promised every assistance – he unfailingly kept his word. Importantly, Stuart also discovered Michael's unpublished autobiography among his papers; and was my primary contact with Jane Ward, who wholeheartedly supported this project and has provided old family photographs.

Next, my thanks to Harriet Fielding, Pen & Sword's production editor, for her advice and support in turning my manuscript into a book, together with copy editor Karyn Burnham.

Sue and Richard Sale shared their transcriptions of Michael's expedition diaries, which was a great help as anyone who's tried to decipher a doctor's scrawl will know. Gordon Sharfe, a handwriting expert in Wellington, offered invaluable tips in this regard.

Also in New Zealand, Pat Barcham and Mike Gill, who were at Silver Hut, made time to be interviewed. Harriet Tuckey emailed me research material from London about her father and the first ascent of Everest, while Sir Chris Bonington readily agreed to write the foreword.

My gratitude also to a number of climbers who read the manuscript and provided me invaluable feedback, including on mountaineering aspects: Colin Monteath (who also engaged Sir Chris), Ronnie Richards and Bryan Scott, all from New Zealand; and Ian Smith in England.

Finally, as with my other books, many thanks to my wife Beth for her never-ending support throughout this process.

# Select Bibliography

Although this bibliography contains only the main works consulted, it begins with a full listing of all of Michael Ward's (known) books and articles, including those to which he contributed.

## Books by Michael Ward


1966. (as editor) *The Mountaineer's Companion*. London: Eyre & Spottiswoode.

1968. (MD thesis) *Diseases Occurring at Altitudes Exceeding 17,500 ft.* University of Cambridge.

1972. *In This Short Span*. London: Victor Gollancz.

1975. *Mountain Medicine: A Clinical Study of Cold and High Altitude*. London: Crosby Lockwood Staples.
> 1989. Republished as *High Altitude Medicine and Physiology* with James Milledge and John West. London: Chapman and Hall Medical.

2003. *Everest: A Thousand Years of Exploration*. Glasgow: Ernest Press.
> 2013. Republished by Hayloft Publishing, Glasgow.


## Contribution to Books by Michael Ward


1953. Appendix VII (with Griffith Pugh) in:
> Hunt, John. *The Ascent of Everest*. London: Hodder & Stoughton.

1982. Introduction and Appendices II and III (with various others) in:
> Bonington, Chris. *Kongur: China's Elusive Summit*. London: Hodder & Stoughton.

1984. Chapter titled 'Accidents and Deaths at Altitude' in:
> Clarke, C. and A. Salkeld (editors). *Lightweight Expeditions to the Great Ranges*. London: Alpine Club.

1987. Chapter titled 'Cold, Hypoxia and Dehydration' in:
Sutton, John., et al. (editors). *Hypoxia and Cold*. New York: Praeger.
1987. Introduction to:
The Royal Geographical Society and the Mount Everest Foundation. *The Mountains of Central Asia*. London: Macmillan.
2003. Preface to (a catalogue for rare books):
*Everest, Chomolungma, Sagarmatha*. London: Henry Sotheran.
2009. Preface to:
Sale, Richard. *Mapping the Himalayas*. Ross-on-Wye: Carreg.

## Articles and Reports by Michael Ward

Note: This listing includes items written with others (et al), but excludes any book reviews.

1952. 'In Eastern Nepal.' *The Lancet* 238–9.
1952. 'The 1951 Everest Reconnaissance.' *London Hospital Gazette* April.
1954. 'High Altitude Deterioration.' *Proceedings of the Royal Society (Series B, Vol. 143)* 40–2.
1956. (with Griffith Pugh) 'Some Effects of High Altitude on Man.' *The Lancet* 1115–21.
1957. (with Griffith Pugh) 'Some Effects of High Altitude on Man.' *Alpine Journal* 507–20.
1958. 'Sarcoma of Vesical Diverticula.' *British Journal of Urology (Vol. 30)* 57–9.
1960. 'Bugaboo.' *Alpine Journal* 18–26.
1961. 'Himalayan Scientific Expedition 1960–61.' *Alpine Journal* 343–64.
1962. (et al) 'Arterial Oxygen Saturation during Exercise at High Altitude.' *Journal of Applied Physiology (Vol. 17)* 617–21.
1962. 'The Ascent of Ama Dablam.' *The Climbers' Club Journal (Vol. XIII)* 271–86.
1963. 'The Descent from Makalu, 1961, and Some Medical Aspects of High Altitude Climbing.' *Alpine Journal* 11–19.
1964. (et al) 'Muscular Exercise at Great Altitudes.' *Journal of Applied Physiology (Vol. 19)* 431–40.
1964. 'The Uses of Adversity: Some Mountaineering and Medical Aspects of the Himalayan Scientific Expedition 1960–61.' In *The Mountain World (1962/63)*, 70–91. London: George Allen & Unwin.

1965. 'Bhutan Himal.' *Alpine Journal* 106–19.

1965. (with Frederic Jackson) 'Medicine in Bhutan.' *The Lancet* 811–13.

1965. (with F. Jackson and R. Turner) 'Report of I.B.P. Expedition to Bhutan, October-December 1965.'

1966. 'Bhutan Himal: Some Further Observations.' *Alpine Journal* 281–84.

1966. 'Some Geographical and Medical Observations in North Bhutan.' *The Geographical Journal (Vol. 132)* 491–506.

1966. (with J.E. Cootes) 'Ventilatory Capacity in Normal Bhutanese.' *Proceedings of Physiological Society (Vol. 186)* 88–9.

1967. (with F. Jackson and R. Turner) 'Himalayan Scientific Expedition to North Bhutan, 1965. Report to the International Biological Programme.' London: The Royal Society.

1967. (with Frederic Jackson) 'The Highest Mountain in Bhutan.' *Alpine Journal* 325–26.

1968. (et al) 'Digital Dematoglyphics of a Lunana Sample from North Bhutan.' *Man* 5–19.

1968. (et al) 'Frostbite: General Observations and Report of Cases Treated by Hyperbaric Oxygen.' *Proceedings of Royal Society of Medicine (Vol. 61)* 787–89.

1968. (et al) 'The Blood Groups, Serum Groups and Haemoglobins of the Inhabitants of Lunana and Thimbu, Bhutan.' *Vox Sanguinis* 31–42.

1969. 'Man and the Mountain Environment.' *Alpine Journal* 133–47.

1971. 'Frost-bite.' *Alpine Journal* 70–87.

1973. 'Periodic Respiration.' *Annals of the Royal College of Surgeons of England (Vol. 52)* 330–4.

1974. 'Frostbite.' *British Medical Journal (Vol. 1)* 67–70.

1975. (et al) *Mountain Medicine and Physiology: Proceedings of a Symposium...* London: Alpine Club. (Ward contributed two articles: 'Everest Without Oxygen?' and 'Frostbite'.)

1976. 'Mountain Literature – Then and Now.' *Alpine Journal* 15–19.

1977. (et al) 'The Effect of Hypoxia on Muscle Glycogen Resynthesis in Man.' *Quarterly Journal of Experimental Physiology* 237–45.

1979. (et al) 'Effect of the Exercise of Seven Consecutive Days Hill-walking on Fluid Homeostasis.' *Clinical Science (Vol. 56)* 305–16.

1980. 'Exercise Oedema and Mountain Sickness – A Field Investigation.' *Alpine Journal* 168–75.

1981. 'Exercise Oedema and Altitude.' *Proceedings of Symposium on Qinghai-Xizang (Tibet) Plateau (Vol. 2)* 1415–21. Peking: Science Press.

1981. (with Chris Bonington) 'The British Mount Kongur Expedition to China.' London (Final report).

1981. 'The Kongur Massif in Southern Xinjiang (Sinkiang).' *Alpine Journal* 7–17.

1982. 'Science on Mount Kongur.' *Alpine Journal* 65–7.

1982. (et al) 'Sodium Balance, Fluid Homeostasis and the Renin-Aldosterone System during the Prolonged Exercise of Hill Walking.' *Clinical Science* 595–604.

1982. 'The Everest Story.' *Geographical Journal (Vol. 148)* 354–56.

1983. (et al) 'Renin-Aldosterone and Angiotensin-converting Enzyme during Prolonged Altitude Exposure.' *Journal of Applied Physiology (Vol. 55)* 699–702.

1983. (et al) 'Cardiorespiratory Response to Exercise in Men Repeatedly Exposed to Extreme Altitude.' *Journal of Applied Physiology (Vol. 55)* 1379–85.

1983. 'The Kongur Massif in Southern Sinkiang.' *Geographical Journal (Vol. 149)* 137–52.

1985. 'The Eastern Himalaya: An Introduction.' *Alpine Journal* 10–17.

1985. 'Medical Notes.' *Alpine Journal* 257.

1986. 'Across Tibet.' *Alpine Journal* 84–9.

1986. (et al) 'Preliminary Conclusions of Royal Society and Academia Sinica 1985 Geotraverse of Tibet.' *Nature (Vol. 323)* 501–7.

1988. 'The Mountaineer at Extreme Altitude.' *Alpine Journal* 191–95.

1989. 'Central Tibet – Tanggula Shan.' *Alpine Journal* 82–83.

1989. 'Sagarmatha–Mount Everest–Qomolungma: Map by the National Geographic Society.' *Geographical Journal (Vol. 155)* 433–35.

1989. 'The Kun Lun Shan: Desert Peaks of Central Asia.' *Alpine Journal* 84–96.

1990. 'Griffith Pugh: An 80th Birthday Tribute.' *Alpine Journal* 188–90.

1990. 'Mountain Medicine and Physiology: A Short History.' *Alpine Journal* 191–98.

1990. 'Tibet: Human and Medical Geography.' *Journal of Wilderness Medicine (Vol. 1)* 36–46.

1990–91. 'The Everest Map.' *Alpine Journal* 246–47.

1991. 'Medicine in Tibet.' *Journal of Wilderness Medicine (Vol. 2)* 198–205.

1991–92. 'Mountains of East and South-East Tibet: An Introduction.' *Alpine Journal* 49–62.

1992. (with P. K. Clark) 'Everest, 1951: Cartographic and Photographic Evidence of a New Route from Nepal.' *The Geographical Journal (Vol. 158)* 47–56.

1992. 'The Exploration of the Nepalese Side of Everest.' *Alpine Journal* 213–21.

1993. 'The Contribution of Medical Science to the First Ascent of Everest.' *Alpine Journal* 37–51.

1993. (with Hamish Nicol) 'Tom Bourdillon 1924–1956.' *Alpine Journal* 62–6.

1993. 'The Everest Sketches of Lt Col E F Norton.' *Alpine Journal* 82 (Plates 15–23).

1993. 'The First Ascent of Mount Everest.' *British Medical Journal (Vol. 306)* 1455–58.

1993. 'The First Ascent of Mount Everest, 1953: the Solution of the Problem of the 'Last Thousand Feet'.' *Journal of Wilderness Medicine (Vol. 4)* 312–318.

1993. 'The Mapping of Everest.' *The Map Collector (No. 64)*.

1994. 'Mapping Everest.' *Cartographic Journal (Vol. 31)* 33–44.

1994. 'The Exploration and Mapping of Everest' *Alpine Journal* 97–108.

1994. 'Northern Approaches: Everest 1918–22.' *Alpine Journal* 213–21.

1995. 'The Height of Mount Everest.' *Alpine Journal* 30–33.

1995. 'Preparations for Everest: Cho Oyu, London and Zermatt 1952.' *Alpine Journal* 222–32.

1995. 'In Memoriam: Lewis Griffith Cresswell Evans Pugh 1909–1994.' *Alpine Journal* 326–27.

1996. 'The Great Angtharkay: A Tribute.' *Alpine Journal* 182–186.

1996. 'The Mountains of Central Tibet.' *Alpine Journal* 209–23.

1997. 'Everest 1951: the Footprints Attributed to the Yeti – Myth and Reality.' *Wilderness and Environmental Medicine (Vol. 8)* 29–32.

1997. 'Exploration of the Bhutan Himalaya.' *Alpine Journal* 219–29.

1997. 'The Name of the World's Highest Peak.' *Himalayan Journal (Vol. 53)*.

1998. 'The Survey of India and the Pundits.' *Alpine Journal* 59–79.

1999. 'The Yeti Footprints: Myth and Reality.' *Alpine Journal* 81–7.

1999. 'Exploration and Mapping SE of Everest in 1954 and 1955.' *Alpine Journal* 197–201.

2000. 'The Exploration of the Tsangpo River and its Mountains.' *Alpine Journal* 124–30.

2001. 'Early Exploration of Kangchenjunga and South Tibet.' *Alpine Journal* 191–96.

2002. 'A Petrean on Everest 1951–53.' *Peterhouse Annual Record 2001/2002* 64–70.

2002. (with James Milledge) 'Griffith Pugh: Pioneer Everest Physiologist.' *High Altitude Medicine & Biology (Vol. 3)* 77–87.

2002. 'The Pundits and the Pamir.' *Alpine Journal* 222–29.

2003. 'A New Map of the Everest Area.' *Alpine Journal* 18–19.

2003. 'The Pundits beyond the Pamir.' *Alpine Journal* 203–8.

2003. 'Everest 1953, First Ascent: A Clinical Record.' *High Altitude Medicine & Biology (Vol. 4)* 27–37.

2005. (et al) 'Tibetans at Extreme Altitude.' *Wilderness and Environmental Medicine (Vol. 16)* 47–54.


## Select Bibliography (excluding works by Michael Ward)

Bishop, Barry. 1962. 'Wintering on the Roof of the World.' *National Geographic (Vol. 122)* 503–47.

Bonington, Chris. 1981. *Quest for Adventure.* Washington D.C.: National Geographic.

— . 1982. *Kongur: China's Elusive Summit.* London: Hodder & Stoughton.

Cox, David. 1973. 'Books of the Year – *In This Short Span.' Alpine Journal* 270–72.

Crew, Peter. 1968. *Encyclopaedic Dictionary of Mountaineering.* London: Constable.

Curran, Jim. 1991. *Suspended Sentences.* London: Hodder & Stoughton.

Dean, Riaz. 2019. *Mapping the Great Game.* Oxford: Casemate, and Delhi: Penguin Random House India.

Denman, Earl. 1954. *Alone to Everest.* London: Coward-McCann.

Gill, Michael. 1969. *Mountain Midsummer: Climbing in Four Continents.* London: Hodder & Stoughton.

— . 2017. *Edmund Hillary: A Biography.* Nelson: Potton & Burton.

Gillman, Peter. 1989. 'The Most Abominable Hoaxer?' *Sunday Times Magazine*, December 10: 39–44.

— . 2001. 'The Yeti Footprints.' *Alpine Journal* 143–51.

Haas, Ernst, and Gisela Minke. 1978. *Himalayan Pilgrimage.* New York: Viking Press.

Hillary, Edmund. 1955. *High Adventure.* London: Hodder & Stoughton.

— . 1975. *Nothing Venture, Nothing Win.* London: Hodder & Stoughton.

Hillary, Edmund, and Desmond Doig. 1962. *High in the Thin Cold Air.* New York: Doubleday.

Horrell, Mark. 2013. Book review: *Everest: The First Ascent by Harriet Tuckey.* Accessed 9/5/23. https://www.markhorrell.com/blog/2013/book-review-everest-the-first-ascent-by-harriet-tuckey/.

Hunt, John. 1953. *The Ascent of Everest.* London: Hodder & Stoughton.

— . 1978. *Life is Meeting.* London: Hodder & Stoughton.

Messner, Reinhold (trans. by P. Constantine). 2000. *My Quest for the Yeti.* New York: St. Martin's Press.

Milledge, James. 2010 . 'The Silver Hut Expedition, 1960–1961.' *High Altitude Medicine & Biology* 93–101.

— . 2017. 'Mountains My Lab.' Unpublished (autobiographical notes).

Milledge, James, and Michael Westmacott. 2006. 'In Memoriam: Michael P Ward.' *Alpine Journal* 373–405.

Mitchell, Ian, and George Rodway. 2011. *Prelude to Everest: Alexander Kellas, Himalayan Mountaineer.* Edinburgh: Luath Press.

Morin, Nea. 1968. *A Woman's Reach.* London: Eyre & Spottiswoode.

Morris, James. 1958. *Coronation Everest.* London: Faber & Faber.

Mulgrew, Peter. 1965. *No Place for Men.* Wellington: A.H. & A.W. Reed.

Murray, W.H. 1952 . 'The Reconnaissance of Mount Everest, 1951.' *Alpine Journal* 433–52.

— . 1967. 'Reviews: *The Mountaineer's Companion.*' *Alpine Journal* 160.

— . 2002. *The Evidence of Things Not Seen: A Mountaineer's Tale.* London: Bâton Wicks.

Noyce, Wilfrid. 1954. *South Col* . London: William Heinemann.

Perrin, Jim. 2005. 'Michael Ward (Obituary).' *The Guardian*, 27 October.

— . 2013. *Shipton and Tilman: The Great Decade of Himalayan Exploration.* London: Hutchinson.

Rodway, George, and Jeremy Windsor. 2008. 'Pioneer of the High Realm: Michael Ward's Life of Medicine, Mountaineering, and Exploration.' *Wilderness and Environmental Medicine (Vol. 19)* 52–8.

— . 2010–11. 'Ama Dablam – 50 Years On.' *Alpine Journal* 193–98.

Sale, Richard. 2009. *Mapping the Himalayas: Michael Ward and the Pundit Legacy.* Ross-On-Wye: Carreg.

Sale, Richard, and George Rodway. 2011. *Everest and Conquest in the Himalaya.* Barnsley: Pen & Sword.

Shipton, Eric. 1951. *Mountains of Tartary.* London: Hodder & Stoughton.

— . 1952. *The Mount Everest Reconnaissance Expedition 1951.* London: Hodder & Stoughton.

— . 1969. *That Untravelled World: An Autobiography.* London: Hodder & Stoughton.

Skrine, Clarmont. 1925. 'Alps of Qungur.' *The Geographical Journal (Vol. 66)* 385–410.

Smythe, F.S. 1937. *Camp Six* . London: Adam & Charles Black.

— . 1942. *British Mountaineers.* London: William Collins.

Steele, Peter. 1970. *Two and Two Halves to Bhutan.* London: Hodder & Stoughton.

— . 1998. *Eric Shipton: Everest and Beyond.* London: Constable.

Temple, Philip. 1969. *The World at their Feet.* Auckland: Whitcombe & Tombs.

Tilman, H.W. 1951. 'The Annapurna Himal and South Side of Everest.' *Alpine Journal (Vol. 58)* 101–10.

Tuckey, Harriet. 2013. *Everest: The First Ascent.* London: Rider.

Turner, Richard. 1968. 'An Expedition to Bhutan.' In *The Mountain World (1966/67)* 88–105. London: George Allen & Unwin.

Ullman, James Ramsey. 1955. *Man of Everest: The Autobiography of Tenzing.* London: George G. Harrap.

Unsworth, Walt. 1981. *Everest.* London: Allen Lane.

Venables, Stephen. 2003. *Everest: Summit of Achievement.* London: Royal Geographical Society.

Vola, Eric. 2012. 'Everest – Michael Ward.' Accessed 9/5/23. https://www.summitpost.org/everest-michael-ward/779004

Waller, Derek. 1990. *The Pundits.* Lexington: University of Kentucky.

Ward, Mark. 2013. 'My Dad on Everest and Beyond – Of God and Science.' Accessed 9/5/23. https://hollywoodandallthat.com/2013/06/16/my-dad-on-everest-and-beyond-of-god-and-science/.

Westmacott, Michael. 2006. 'In Memoriam – Michael Phelps Ward.' *The Himalayan Journal (Vol. 62)* Unpaginated.

Dear Reader,

We hope you have enjoyed this book, but why not share your views on social media? You can also follow our pages to see more about our other products: facebook.com/penandswordbooks or follow us on X @penswordbooks

You can also view our products at www.pen-and-sword.co.uk (UK and ROW) or www.penandswordbooks.com (North America).

To keep up to date with our latest releases and online catalogues, please sign up to our newsletter at: www.pen-and-sword.co.uk/newsletter

If you would like a printed catalogue with our latest books, then please email: enquiries@pen-and-sword.co.uk or telephone: 01226 734555 (UK and ROW) or email: uspen-and-sword@casematepublishers.com or telephone: (610) 853-9131 (North America).

We respect your privacy and we will only use personal information to send you information about our products.

Thank you!